Table o

GW01458012

ITS ONLY GOT FOUR STRINGS

ITS ONLY GOT FOUR STRINGS

MISHAPS, MISFIRES AND MISADVENTURES OF AN UNPROFESSIONAL MUSICIAN

STEVE STEELE

Steve Steele?

Chances are you've never heard of him.
As an unprofessional bass guitarist, He has successfully avoided any visible form of international acclaim since the late eighties.
Over three decades upon stages of various sizes spread across two continents he shares, his mishaps, mis-fires and misadventures.
This isn't a cautionary tale, nor a rags to slightly better rags story. It's not rocket science, this is rock and roll and his only excuse?
...It's Only Got Four Strings

"Every Breath You Take"
The 1983 global hit single by The Police.
With fifteen million air plays as of March 2019, its one of the most
played songs in Radio History and still nets its chief songwriter Sting
around $2,000 in royalties...a day.

PRELUDE: CRUSHED... BY A DWARF

TUTTS CLUMP UK 1991

"Oi, mate, that song was SHIT!"

After a brief, confused silence my bandmates and I collapsed into fits of laughter.

Grinning up at us from the muddy field, the pint-sized critic can't have been more than twelve years old.

Alfie our volatile lead singer did not share in our amusement and fixed the cheeky punk with a thousand-yard stare.

Red faced and rigid with rage he now bellowed into the microphone...

"Well, don't blame me, he spat.

Blame fucking Sting he wrote the fucker!"

Maybe the kid had a point as my band, Incognito, had just assaulted both his and the audiences ear drums with a piss poor rendition of "Every Breath You Take."

In keeping with the moodiness of the tune, the band with the exception of our vocalist had decided it would look cool if we smoked cigarettes during the song.

What we hadn't considered was the beat of the song, which is constant.

At no point could we remove our cigarettes and take a breath at least, not without risking a major musical train-wreck.

So, we looked cool alright, playing a song about breath as we collectively asphyxiated.

Meanwhile over at the microphone, our lead singer was having his own problems with air supply.

It being an outdoor show, acrid smoke from the nearby campsite bonfires had been wafting across the stage for most of our set which was now causing Alfie to have issues with his vocals.

Angered by the crowd's tepid response and the fact his voice had rapidly gone downhill he'd resorted to simply shouting the final refrain.

"I'll be watching you...

He roared, pointing at random people in the crowd.

And you, and you...and YOU!

Well... why won't you watch ME?!"

He asked angrily.

The last chord rang out, the four of us gasped for air and the crowd went... mild.

With the mini critic still laughing at Alfie's foul-mouthed rebuttal I signaled for our drummer, T-Bone, to kick off our closing song which had also been written by someone else.

Judas Priest's "Breaking the Law" was a tune the entire band enjoyed playing and we gave it some extra welly.

But, with smoke inhalation, an indifferent audience and a mouthy tween conspiring against Alfie, he wasn't in the best position to actually sing it.

Pointlessly he reached for high notes that even operatic vocalist Rob Halford hadn't sung on the original version.

His unnecessary rhythmic screams synched with T-Bones cymbal hits during the finale sounded like a bullfrog being run over by a steamroller.

Overall, Incognitos debut show had been a minor disaster piece with our performance leaving most of the audience more annoyed than entertained.

After the crash, bang, and squealing feedback of the song's crescendo, Alfie left the crowd with a snide parting shot.

"They said music like ours couldn't die...

He seethed sarcastically.
Thanks to you lot, I think it probably just did!"

THE BANJO, THE GOTH & THE ODEON

WOODLEY UK 1979

My grandmother, Joyce was church organist for the parish of Ludgershall and in the front room of her home on Pretoria Road she had an old piano.

As a child whenever the family paid her a visit, my younger brother and I would be magnetically drawn to it.

Both, wide eyed in wonder, like flies flocking to an open jar of honey.

Not that there was anything remotely sweet about the subsequent shitty racket we would generate.

Grandma never seemed to get cross with us, she probably told us gently once or twice not to hit it quite so violently.

More often, though she would just smile sweetly in saintly tolerance.

I was fortunate enough to once see Grandma in her element playing the church organ in St James.

Her hands moved effortlessly like they were being guided by a higher power.

Fingers darting between the keyboards as her feet independently operated the pedals that generated the deep accompanying bass notes.

My impressionable young mind was wowed by Grandma's musical skills and even more impressed that most of the time she played with her eyes closed!

Having inherited her musical ability, my dad had taken up guitar in his teens and formed a skiffle band called.

The Temperance Seven who played at the local village fairs and school dances.

One rainy Sunday afternoon a long time ago, Dad brought a small case down from the attic and placed it on the kitchen table.

With theatrical flair he blew the dust from it and opened it in painfully slow increments.

I imagined there was some ancient artifact within sealed for centuries and if exposed too soon to the twentieth centenary, it would instantly dissolve to dust.

Inside the case was an odd-looking stringed instrument, like a tambourine with a thin piece of wood attached to it.

I thought it looked silly, like something a circus clown would bash himself over the head with.

Dad began to enlighten me as he removed it gingerly from the case.

"Son, this is a Banjo, he said, removing some more dust.

It's very old and once belonged to Reg Presley."

Reg was from the same town as Dad in the sixties he had been the lead singer for a band called The Trogg's

In 1966 the band had scored a #1 single with the song "Wild Thing"

Turning the five small pegs set on the small block of wood at the end of the neck, he slowly tweaked the creaking antique into tune and strummed up a few melodies.

Over the next couple of hours, Dad patiently tried to show me how to form a simple chord.

Just trying to hold down one of the rusty strings was painful enough and it left a filthy groove of grime on my fingers.

Despite his efforts and patience another trait he'd inherited from Grandma.

His eldest son wasn't going to be sat on the front porch bashing out *Dueling Banjos* anytime soon.

Bulmershe Comprehensive School, Woodley UK, 1985...

School days... weren't these supposed to be the most carefree and the happiest of my life?

I don't think so.

In secondary school I was painfully shy, below average academically and totally useless at sports.

Having been blessed with pitiful hand to eye co-ordination.

All of which made me an easy target for ridicule from the smarter more popular students.

Thankfully I wasn't alone though and soon befriended similar outcasts.

In my year was a mysterious misfit, who also didn't fit like me and my fellow weirdos.

What puzzled me though, was he never seemed to get any stick for being different, what passed for normal kids wanted to hang around with him and even the bullies gave him a wide berth.

This curious creature's name was Knobby and he was a Goth.

Tall, painfully thin with a pasty, vampiric complexion.

He wasn't especially good looking, dressed constantly in black with a shock of dyed hair to match and spoke with an effeminate lisp.

The Gothic musical sub-genre he represented was into had emerged after the death of Punk Rock, bands that had spearheaded the movement, Siouxsie and The Banshees, The Cure and Bauhaus their lyrics dealt in sinister subject matter coupled with sparse moody soundscapes and the subsequent fashion that complimented the music was just as dark.

Self-assured but far from arrogant Knobby didn't need to fall in line with any cliques, he was already part of a tribe and unique in school as the only one of his kind.

Still, this didn't explain how he'd escaped being bullied by daring to express his individuality.

How come, the whole school considered him as to be...well cool?

One afternoon, in the playground, I overheard a couple of girls talking about him in hushed awe and learnt his secret.

Knobby, was a musician and played the bass guitar in a band called, The Coughing Nails.

Dad told me that a bass was similar to a guitar but tuned lower and instead of having six, it only had four strings.

Which led me to assume bass must be a lot easier to play over guitar and it didn't matter if you were different as long as you played in a band you'd be universally accepted.

I shared one class with Knobby, woodwork.

Each week, I'd look for an opportunity to strike up a conversation with him not being outgoing, there never seemed to be a good opportunity and there never would be as he suddenly stopped showing up at school.

As to where he'd gone depended on who you asked.

One rumor was he'd been expelled after having a drug overdose in the girls changing room.

Another doing the rounds in the playground was he'd done a runner after knocking up a girl in the sixth form.

Then the third which was the most far-fetched of all but despite that, I desperately wanted to believe it was the truth.

Knobby's band had landed a record deal and he'd quit school to become a full-time rock star.

Woodley, UK 1980...

I'd discovered a love for music via the BBC's weekly run down of the Top 40 singles chart on Radio One and its TV counterpart on BBC One, Top of The Pops.

7pm every Thursday night I'd be glued to the box for the half hour show, one cold November evening a band called Adam & The Ants were performing.

They looked like a gang of cutthroat pirates.

The leader, Adam Ant wore a civil war infantry man's coat, leather trousers and had a white stripe painted across his face.

This was his war paint and Adam and his ant warriors meant business.

Their song "Ant Music" was a blend of seventies glam rock, sixties twangy guitar backed with a heavy tribal beat provided by the band's duo of drummers.

Saving up my pocket money for weeks to buy the seven-inch single, it was the first record I paid for with my own money and I played it over and over again on my cheap record player with a built-in speaker.

The song on the B side was a complete contrast, an up-tempo punk rock track "Fall in" it didn't have that many words but those it did, stuck in my brain,

"Ten, nine, eight, seven, six, five, four, three, two, one
You'd better listen to the ants now!" Adam sang.

My ears were now pricked up and I wanted to hear more.

A few months later, still a couple of years shy of the minimum age of to apply for a paper round, a family friend who knew the manager of a local newsagents Knights agreed to bend the rule and give me a week's trail.

Mr. Hart was a kind and fair first boss, he paid me off the books, I showed up on time and did as good a job as I could.

At the end of each week, I'd end up blowing most of my wages on 45's from the small record department in the back of the shop.

My pay ending up going right back where it had first come from, the cash register.

After earning a few extra quid, by filling in for when the other paperboys didn't show up, I purchased my first Album, the latest by Adam & The Ants

"Kings of The Wild Frontier"

The record contained twelve songs, including the single "Ant Music" there was a mixture of musical styles on the album, a homage to the Wild West, a creepy sounding song with terrifying lyrics about an imaginary invasion of killer ants and even a sea shanty sang by the whole band.

This was quite a lot for my 11-year-old brain to process, slowly I gradually picked up on the band's musical hallmarks.

Marco Pirroni's reverb soaked, cowboy sounding guitar for example, I loved the booming depth of it, he didn't play solos as such, instead he strung together memorable melodic passages that I could hum along to.

Spinning through the racks at Knights after making my deliveries one morning

I came across a cassette "Dirk Wears White Sox" the first album by Adam & The Ants, it had been reduced for clearance, I blew my weeks' pay on it and rushed home to listen.

Instantly, I was disappointed.

Aside from Adams vocals there was a different gang of Ants playing on the record and there was little that sounded like anything on Kings of The Wild Frontier

The songs were quirkier with lyrics about the assassination of John F Kennedy, the Egyptian queen, Cleopatra, and a real head scratcher called The Day I Met God which told the story of a chance meeting Adam had on his way back from Milan...in a van and being impressed by the size of the big man upstairs'...Knob!

Just one song on the album appealed to me, the opening track "Car-Trouble" as it had some decent drumming and a catchy chorus.

My cousin Michael also loved music and bought a lot of singles and whenever he purchased a subsequent album that contained the singles, he owned he'd give me his old 45's.

Thanks to his generosity my collection expanded rapidly,

Still, I craved more music, so he taught me how to record the weekly chart show on Radio 1,

Listening to the broadcast by his impressive boom box, his finger poised to release the pause button once the DJ had finished introducing and record a song he liked.

Using his method, I was able make a seamless mix tape of the songs I liked for free.

Having not seen my cousin in a while I was excited to share with him my newfound obsession with Adam and his Ants.

On my next visit, my Aunt Val stopped me before I could burst into his bedroom.

"Oh, don't go in there yet my boy, she smiled

He's in there with his friend, they are trying to work something out, best leave them to it for a little bit"

Music was coming from behind the bedroom door, only it didn't sound like they were listening to a record It was a lot louder plus there were no drums or vocals.

Suddenly the music stopped, and the door opened.

My cousin poked his head out, saw me and smiled.

"Hey Steve, we've just been jamming, would you like to have a listen?

My cousin picked up his brand-new bass and sat on the bed next to his friend who had a guitar.

They started to play,

I could hardly believe it when they broke into "Cartrouble" by Adam and The Ants.

I'd only ever seen bands playing live on TV before, this was a lot louder, far more powerful, and goddamn was it ever exciting.

Nodding my head in time to the rhythm, all I could think was...I really, really want to be able to do this.

It wasn't long before Michael was playing bass in a successful local band called "Hammerhead Sparks."

The five-piece played boisterous bluesy rock n roll.

They kitted themselves out in dark glasses and trilby hats like the Blues Brothers.

I got to see them play live in a local football stadium as one of the opening acts for the Australian band Mental as Anything who'd recently had a top ten hit with "Live It Up"

It was staggering how loud The Sparks were but also how clear, naturally I paid close attention to what Michael was playing.

Bulmershe School, Woodley UK, January 1986...

I'd just turned sixteen and was counting down my last few months of school life, with Nobby either in rehab, on the run from a shotgun or on tour in Japan, there was a new bassist on the school campus.

Only Matthew wasn't anything like Knobby, he was full of himself and a complete wanker

"He got a detention for playing U2's New Year's Day on the double bass in music class!

I heard a girl coo during registration, The school's head of music, Mr. Dobbs was notoriously hot headed and would dole out several detention slips per class for the most minor of offenses.

I'd received two detentions in the past, one for chewing gum in what he'd told me was an aggressive manner.

The second for accidentally hitting the wrong note on a glockenspiel.

On the slips reason for punishment section he'd written,

"With deliberate and disruptive intent Mr. Steele sabotaged an otherwise sublime group performance of London's Burning by playing a plethora of incorrect notes.

After his class one afternoon, I was scanning the pupil bulletin board when my attention was drawn to a poorly written note.

For Sale: Bass Guitar

Thirty Pounds

With the cash I'd received for my sixteenth birthday, I had enough to afford it.

Taking the note, I called the number scrawled on the note and was given the address.

Oh, deep joy... I thought when the door was answered by Matthew the Wanker.

"I just called about your bass" I told him, he frowned.

"I don't think I want to sell it anymore,"

He frowned and started to close the door...

"Hang on a minute" I said producing the note.

Look, it says here you want thirty quid for it"!

He told me someone had just offered him fifty for it, as it was rare and considered a collector's item.

"But Ive only got forty quid to my name" I protested.

And...it's my birthday."

Hoping it would make him drop the price.

"Well, if it really *is* your birthday...

He said sneakily.

It shouldn't be too hard to blag another tenner from some distant relative."

With a cruel grin he shut the door, leaving me to walk home, more upset than angry.

The bastard knew he had me on the hook.

After persuading my parents to lend me the extra money

I was back on his doorstep,

Matthew snatched my cash and told me he'd be right back.

A few minutes later he handed me a dusty, ugly looking instrument, along with a strap and a cable.

"Here you go, have fun"

I could hear him laughing as he slammed the door in my disappointed face.

The bass was made by a Japanese company, Kay who specialized in low budget lookalikes of more expensive models by manufacturers like Fender and Gibson

My new questionable pride and joy looked like a Gibson EB3 bass; a model made famous by Jack Bruce the bassist for Cream in the late 60's.

In 1986 however its look was well and truly out of fashion.

The instrument was not only ugly but as it was made mainly from mahogany it weighed a bloody ton.

Sitting on my bed, trying to push the strings against the finger board like Dad had shown me on his dusty banjo years ago was a lot more painful than I remembered.

The space between the strings and the neck/fingerboard was huge, I came to learn this was called the instruments, action.

Inside the neck was a metal truss rod which used with an Allen key to lower or heighten the strings, but the wooden neck had warped significantly over time, and it couldn't be adjusted to sit any lower.

What that Wanker, had called a *collector's item* was far from it and even worse, almost unplayable.

Not that I held out much hope, but perhaps it would sound ok when it was amplified.

Plugging the cable from the bass into my Hi-Fi's headphone socket I switched to auxiliary output, which in theory should amplify the bass via the speakers.

Adjusting the volume dial on the bass to what felt would be fairly quiet, I took a deep breath and hit the lowest and thickest string as hard as possible.

BWAAAAAAAANGGG!

The deafening deep dull boom gave way to a flapping sound as one of the speaker cones blew.

My first musical *performance* sounded nothing like a bass guitar at all, it was more akin to an elephant farting itself to death.

Determined, by hook or by crook to learn how to play the unwieldy thing, I bought an instructional book from the local music shop.

"How to Play the Bass Guitar" came packaged with a cassette of audio examples of the terminally dull exercises

The bloke on the cover holding a bass didn't accurately depict a rock star.

With sensible short hair, dressed in a conservative looking jumper, he looked like he sold double glazing.

On the back cover was a series of film strip shots of the Salesman accompanied with cartoon speech bubbles

In the first shot, he looked deep in concentration.the bubble read *You Listen...*

The second, he looked a little less uptight.

You understand...

In the last he sported an awful cheesy grin

You play!

Of course, it was never gonna be that easy.

It took me two weeks alone to figure out how to tune the bloody thing.

Then I spent even more time on a tedious chapter that dealt with "Digit Independence"

My fingers refused to work independently of each other and seemed to be fused together like a bear paw in a boxing glove.

After another month I could just about prize them apart, but the high action of the bass added to my difficulties.

All that the book had taught me so far was the bass or mine in particular was not fun to play at all.

The next chapter detailed how to play various scales, but they didn't sound musical, I wanted to learn something I'd heard on a record, just show me how to jam goddammit!

I must have driven Dad half mad with the non-musical elephant farts vibrating through the living room ceiling, he came into my bedroom and told me.

"You need to learn to play something musical"

He grabbed the bass and taught me my first riff,

The Peter Gunn theme by Duane Eddie which had originally been played on guitar but then, Dad wasn't a bassist.

After a week of me playing it.... loudly and terribly, he came back upstairs and finally taught me my first proper bass-line.

John McVie's classic bass hook from the coda to Fleetwood Mac's "The Chain" was far more complex, as it was played on two strings, it was hard enough managing just one, now I had another musical mountain to climb.

But Dad had faith.

"Now, son listen to your records, the radio, watch the music shows you like so much on TV and absorb as many different types of music as you can, he advised sagely.

Over time your ears will adjust, and you'll be able to pick up what the bass is playing.

My best friend during my last few years in school was Rick, three months older a few inches taller and slightly better looking than me.

The pair of us had been all over the shop with conflicting musical tastes ranging from pop to hi-hop, rap, and jazz funk.

Then in the spring of 1985, a guitar driven, psychedelic rock tune with a tongue twister of a title hit the Top Twenty of the UK singles chart.

The Cult's "She Sells Sanctuary" became a cross-over hit, even with the record buying public that didn't necessarily like rock music.

Both Rick and I loved it, you could dance and bang your head to it at the same time, the track galvanized our musical tastes, The Cult acting as ambassadors into our embracing the genre of Hard Rock as our preferred music genre.

After I'd been struggling with playing the bass for a few months Rick decided he wanted to have a bash at guitar.

Not that I'd inspired him, in his case the impetus came the waist down and via an advert in the back of one of my music magazines.

Underneath a picture of a perplexed looking bloke with a guitar, it listed the 10 reasons for playing in a band.

1: To Attract the Opposite Sex

2: To Attract the Opposite Sex

3: To Attract the Opposite Sex

As so forth until number ten...

10: Drinking and having a laugh down the pub with your band mates

"I'll have some of that!" he smiled assuming that if he took up the guitar, he'd automatically get laid...a shit load.

The pair of us were of the same mindset as most teenage lads when it came to girls.

Devising ways to attract them was frequently on my mind and it was never off Ricks.

Rick got his first guitar via mail order, it was a white Epiphone Flying V, a budget version of the Gibson model.

Unlike my unfashionably ugly plank, his six-string looked more like something an actual rock stars would play, albeit one on a shoestring

With the pair of us facing steep learning curves, we'd often argue over which songs we should learn.

My musical tastes had got really dark and well suited to the angry petulant teen I had become of late.

The gateway provided by The Cult had led me to explore their earlier material, which had shades of post punk goth this led to me getting deep into the genre especially the more successful bands like Siouxise & The Banshees and The Cure.

I started to dress all in black, dying my hair to match and adding a red stripe on the left-hand side.

Most of the goth bands songs featured bass as the lead instrument, like reggae.

My three most admired bassist's Steven Severin, Simon Gallup & Jamie Stewart all played a Music man Stingray Bass and used a Chorus pedal.

A modulation effect designed for use on guitar, but when employed on bass it gave the lower frequencies a metallic shimmering and sinister sound.

I bought myself a cheap off brand Chorus the poor quality and cheap circuits in the device generated a lot of white noise and the sound I got was sort of what I'd liked but with a loud hiss on-top like I'd left a blank tape playing at high volume.

Rick wasn't quite on the same dark wavelength as me, he tolerated some of it, but heard little in it he felt was worth learning rarely, if ever would you hear a blistering guitar solo in the gothic genre.

Led Zeppelin, Metallica, and early Ozzy Osbourne were his faves and in all of Rick's preferred bands, the six string was king.

In an issue of the NME, The New Musical Express was an article stating The Cult would be releasing a new album and going on tour the following spring.

We had to go I decided as neither of us had been to a proper rock n roll concert.

Taking a trip down to London the weekend the tickets went on sale, we queued up in the rain outside Hammersmith Odeon's Box office.

A month before the show, The Cult performed their new single live for the first time on the BBC2 music program "The Old Grey Whistle Test" the presenter introduced the band the camera panned across the studio, and I almost didn't recognize them.

The Cult had gotten a complete makeover, ditching their previous psychedelic rock attire, they had grown out their hair and were now decked out in denim and leather.

They looked like a bunch of greasy bikers.

The song, "Love Removal Machine" started with a stark three chord progression from guitarist Billy Duffy

The song had none of the swirling effected guitar tone of the band's previous album.

The creepy vocals, prominent bass lines and tribal drums of their previous two albums had also been jettisoned.

Almost everything I'd loved about the band sonically had been stripped away.

They now sounded like AC/DC or The Rolling Stones, no more gimmicks or frills just nasty rock n roll.

For months I'd obsessed over The Cult's "Dreamtime Live at The Lyceum" album on it bassist Jamie Stewart played a Music man Stingray Bass with a Chorus effect pedal and his nimble playing leapt out of the mix

Now, he was on telly looking like he hadn't had a bath in weeks, dressed head to toe in black leather playing a beaten-up old Fender Precision Bass, straight into an amp with no effects at all.

He's sold out, I thought, thrown his low-end lot in with all the bassists, that played a boring old Fender Basses.

Even when they played the first hit "She Sells Sanctuary" later in the show, it was a lot more rough and ready, and I was pissed off as they only played half of it and went into a cover of Steppenwolf's "Born to Be Wild."

Hammering the point home that they were now a very different band.

Once I'd got over the shock, The Cult's new sound grew on me and by the time the concert came around, I was fully onboard.

Boarding the bus with Rick from the town centre to Central London, we then took a tube to the Hammersmith Odeon

My first visit to what we'd soon come to know as The Rock N Roll temple, or good old "Hammy O" would be a pivotal one.

Opened in 1932 as an art deco cinema, it had been converted to a concert venue with a capacity of nearly three and a half thousand.

A myriad of legendary artists had performed there in the past, including The Beatles.

Dad had a framed ticket stub in the downstairs loo from when he saw them play there in late 1965,

His recollection of the experience wasn't of it being exactly life changing,

"I couldn't hear a bloody thing!" had been his one-line review.

This was likely due to the bands underpowered amplification being drowned out by the audience, the majority of which was made up of screaming teenage girls.

Twenty-two years later, on a mild spring Saturday evening we arrived at what would become my venue of choice.

The Marquee outside emblazoned with

The Cult Electric Tour March 12th, 13th 14th SOLD OUT

Underneath was a suggestion on how attendees might conduct themselves.

"Boogie Til You Blow Chunks!"

Did I really want to be rocked out to the point of vomiting?

Possibly, it put a smile on my face as we presented our tickets and were admitted through the lofty double doors.

The sights, smells and sounds that we found inside, were equally intimidating and exciting.

Our tickets were towards the middle of the upper balcony, heading upstairs to the circle bar, we ordered up a pair of pints, nearby a group of die-hard fans had gathered.

They were tall, dark, and gruesome dressed and cut from the same the blackened cloth as Knobby from back in school.

Standing in the shadows they nursed pints of Cider mixed with Blackcurrant juice, reeking of patchouli oil.

A few were complaining that the band had sold out to the man, altering their sound to be more commercial.

They'd forsaken their old sound ergo abandoned them, those that had made them a success in the first place.

Which made me wonder me why they had bothered paying to get in, if they only wanted to slag off the band

Not, that I really cared what the old guard thought, the band probably didn't either, having got made out like bandits with all three shows having sold out.

The support act was Crazyhead, a garage punk rock type combo, who'd recently had a hit on the independent charts with the brilliantly titled "What Makes You Think Your So Amazing Baby" they were entertaining. especially their bassist, a tubby lad by the name of "Porkbeast"

His heft didn't hinder his performance and he ran around the stage like a leather clad pig in dark glasses banging his afro like a maniac.

When at the last the lights went down for the main attraction, the volume, vibration, and roar of anticipation from the sold-out crowd was electrifying.

Multi-colored searchlights circled the venue, the sound of helicopters buzzed between the Massive PA speakers and Wagner's classical piece "Ride of The Valkyries" began.

Building to a its crescendo, the music suddenly was cut, replaced by a four count on the hi-hat sounded and the stage exploded into life.

Flash bulbs and a burst of pyrotechnics marked The Cults arrival and they launched into my favorite song "Nirvana."

The show was intoxicating, I found it mind-blowing simply being in the same building as the band.

The setlist, structure of the show and the crowd interaction was unlike anything, I'd ever experienced.

Before playing their latest fanbase polarizing single "Love Removal Machine" lead singer Ian Astbury addressed what the Older Goths had been bitching about back at the bar.

"You know, some people have said how we've gone all American, sold out and shit, he began.

I'd like to point out that this next song is the song that the BBC chart system put down because it was too heavy for the radio and got in the way of the commercial system."

What Astbury was ranting about wasn't true the single had entered the top 20 the week of release and then dropped like a stone.

This wasn't, however, due to some high up executive thinking the single's existence might spark some sort of countywide teen rebellion rather, the reason for it dropping chart positions was the fact most of the band's fanbase had bought the single during the first week of release.

Not that any of that mattered, not tonight anyway and his rap received a rapturous response.

The Cult's show concluded with a second encore which brought to mind Dad's Dusty old Banjo and its former owner's Band, The

Trogg's when the band performed a ramshackle cover of "Wild Thing."

Once the dry ice dissipated, the feedback faded, and the house lights came up.

I was left with a single purpose, my goal was to get good enough at this four-string malarkey to be able to play on the stage, any stage.

By the time Guns N Roses released their debut album that summer "Appetite for Destruction" I was fully devoted to my dream of becoming a proper grown-up musician.

They looked so cool and dangerous in the group photo on the back cover.

Duff McKagan their bassist looked especially badass, there was no way he had ever sold double glazing, fuck he'd probably overdosed twice this month already.

Duff bass was high in the mix on the record, this proved invaluable in my studies as I could hear every note, lick, and riff he was playing.

Every day for hours, I'd put the record on, pulling the needle back dropping it haphazardly back down in an attempt to master, a riff, then an entire song and eventually the whole damn record.

By a minor miracle Rick also loved the album

Along with Axl's edgy vocals, Izzy & Slash's Guitar were the stars of the album, I'd been hoping Rick would be as inspired by the album as me.

However, he flipped out when I brought it up.

"Oh, big whoop, he said sarcastically learnt how to play all the bass parts did you?

Well, it's only got four strings so it's a piece of piss for you" he complained,

Did you forget the band has two guitar players?

That WAY too much for me learn!"

"Well, what do you bloody want to play?" I snorted.

He wanted us to work on a Led Zeppelin song, oh bollocks, I thought and gulped at the prospect of learning anything by their bassist John Paul Jones.

His playing was way above and beyond my current level, matching Rick's bitchiness I argued that Jimmy Page's guitar parts were even more intricate than Izzy & Slash's combined.

After much sulking, not speaking to each other for a day or two, we made a compromise and agreed on a Zeppelin song we'd both learn.

The song was fairly simple by their standards, soon we realized it was too tricky to tackle the entire song and we scaled it back to just the verse section.

Sunday afternoon, we set up in my parent's double garage and played an excerpt from Led Zeppelin's "Dazed & Confused" the slow descending blues riff from the verse.

The same damn riff in a loop for... hours.

As we played, I felt lightheaded, a sense of elation.

I'd felt a similar sensation at The Cult show, only this was far more intense.

Eventually we noticed an intermittent pounding on one of the garage doors, Rick put down his guitar, he was smiling...

"There here... he said in the singsong fashion of that irritating blonde kid from the Poltergeist movies.

Just listen to them man, he grinned beating down the door they can't get enough,

Go ahead, open it up but you'd better brace yourself for a tidal wave of wall-to-wall women!"

Personally, I very much doubted that was about to happen, I took off my bass walked to the double doors and pulled one of them up.

Blinded momentarily by the sun, I squinted, our jamming had drawn a very small crowd but none of their number were lust crazed females.

Our very first audience was made up of four angry looking adults, a couple of kids on bikes and an annoying yapping Yorkshire Terrier

One of the dad's now marched towards me,

Clearly looking to give us a right bollocking.

"Would you turn that racket down before I'll call the police!" he ranted.

I grinned nervously, while Rick held up his hands and shrugged his shoulders.

"Sorry, man, I said nervously.

We thought the garage was soundproof."

"I wouldn't bloody well be standing here if it was now, would I?! He shot back.

"Look... I'm a patron of the arts, I realize you lads need to practice but you pair of jokers are taking the piss, playing the same crap over and over again, it's like listening to a broken record.

He took a breath, a deep sigh and asked us again more calmly.

So, please would you turn it down and while you're at it, how about you play something...

Fucking, anything else, instead?!"

STONERS, SHREDDERS & EGOS

WILLIAMSBURG BROOKLYN 2004

Entering the US with a Finance Visa stamp in my passport and without a return ticket had got me instantly red flagged as a person of interest.

I'd half expected JFK to have been notified ahead of my arrival and a fully gunned up swat team been on hand to apprehend me for being a no-good limey lone wolf terrorist.

They didn't go to that much trouble, instead I was detained and sent before a high ranking official.

Taking his time inspecting my passport, it looked as if he'd never seen such an endorsement before and so called a colleague over to confer.

The pair of them disappeared into an office with my passport, while I was instructed to wait on a wooden bench outside.

Eventually a third officer arrived to grill me.

She was stone faced in an immaculately pressed uniform around her waist was a belt with a gun, taser and handcuffs.

Her questions came fast giving me little time to respond.

Did I pack my bags myself?

Was I affiliated with any terrorist organizations?

The address at which I'll be living?

The date I plan on getting married?"

Who am I planning to marry?

What's their full name, date, and state of birth?

Answering each as politely as possible, nodding she turned my passport over in her hand but seemed hesitant to hand it back, now in my head my Paranoia took over...

Oh dear, you've blown it at the last second.

Tuck your tail between your legs and brace.

She's gonna kick your ass all the way back to Heathrow.

"You understand you cannot legally work with this type of Visa?

I nodded, she forced a smile and finally handed back my passport.

Welcome to the United States of America, Sir"

The visa was valid for ninety days and allowed me to do one thing, the right to marry an American Citizen.

Paranoia had me tying the knot within ten.

Now married, I could apply for a social security number, nt long after I was the bearer of a numbered card stamped "Valid for employment only with INS authorization."

Great, still I couldn't work legally and to do so, I needed to file for employment authorization

Two years post 9/11 in New York City, meant my application would be subject to extreme scrutiny and the longest processing times in the entire country.

The website listed an ETA of at least eight months.

Beyond being a domestic goddess and walking the dog to exhaustion, after a couple of months without a workday routine I starting to go a bit mental.

Until my inner teenager put an idiotic thought in my mind...

You don't need a job...

You play the bass!

Genius, all I had to do was hook up with an established and lucrative band in this brand-new town of mine.

Craigslist's classifieds musicians section seemed the best place to look.

"Dude, we totally rock with our cocks out" one ad proclaimed, I gave that one a miss,

Another was a smidgen more sensible.

"Totally committed to seeing this through to conclusion, have material, management and the talent to take it the whole way, the real question is are you good enough for us?"

Oh dear, instead I decided to draft my own "Rock Bass player available" posting.

Hoping it would generate a landslide of responses, ok, maybe a steady stream or at least a slow trickle.

Two days later, I'd received one reply, The responder came across as fairly sane in his emails and seemed keen to meet me, plus it was a good excuse for me to learn how to navigate the subway.

New York City's glorious alphabetical, numerical mass transit system owned by the city and leased to the NY Transit Authority.

A subsidiary of the Metro Transit Authority, the MTA, most locals thought of it as being short for More Trouble Ahead.

Being one of the most extensive systems in the world, with 468 stations, 656 miles of track that run 24/7 365 days a year and with a daily ridership measured in the millions,

Which can often cause delays due to the never specified Police Activity, mechanical failure or King Kong derailing a Queens bound N train in search of his bride.

When I first unfolded a map of the system, I couldn't imagine ever making any sense of it.

Ok, the 1 train that probably goes up and down First Avenue nope it was tunneled under Seventh.

The E Train then, well part of it served Eighth Avenue, which sort of made sense but then the A and C also ran on the same track.

Trains ran local or express confusingly but then a local service may not always make every stop.

The term Rush Hour did not apply to New York City, peak times were considered from 5am to 10am and 3pm to 8pm.

Being used to the London Underground and the sonorous announcement to *Mind the Gap* between platform and train, now I had a new monotonous mantra to heed.

Stand clear of the closing doors, please.

Never mind falling and getting fried by the third rail, just don't hold up the train, dammit!

The day of my first craigslist encounter a vicious thunderstorm had been battering the city the pour was still torrential when I set out, bass in a gig bag on my back and carrying my practice amp wrapped in plastic.

Almost slipping on my way down the stairs to the Lorimer Street subway stop, I double checked the route I'd written down against the system map on the wall.

To get to 62nd Street in New Utrecht, Brooklyn, first I had to take the L train under the East River to Union Square in lower Manhattan then change to a Coney Island bound N train which would take me back over the same river and into Brooklyn via the Manhattan Bridge

It made little to no sense to me, I walked to the platform, boarded a Manhattan bound L and glanced around pensively.

Feeling uneasy, soon I realized no-one was paying attention to me at all.

Just like the Gym, ignorance was key in this environment avoiding any form of bodily contact and adopting a stare of indifference.

A disheveled looking vagrant began to shuffle through the carriage, stopping in the middle of the car he told his questionable sob story.

"Ladies and Gentlemen, I'm sorry for the interruption, I recently lost my arm in a fire and I'm looking for any way you good people can help me out, I take coins, bills food stamps."

The beggar was clearly a junkie, and his speech did nothing to win over any of the riders hardened hearts.

Reaching the end of the carriage, he spun round before opening the door to the next car.

"I can't believe a single one of you motherfuckers won't even give me a fucking dime!"

A heavy-set guy in shades looked up from his seat.

"That's coz you got a bad attitude, so you don't get shit!"

The Junkie started screaming and dropping F-Bombs as he headed through the door to the next car while the dude in sunglasses exchanged a high five with his buddy.

Making the switch to an N train at Manhattan's Union Square Station was easy enough, until four stops later I realized I was heading in the wrong direction.

Back over the east river into Brooklyn after an hour the train broke cover.

Continuing above ground, each station it passed looked more derelict and desolate than the last.

Ninety minutes after setting out, I arrived at my drenched destination.

A good fifteen miles from home, the neighborhood of Bensonhurst was closer to the Atlantic Ocean than the East River.

Moderately miserable, I headed toward the address a ten-minute walk away.

Squelching onto the front step the rain miraculously ceased as I knocked on the front door.

Hey man, its Steve, right?" a

A waft of weed smoke escaped the open door, I nodded.

Jimmy shook my hand, ushered me in and offered me a hit, I declined.

He didn't seem that concerned with his appearance, unshaven, stained olive t-shirt stuffed with a pot belly and a shock of curly hair like an electrocuted Art Garfunkel.

"I'll be honest I'm not exactly sure what a bass player does, he said cheerfully, I just know that I need one."

After this statement of low-end ignorance, I was pretty sure this was gonna be a dead loss.

Having travelled so far, I decided not to leave right away.

Petting his stoned looking cat while he fumbled with a filthy archaic looking cassette player, he put on a Neil Young album whom I hated.

"Are you able to pick out what the bass is doing here?" He asked. I plugged in my bass and after a couple of minutes I'd sussed out the simple part and started playing along to the tape.

Initially he looked confused then started bopping his head in time with the rhythm and smiled,

"Cool man, clearly you know a lot more about the bass than me!"

I couldn't really dislike the guy, but this wasn't going to work at all, so I lied.

"Shit, what time is it?" I asked, he looked at the clock on the dusty VHS recorder in the corner.

"It's early, three forty-five, man."

"Sorry, I gotta split, I have another audition in the city at 5pm

"In Manhattan?"

he asked, I told him yes and he smiled a little sadly.

"Well, it's been great meeting you, just let me know if you want to jam again!"

One positive outcome to our meeting was Jimmy now knew what a bassist actually did.

Back at home, I reworded my ad in the hope of weeding out any more four string ignorant stoners.

Later that week I had another bite and took an N train again but to the other end of the line, Astoria, Queens.

The band known as Vodka Bath were suspect of my English accent and one of them remarked.

"I bet you're from Minnesota really."

I replied It was on loan from Spinal Tap.

The band seemed to like me until I accidentally let slip, I didn't have a job, after which their enthusiasm waned.

They had no interested in me trying to take a free ride on their coattails.

A day later, another response which sounded the most promising yet.

Setting up a meeting in a studio in Midtown Manhattan, I met Robby, a gifted but unrepentantly arrogant guitarist after shaking my hand and blowing his foppish hair out of his eyes he laid it out.

"I'm not so much part of the local music scene as such" he picked up his Gibson Les Paul and switched the Marshall stacks control to on.

"While I'm my own man, I'm really looking for this band to be a democracy."

The door opened and an auditioning drummer walked in, the three of us then spent fifteen minutes jamming Led Zeppelin's Trampled Underfoot, straight forward for both the drummer and me.

The jam acted more as a showcase for his soloing prowess, Robby had his head thrown back wailing away for most of it.

Maybe his angle was to ascertain if the drummer and I could hold it down, be content to take the back seat while he manned the wheel and took all the glory.

Afterward Robby laid it on even thicker.

"You know, I'm a face man and well known in this town, I just have to make one call and the band gets booked."

"CBGB's the Continental, Arlene's no shitty slots either, prime time Friday and Saturday nights

He didn't want this new project to be lumped into the local rock scene, he wanted the band to define a whole new genre, which was confusing to me, wasn't he also relying on his reputation within the scene to get it off the ground?

"One question you guys gotta ask yourselves if I did happen to offer you the spot, are you really ready for this?"

Continuing to blather on about how with the right dudes the band would blow up real fucking quick.

This desperate dude was stuck fast up his own arse which for me, was a dealbreaker.

The two of us were dismissed after half an hour as he still had a bunch of what he dubbed world class players to see.

Once-inside the elevator the drummer broke the awkward silence and read my mind.

"God, that guy was a real dick!"

Laughing I nodded my head in agreement.

"Take a solo" the guitarist said, assuming I'd misheard I asked over the microphone.

"Er...what?!"

Friday night, I'm auditioning in some cavernous nameless equipment rental warehouse on 34th and 10th Avenue and I'm WAY above my musical pay grade.

Spoonful was the name of the collective of top draw musicians.

The guitarist was Japanese, his guitar was named Mothra after the giant moth from the Godzilla flicks.

And he had just asked me to perform the one thing more boring than a drum solo.

I hoped he was joking dude, you want me to play a bloody bass solo, I thought, trust me, nobody wants to be subjected to that.

Having no clue what to do, I ignored his request, so he asked again,

Over the course of the past half hours jam, the drummer, keyboard player and Mr. Mothra had taken several each already.

His third request took on a more demanding tone.

"Just, take a damn solo man!"

Tacking together a few phrases that were sort of in the same key I delivered a poor forgery of a solo, which immediately caused the jam to fall apart, and I was gently dismissed.

While this process was increasingly frustrating at each, audition, try out or jam I usually learnt something.

Often it would be the type of people I didn't want to play with.

After a month I had become proficient at navigating the subway arriving at auditions with a non-committal attitude of lukewarm water, not appearing too keen nor too laid back.

"You got a great facility" that was I assumed a technical term for me being good with my hands.

The remark had been administered by a drumming Doctor in training who lived in a tiny dorm in Greenwich village.

He had a crappy sounding electronic drum kit set up in the kitchen, next to the oven.

We jammed on a couple of Rush songs but the prospect of having to find a singer and guitarist to round out a potential cover band didn't appeal to me.

My desire was to get onstage and at em as soon as possible, so I blew the guy off.

We rock like hell!

We are heavy as fuck, and you should be too!

We... are... "Monster-Christ!"

The ad and band name had made me laugh so I replied turned out they were even more ridiculous in person.

A duo of a guitarist and drummer ten years younger than me, who initially seemed a bit in awe of me, maybe I'd overdone it with the accent.

After a quick jam on a Metallica song, the drummer complimented me on my bass.

"Hey man, that bass is fucking cool.

"This old thing?" I asked him nonchalantly.

"Yeah...but, can you *TUNE* down that bass?"

I shrugged my shoulders at what was a pretty stupid question.

"Should the song require it...Yes"

I replied.

"Can you *SLAP* that bass?! he grinned.

"Well... I can, but only if it's really necessary"

I rationalized.

Cool man, but what I really wanna know is ...

can you MELT faces with that bass?"

Dio in Heaven, I thought,

How about I just play the bloody thing instead of weaponizing it!

Onto the next audition, which was in the same rehearsal complex, an hour later.

They were older than me and a little bit too much love, peace and understanding for my taste.

The band knew how to play but were frightfully dull and there was no chemistry.

The guitarist, contacted me months later, he was looking to put a new project together as the lineup I'd auditioned for had since fallen apart, let me guess, you want me to melt some faces, right?

Demon's & Debutants a duo made up of a singing drummer and fractious guitarist, they rehearsed next door to the local hell's angels chapter house.

Which was less than five minutes' walk from my front door, perfect, I had nothing to lose, not even a swipe of a Metro card.

Their material was diverse ranging from ballads to straight up Heavy Metal.

They were a mismatch, the drummer an uptight hipster with a huge Afro, the guitarist bald with a goatee looked like he'd just been released from San Quinten.

Jamming on some of their song's, one of which was oh so cleverly titled "I forgot to remember" soon it was apparent there was no chemistry they simply didn't like me, nor did I them.

Shredder is a term given to a particular subspecies of guitarist, who's main musical goal is to play as many notes as quickly as possible.

From a technical point of view those of this ilk are brilliant but frequently their bid to become the fastest six strings since Eddie Van Halen will cause them to neglect to inject any sense of melody or emotional feel into their playing approach.

To me when a shredder started to play a solo, they made a sound I imagined was a lot like a beehive getting struck by lightning.

It was inevitable, at some point I'd run into one of them.

I now had a standard question to ask at each audition, what was the band they/he/she is looking for in a bass player

This query I had just posed it to the Morgan Avenue Shredder.

Stroking his stubbled chin, he ran his fingers through his tight curly oiled hair.

Dressed in faded blue jeans with the waistband stationed halfway up his chest, unruly hair sprouting from his pristine white tea bag muscle shirt.

He began to answer.

"I want" he paused to wipe a speck of drool from his guitar which was hung on a strap so high it was closer to his chin than waist.

"I want YOU to lay down a rock-solid foundation while I take off fucking heads!"

Flicking on his Amp, he pointed at me to start playing as he unleashed a volley of unconnected phrases, notes, and licks with blistering velocity.

Soon, The Shredder was out of control, unstoppable in his need to exceed his personal speed limit.

Fifteen minutes had passed my fingers started to cramp and he had yet to throw out a single chord, riff, or melodic hook.

All flash, All speed and all the time.

He sought to satisfy only his own ego, eyes closed, head thrown back and mouth agape.

A sliver of drool began to roll down his chin as he reached a new level of self-gratification.

This was a fucking nightmare, surreptitiously I pulled the cable out of the Amp and made it look accidental.

The Shredder was so far gone, it took him a full minute to notice I was no longer playing.

"Oh, shit I was just starting to really cook, he gasped.

But, man, you had that low end down solid, brother."

Making some excuse or other about my apartment being on fire, I got me the hell of there.

I hoped he'd be the last of his kind I'd have to endure.

New York City, I had heard was suffering from a shortage of decent bassists, or was it a case of there were too many bands and a drought of decent ones worth my effort?

Now, I was about to really dredge the depths and truly hit Rock Bottom.

Bikini Bottom, in fact a quartet punk's now into their forties, with kids, mortgage and I assumed decent jobs.

Funny thing was they were all of them, still furious.

A cloud of toxic hostility smothered me, as I walked into their rehearsal room.

"Who the FUCK... are YOU?!" a red-faced angry hockey dad of a guitarist roared.

Calmly I told him, which did nothing to alleviate his anger.

"What. well, WHY are you here?!"

I am contemplating walking out, then the drummer I'd set the meeting up with walked into the room.

A tad less fractious, but equally red faced, he half assed an apology how he'd neglecting to tell the band I'd was auditioning tonight.

Now very uncomfortable and extremely pissed off, I dutifully played a few of their songs with them, as a professional courtesy

Ten minutes, four simplistic, rage filled rants later, I half thanked the bitchy bastards for the opportunity, wished them the best of luck and could they point me in the direction of nearest subway stop.

The room went silent, until the now beyond furious drummer, snarled.

"No fucking idea, we all drove here"

SUICIDAL STUPIDITY &
TWENTY-EIGHT STRINGS

WOODLEY UK 1986

After leaving secondary school, for six weeks Rick and I did a lot of next to nothing.

While I was still getting up each day for my paper round the idea of having to get a full-time job was, frankly, terrifying.

We weren't desirable employees as school leavers with no work experience and most of the situations vacant at the local Job Center were for YTS placements.

The Youth Training Scheme was a government subsidized program which paid half of a trainee's salary while their employer made up the difference the idea being to encourage more companies to take on school leavers.

YTS schemes ran for two years after which your employer could decide to take you on as a fully paid worker or in many cases having to shell out significantly more for your services meant you'd receive a P45 and a letter of reference for your next employer.

After a few fruitless trips a week to the Job Center, we'd hang around Woodford Park supping from a four pack of Fosters or if we had enough dosh go halves on a small bottle of rock n roll mouthwash Jack Daniels.

Most days we'd have no money at all and would waste our time walking, over to the woods, around south lake or up to Warren Road.

At the end of the leafy street stood Suicide Bridge crossing the railway sixty feet below that ran through the mile long Sonning Cutting

That afternoon Rick soon tired of our usual time suck of watching the trains pass beneath.

"I'm sick of doing fuck all...

He sighed his gaze wandering to the fence at the far side of the bridge.

"Hang on... I've got an idea."

Rick had spotted a small hole in the fence on and after some casual vandalism the pair of us had wrenched it into a gap large enough to squeeze through.

We beat a path through the wood, clambered down the embankment and stood beside the first of the four tracks.

After watching a few trains go by Rick decided that this was also pretty fucking boring.

Let's run to the other side" he suggested.

Rather reluctantly, I started to step onto the track until he stopped me.

"Nah, he smiled.

Now that...

Would be way too easy."

Rick wanted to wait until a train was within sight.

This act of suicidal stupidity began with listening for a hiss to emanate from the rails, followed by a faint horn in the distance and finally the growing vibration of the track as the train came into view.

"Right... marks" Rick ordered.

I braced, feeling the growing vibration of the track as the dirty yellow nose of the express appeared in the distance.

"Fucking GO!" he shouted,

We gave it toes legging it as fast as we could across the tracks, making it to the far side in time to wave as the train blasted by.

This went well for a while; a train would enter the cutting bound for Reading we'd race to the right-hand side.

Then when a London bound one came into view, we'd leg it back.

The arrogance and complacency of youth soon set in and for our next death wish dash in front of a Reading bound train we forgot to look in both directions.

Reaching the other side, we waved like idiots while the train zoomed by on the far track, seconds later it vanished behind a fast-moving freight train on the track mere feet in front of us.

"Fucking Shit!" Rick screamed.

My heart racing, it rattled past, blasting its horn multiple times, calling us out for being a pair of total dipshits.

Thankful to be able to breathe several sighs of relief, in shock I gazed at Rick whose mouth was wide.

"Fuck me...he gasped.

Maybe... he said soberly we should knock this shit on the head.

With no trains in sight, we crossed, climbed the bank, and squeezed back through the fence.

After dusting ourselves down we started to head home.

However, our suicidal stupidity hadn't gone unnoticed and waiting for us on the other side of the bridge.

Was an idling cop car.

"Afternoon gentlemen, would you mind telling me exactly what you've have been up to down there?"

Turned out, the Pigs had collared us by accident.

They were casing the bridge in response to a call that a gang of kids had been lobbing bricks onto the passing trains.

Suicide Bridge was one of four crossings that spanned the cutting, this was the first one they'd checked and after finding no brick dust on either of us they let us go with a verbal clip round the ear.

Our reckless summer was about to be over when we both got accepted for employment as Postal Cadets for The Royal Mail.

Unlike other employers the Post Office paid a lot more for YTS trainees at the end of the two-year program it was pretty much guaranteed you'd get taken on.

As part of a new batch of trainees we were given the same start date, we were assigned to the early shift from 6am to 1pm.

With no intention of curtailing our evening activities and with Red Bull years from being created we made do with a potent blend of instant coffee mixed with a can of Dr Pepper to be alert enough for the workday.

After an average of four hours shut eye, the alarm would blast through my brain at 4:30am.

Heading out in the dark on my bike, I'd pedal frantically down Fairwater Drive to Rick's Dad's house on Oak Way.

Rick was running late and frequently not even awake, my knocking would rouse his grumpy father who'd drag his royal tardiness out of bed.

Eventually he would emerge in a foul mood, fetch his bike and our laborious commute began.

Through the creepy echoing underpass beneath the M4 Motorway and the Railway, up onto Henley Wood Road past my old house then left onto the Wokingham Road.

Next, was an incredibly boring five miles in a straight line.

Half an hour later we pedaled into a dark deserted industrial estate at the far end looming from the fog and eerily floodlit stood our final destination.

The Love-Rock Road Sorting Office.

Racing to our desks, we sorted the overnight mail as swiftly as possible bundled and packed our bags and awaited the cut off time of six thirty when we could leave for delivery.

Three miles west of Love-Rock was Fords Farm a new housing development, its entire area was broken up into postal routes for us cadets.

Residents would often get their mail mis-delivered, damaged, or not get any at all.

Unaware their shiny new neighborhood was being serviced by a gang of fresh-faced irresponsible idiots

The clock struck six thirty and the mass exodus began.

Along with our fellow trainees we'd get a lift to the Farm from Barney a former cadet who'd just turned eighteen.

That wasn't his real name, it was derived from rhyming slang, Barney Rubble denoting Trouble.

He'd gotten named it as he was always in it with the supervisor.

At seventeen Barney had applied to become a driver as the Job provided lessons and a road test for free during working hours

Failing his test six times he was set to make it seven, until the examiner took pity on him.

He was likely sick of the sight of him, and passed him regardless, unleashing a total fucking maniac upon the town's unsuspecting motorists.

Driving was a riot to Barney and paying any attention to any signage or adhering to posted speed limits was for pricks and squares.

His recklessness behind the wheel hadn't been considered when he'd been assigned the position of cadet transport specialist and responsible of driving us safely out to our routes in a designated minibus.

After dropping us off he'd head back to base and switch to sherpa van to make his parcel deliveries.

Once he'd finished, Barney would drive back to The Farm.

Making a few circuits of the main road in search of any cadets that had finished their routes.

Personnel were not permitted to hitch a ride in the back of a parcel van, which was no concern to Barney, his rationale for bending the rule was flawless...

"No windows in the back of a sherpa is there, so... who the fucks gonna know?

At six thirty we piled into the minibus, Barney jumped in roared off up Portman Road, tires squealing as he navigated the roundabouts as fast as he dared.

Ten minutes later, we were nearing our drop off point, but he didn't slow down and skidded into a sharp right turn onto Carters Rise, despite bracing ourselves we were still thrown violently from our seats, which Barney found hilarious.

Posties and cadets got to ride the towns buses for free but that was no fun, the ride took half an hour from the farm to the nearest stop on Oxford Road, which was a ten-minute walk from the sorting office,

Once I finished making my delivery how I got back was a matter of who showed up first.

The chuckle bus or Batshit Barney.

Today looked like it was a bust as I stood by the Bus stop, and it appeared in the distance.

The bus was less than a hundred feet away when Barney's Van overtook it at high speed, narrowly avoiding a head on with an approaching car and squealed to a halt alongside me.

Squeezing into the back with Rick and two other Cadets. Barney blasted off out of the estate, gunned it to the main Road, grinding the gears as the transmission noisily protested his haphazard technique.

Next was the steep incline of Cockney Hill, Barney's fave gag was to floor it to the top, switch off the ignition then freewheel down the other side.

Playing a personal game of chicken, he'd leave it until the last second before re-starting the engine and avoid sailing through the intersection to an inevitable collision.

Halfway up the hill, I noticed a chink of daylight appearing between the back doors.

Soon it became a crack, then one door swung ajar, temporarily blinding us with daylight.

The steep incline coupled with Barney's breakneck pace had us sliding in a screaming pile towards the open door and certain death upon the black top.

Rick grabbed the doors interior handle, but it wouldn't budge, all his effort did was cause the other door to fly open.

The last thing Barney would have thought to do was ensure both back doors were properly secured.

Thanks a lot man, I mused thinking at least one of us is about to get a tarmac fascial.

Our screaming had gotten his attention he banged on the divider, and I heard his muffled shouting.

"The fucks going on back there, Barney yelled.

You sad sacks scared of a little speed?"

Cresting the summit, we coasted over the top as we sailed silently down the other side, we were now able to pull the doors closed.

Five minutes later, Barney skidded to a halt at Love-Rock swerving into a huge puddle plastering the wall with mud.

Once he threw the back doors back open, he found four shivering, scared looking boys.

"Look at you sorry fucks, he laughed, I floors it and you pansies shit yourselves"

Luckily not everyone in the cadet community was as mental as Barney and over time we even discovered a few fellow members of our Rock N Roll tribe.

I met Sean in the canteen one morning, he sat my table after he told me he liked my shirt pointing out the Cult logo under my uniform jacket.

He dug rock, Kiss especially and played guitar.

"I've got a sunburst Epiphone Les Paul, couple of Boss Effect Pedals, that I run through a Marshall Stack."

He boasted.

It took me a few seconds to grasp the sheer volume what he'd just said.

"What the, you've got a Marshall?! " I blurted out.

Sean nodded slowly with a cocky grin.

Bloody hell, I thought, this dude is one serious heavy hitter,

Sean kept up this pretense that he was until a few weeks later when invited me over to his place after work.

There he revealed his "Stack" made by Marshall and almost identical to the Industry Standard 100-watt version that graced stages and had given tinnitus to millions the world over.

Only Sean's was the pint-sized practice version that belted out just 12 watts.

"What the fuck is this training wheel shit?" I was moved to ask Sean burst out laughing having successfully had me thinking he was a big shot for over a month.

During a weeklong course in Introductory word-processing that the Job had us take, which was a flowery way of saying,

We are going to teach you to type using two hands.

Rick and I met Sean's friends, Blackwell, and Bob.

The pair also played guitar and were big into Thrash metal, that was cool as I'd already dipped my toes into its visceral waters and owned albums by Metallica & Overkill

All three were fans of Slayer and the trio were going to see their London show that night.

"Man, it's gonna be EVIL!" Bob bugged his eyes like Igor's in Young Frankenstein.

He speculated that the show at Hammersmith Odeon was going to be so brutal and violent that they may just get themselves deceased in the mosh pit,

"You never know man, Blackwell added.

Slayer have snuffed chickens and goats onstage before, tonight's their only UK show, maybe they'll make a human sacrifice!

This all sounded utterly terrifying, well it would have been if a word of it had been true.

The band's devil worshipping Image was a front, a darker shade of Window dressing, the band weren't practicing satanist rather four fairly levelheaded laid-back Californians.

The day done, we bid them farewell and hoped they enjoyed their inevitable, gruesome demises.

Tonight, Rick and I had our own gig to attend at Reading's Majestic Nightclub.

Zodiac Mindwarp & The Love Reaction a gang of crazy looking bikers that were pedaling a similar form of Biker rock that The Cult had been of late,

Id bought tickets to the show on the strength of one song "Prime Mover" which was pretty good and other than that I knew nothing more about the band other than vocalist Zody had a scruffy beard and often wore an army helmet.

We had been waiting for ages in the venue and I was bored beyond belief when the lights finally went down, and dry ice filled the stage.

The stinky mist flowed into the audience, so thick that the band that took to the stage arrived as silhouettes.

A minute into the first song, I was confused, this sounded nothing like the Prime Mover, the thick, fake fog slowly dispersed to reveal a five-piece band dressed for the wild west.

Duster coats, cowboy hats all the entire band were doused in flour.

Who were these jokers? I thought, it looked like someone had dug them up from the Graveyard behind the club.

The lead singer was wearing a hat and sporting a beard, but this was not Zodiac this was spaghetti metal, good time goth rockers Fields of The Nephilim and soon enough I found their bass heavy creepy tunes appealing.

Zody and his greasy gang of cohorts finally took to the stage after Midnight, bludgeoning the crowd with the riff hammer of the "High Priest of Love."

I recall little else as I was right next to the PA's bass bin, being squashed into the guard rail and looking up the bassist, Trash D Garbage's beer gut.

The following morning Sean and company had survived the Slayer show but all three were suffering extreme, self-inflicted pain.

Hungover with chronic cases of Whiplash, or total neck fuck as Bob branded it brought on by ninety minutes of synchronized, relentless head banging.

My neck was fine, but I couldn't hear out of my right ear, I'd have to wait a couple more days before it returned.

All week I'd been nagging the trio to come Jam with us, Sean kept telling me how he was about to join a band tied up trying to learn their material,

Today probably as they were in so much pain and wanting me to just shut the fuck up, the three of them agreed and we set a date for the following week.

Early on a rainy Wednesday afternoon, the house was ours, my folks wouldn't be back for a couple of hours, taking over the living room we set up our amps and guitars.

Assigning myself as Archivist, I set up a mic, tape deck and two fresh TDK blank cassettes to document the beautiful noise we were about to create.

First, a quick intro "Greetings Planet Earth, I said into the mic, what you have just uncovered was rock history in the making, I give you the birth of the almighty, Blitzspear!"

My first ever band we had a name but no drummer or a lead singer and between the five of us we had twenty-eight strings.

Within five minutes both Rick and Blackwell were arguing as they both wanted to play lead.

Bob was happy doling out a steady rhythm guitar while Sean ignored everyone, he was his own little world.

Over the weekend, he'd renounced his love for Slayer, thrash metal in general and all that bubble gum Kiss shit.

Today the heavy metal turncoat was wearing a cheap cowboy hat and had a blues slide fixed to his finger

He was now all about the southern rock.

Jamming parts of Metallica and Zeppelin songs we would stop once we exhausted our knowledge of the song.

Sean didn't so much play with us, he played whatever the hell he wanted his bottleneck drowning out what most of us were playing.

He didn't care if he was in the same key, his eyes closed, head looking heavenward and slip sliding the fuck away.

Then, Bob abruptly threw down his guitar.

"Fuck this, bullshit" he shouted.

"I fucking quit!

A dozy looking Sean now opened his eyes and asked.

"Er...why?"

No, this can't be happening, I thought, the band was less than an hour old and Bob already wanted out.

He was pissed off as he'd hardly had a chance to play as he didn't know any of the songs we'd been jamming.

"You're a bunch of selfish, elitist arseholes" he complained.

"Alright then" I suggested.

"How about you play us a song you do know?"

Bob picked out the intro to AC/DC's "Hells Bells" which of course we didn't

"I fucking rest my case" he bitched.

Sean broke the tension by playing the intro to "Sweet Home Alabama."

Three simple chords, D, C and G.

Bob knew these and happily strummed along until Scott hit a section beyond his knowledge and he threw another tantrum.

In the space of a single afternoon, my first band had formed, fallen out and spilt up.

The mighty Blitzspear, with its four man twenty eight string axe attack was also its highly strung downfall.

LIGHTS, CAMERA, ASSHOLES!

SOHO NYC 2004

The chances of me landing a lucrative spot in a successful band was looking like a non-starter.

Seriously disillusioned and in dire need of a routine, I reached out to a friend who was also like me, a permanent US Resident.

She suggested I try filling my time with volunteer work and put me in contact with a production office in Soho that may be able to offer me some.

After setting up an interview, I took the elevated J train into the city, over the Williamsburg Bridge to Canal Street, after exiting the station I immediately got lost in Chinatown.

A strange, unique neighborhood and one I'd only found myself in once before, with strange stores and tanks of live toads, lobsters and other deep-sea frights lining the streets.

After calling the office number several times, the defeatist in me told my contact.

"It's no good, I'm still lost,

I don't think this in gonna work."

She told me to relax, take a deep breath and simply walk two blocks north.

The companies' offices were housed on the fifth floor of a narrow building on a cobblestone street,

Kathy, the volunteer manager met me at the elevator, she broke the ice by making fun of my accent and my directional difficulties.

Skinny with short dark hair a few years older than me she was originally from New Orleans and swore like a sailor.

My interview was more a getting to know you chat, I was offered me the position on the spot and set my first task, drafting an email to recruit more volunteers from the companies database.

Film industry working practices, I was soon to find were very different from what I'd been used to.

People usually skipped lunch or stayed late until a project was completed instead of picking it up the next day.

Not getting paid was a bit of a head fuck at first but, at least I now had a weekday routine and soon would be able to add production assistant to my CV.

The office was in prep mode for an annual film festival, for which they handled the big-ticket events, red carpet movie premieres and award shows.

The festival was now in its third year and staged in and around Lower Manhattan

My first assignment was to research movies set for release over the the next year and type up proposals on how to present the premier in an eye catching way that tied in to the look, message or vibe of the film.

For The Aviator a stylized bio pic starring Leonardo DeCaprio as Inventor Howard Hughes, my outline was to stage the premier in the museum that exhibited the Spruce Goose, the enormous flying boat Hughes had designed.

Piece of piss I thought, it's in a huge hanger, which could easily double as a cinema.

Roll out some red carpet, set up a couple hundred chairs and project the flick onto one of the vast walls, Job done.

Kathy thought it was great idea until I mentioned the museum was in Oregon, as a location that wasn't gonna fly.

Bollocks... on to the next, then.

Finding an authentic looking Castle for the premier of action horror flick, Van Helsing within spitting distance of Hugh Jackman's Hollywood Mansion.

In the weeks that followed, the place soon became a madhouse with the number of staff in the office doubling

With all desks and chairs taken the overflow of employees spilled into the entrance hallway.

Everyone was dealing with some sort of world ending crisis, yelling into cell phones, or hammering away frantically on laptops.

"What fresh hell is this?" I had asked Kathy referring to the sudden and ongoing deluge of extra staff.

She explained the permanent staff were always augmented by freelancers and temps as it got closer to the Film Festival.

"Now, let me ask *You* a question" She grinned,

How, many people do you think in here right now are not getting paid a single fucking dime?"

Looking around the space, I took a quick head count of twenty.

"Including my exploited ass, maybe... four?"

"Oh, you suck she laughed, Including the freelancers in the hallway, try thirteen!"

My experiences so far within the music field paled compared to utter lunatics, I'd was going to be dealing with in the film industry.

Diva like temper tantrums, screaming matches, borderline physical altercations were all tolerated.

A toxic, hostile working environment was just par for the course in the Movie Business.

Kathy had long since learnt to float above it and told me sarcastically that...

"You see, he, she or non-binary is an artist they have to feel free enough to express themselves with no limitations, in order for them, to share their genius artistry with the world"

Learning to not take anything personal at all was key,

I still had to bite my lip and hold my tongue multiple times a day, finding it hard to believe how much abuse the floating staff would put up with.

But then of course they all had, an idea for a movie, an outline, or a script they were dying to get into the right hands

As Prep for the festival ramped up, I was given assignments with different members of the permanent staff, such as the event producers, Joel and Kyle who were funny guys but prone to flipping out.

Above their desk was a Mission board, scrawled in black, block capitals was a reminder to powder their noses...

GET DRUGZ!!

One afternoon, out on the fire-escape which was ironically the designated Smoker's corner Kyle mentioned that he and Joel may have to borrow me soon for a new assignment

"You're a bassist, right?" he asked, I nodded.

Cool, man you know Joel both play, our little musical group is called Julius Seizure and we could use a good bassist"

Bloody hell what a rubbish name I thought.

Sounds interesting" I fibbed.

Kyle smiled.

"Do you slap that bass, man?"

Fuck, here we go again, I thought and began to cringe.

The next day, they gave me my next assignment I was to curate the clips for the awards show, the glitzy closing event of the festival.

First, locate the media be it VHS, DVD, or some weird obscure format, at a film library downtown.

The festival being an international event, many of the films weren't in English and most didn't have subtitles.

Going from a list that were up for nomination, I'd watch the first twenty minutes and pick two short clips for potential inclusion.

Joel had given me an outline on how to approach such a prestigious task.

"Your mandate is to capture in thirty seconds or even less, the very essence and scope of vision that the filmmaker is looking to convey."

Steady on son, I imagined the cocaine was pretty banging that afternoon.

Problems soon arose, the library didn't have a copy of half the flicks on my list I was told by the staff there was usually three copies before a film went to duplication and distribution, a work print, final cut and the directors' personal copy."

Next step get hold of the director or preferably their English speaking assistant, tell them their film was under consideration and no I wasn't just trying to steal a copy of their precious movie.

Should I convince them to part with their precious art, then pretty please could you FedEx us a copy?

A fortnight before the festival my work rate increased, Now I was also having to interview prospective volunteers, sometimes two at a time, in the entrance hallway by the elevator.

Kathy ensured I got a few perks, tickets to previews of Broadway plays a few movie passes and upgraded my lanyard to give me access to the free catering once the festival was in full swing.

A month later, its Saturday evening and the star-studded awards show is just twenty-four hours away and it seems everything planned for months in minute detail is being changed at the last minute.

Kyle had got a tipoff that a documentary on New York's early punk movement had won best doc.

The library didn't have a copy, my messages to the director's office hadn't been returned and we needed a copy of the flick, like fucking yesterday.

Picking up his Nextel, he soon became a trifle miffed by what the person on the other end had to say.

"What the actual fuck, let me get this clear maybe I'm a bit of a fucking idiot..because,

I can't quite believe what you are telling me.

Briefly taking the device away from his ear he mouthed to me...

Motherfuckers!

"So, the fucking director brought one, fucking copy which is tied up right now at a public fucking screening?!"

Snapping the phone shut, he composed himself and went into fireman mode.

As Event Producer, he'd mentioned to me several times that all he really did was to put out fires, this being a five alarm one.

He put his feet on his desk and laid out his plan.

"Ok, Kill Your Idols has won, best documentary, I need a thirty second clip of it within the next hour, the screening finishes at Stuyvesant High School in ten minutes, get down sharpish ask for Tony, he'll give you the copy.

He paused to finish his can of Red Bull,

"Bring it to the HD truck outside the Conference center, we'll duplicate it, I'll have someone take the original back to the director and send you to the Editing Suite up on Sixth Avenue with the copy.

Twenty minutes later, I arrived at the screening only to be detained by security, as it was in fact an industry only affair.

I called Kyle, who then asked me to put Security on.

"Stop fucking around with my PA!"

Kyle's disembodied voice screamed from the speaker.

Now, get me the mother fucking director right fucking now!"

Five minutes later, the auteur appeared carrying a leather bag.

"Name he asked, condescendingly.

And who do you work for."

Then he called Kyle back to confirm

Handing me the bag he snarled

"You've got it for fifteen minutes."

Sprinting the short distance to where the truck was parked, Kyle was outside smoking, pointing at me he yelled "You are a fucking Monster!"

He opened the door and followed me inside.

Snatching the tape, the HD director said "Lemme see that, oh great, it's a shitty format, she complained.

Going to be tricky upscaling this to look half decent."

Slotting it into one of the duplicators she copied the first twenty minutes of the flick on high speed.

Up on Sixth Avenue in the Editing Suite, I was seriously impressed with the way the editor and her assistant cut, cross faded and spliced the clips for the award show into a seamless reel to play in-between the presenters handing out the trophies.

Out of my list of suggested clips I'd spent weeks curating, only ONE had made the final cut.

A frustrating fact, anything I did was double checked and if necessary, re-done by other unpaid help,

Rubbing my eyes, I went over my notes and cheat sheets to see if there was anything else I had to do.

On a dog-eared sheet of paper, I had the contact info for presenters, managers, and agents.

Some of the talent, preferred to go it alone and the list contact a handful of direct numbers, it was cool to have Christopher Walken's cell phone on the list, but his agent had called earlier to cancel his appearance.

It was now 4am, Kyle and Joel were still supervising the editing process in the suite, Joel told me he could send out for coffee or even better he had some "Enhancements" about his person if I needed any.

Declining his offer, I curled up on a couch in a conference room to catch a couple of hours kip.

Sunday, 7:00am and I was in a yellow cab heading back downtown, I've changed into a black suit for the evening's grand affair.

My mission to get to an art gallery downtown, several pieces were being displayed in the green room at the show, as well as a gang of volunteers I'd need assistance from the festival's drivers, Tony, and Ron.

Tony's last name was Lobo, so everyone called him The Wolf.

Unlike most of us, they were paid a salary and a pair of total lunatics.

Thinking their all-access passes gave them carte blanche to race their truck around Manhattan, jump red lights and park anywhere they wanted, all in the name of entertainment.

Word would get around the office of their capers,

A week ago, The Wolf had been detained by the NYPD after he decided to block a busy intersection with his carefree parking and neglected to display his Industry Pass on the dashboard.

He'd told the cops he was Robert di Niro's personal assistant and if they didn't take off these cuffs, he'd be forced to call his boss, who would then have the entire precinct fired.

Kyle had to call the captain to put out this particular fire, the company paid the ticket, and The Wolf was let loose with a stern warning.

My Nextel chirped in reply.

"YO" The Wolf boomed in a gravel filled baritone.

Telling him who I was and confirming where we would meet to pick up the artwork, He was already there when I arrived,

He certainly lived up to his nickname, with prominent incisors and a lupine grin.

He stood a towering six foot eight, his height enhanced by and impressive Elvis type quiff.

My team of volunteers wrapped the fine art in bubble wrap and loaded them into the back of the truck.

The Wolf only had to transport the pieces just over a mile and assured me they would get there in one piece, due to road closures his only route would be to go a couple of blocks across town and then down the West Side Highway.

As his battered truck roared off up the street, I imagined him running a red taking a hard left, the back doors flying open and a million dollars' worth of artwork colliding with three lanes of speeding traffic.

But the pricy cargo arrived intact.

Then I was off on another mission of mercy with another volunteer, the show's script had been in last minute re-writes and now needed to be photocopied back at the office.

My Nextel would not shut up.

"Any word on who's got the script?

"Who last had it?

"Go, for Steve, ETA on the script?

"How long for the script?"

"Dress rehearsal, three minutes, script now please!

This was seriously pissing me off, if they needed it so bloody fast why hadn't they just sent the Wolf?

Three copies done, dusted and stapled, I tucked it under my arm and ran.

A big no no, Kathy told me after I'd delivered it and caught my breath,

"You never run in this Industry, feel free to panic frequently but never, ever show it."

An hour before Showtime I took on the job of an usher to guide the actors along the red carpet to the press and photo corridor.

Everyone on staff was under the threat of instant dismissal should we interact with the talent beyond a clipped "this way please."

Yes, most of them their famous people were shorter than I imagined, and while the sneering Bill Paxton was a bit of a dust mite, his grin was borderline demonic.

Sarah Jessica Parker was minuscule, very sweet and broke protocol by saying hello.

Will Smith was way taller than I'd been expecting as was the stunning Sigourney Weaver, who didn't walk, she glided past me, shiny and regal like the Chrysler building only with more curves.

The man who had started the whole damn film festival in the first place arrived fashionably late, just a few minutes before the curtain was due to go up.

Like most of the celebrities tonight, he didn't pull up in an audacious stretch limo arriving instead in a nondescript town car.

For weeks I'd been warned repeatedly by numerous staff that should our paths cross, to not even entertain any thought of making eye contact with him.

Do not speak, unless he addresses you directly which of course is not gonna happen.

Now, as his taxi driver opened the rear door, from the corner of my eye the outline of a bona-fide movie star emerged.

Frantically, I told myself...

Don't look, just DON'T look at him!

I was weak and unable to resist taking just a quick peek.

My eyes briefly beheld Robert DeNiro who rewarded my reckless curiosity by fixing me with a thousand-yard stare.

He was swiftly whisked into the auditorium by two security guards as I resisted the urge to shout after him...

"You looking at me, You looking at ME?!"

All celebs accounted for I next headed backstage to meet with the rest of the production team.

Three of us were assigned the simple task of manning the curtain.

Drawing it back when the celebrity presenters left the stage and directing them back to the green room.

Most of the celebs were far too aloof and didn't even acknowledge me or any of my fellow unpaid help.

Then came the category that featured the sole clip, I'd curated, which was supposed to have been presented by Christopher Walken.

I'd been disappointed he had cancelled until his last-minute replacement, one of my favourite comedians, Eddie Izzard walked out.

Which gave me a brief, proud moment that the last six weeks of working for free almost worth it.

On the podium Izzard started ad- libbing going off on a tangent about... A curtain.

"If I may draw your attention, Ladies and Gentlemen and yes indeed that pun was intended to this imposing curtain to my right which is to your left of the stage.

The material used in its manufacture is so dense and cumbersome, that it takes, not one, ladies and gentlemen but three...

Yes, three people all dressed in black to pull that big red bastard back!"

I grinned; it was nice to finally be publicly acknowledged.

Eddie came offstage, paused briefly to admire the curtain smiled at me and in a mock panic asked.

"Which way, which way do I go?!"

We shared a laugh as I gestured towards the green room with a theatrical bow.

With the show over, it was onto one last event, the afterparty, where I was planned on taking take full advantage of the top shelf catering and booze.

Kyle was at the bar when I walked in and already well oiled.

"You...are a fucking rock-star!" he slurred.

I told him If he should pay me like one and buy me a case of Jack Daniels, he said he'd have to owe me and handed me his half-finished glass of red wine and staggered away.

Many wines later I sat outside on the steps in the cool night air enjoying a cigarette.

Kathy was already outside talking to someone whom she introduced as a photographer for Rolling Stone.

Tipsy, and exhausted, I shook her hand.

"Pleased to meet you, I said, belligerently.

Sorry to say, I've never heard of you"

She told me how she liked my washed-up Gary Oldman look; I couldn't decipher if she was being insulting or complimentary.

Either way she wanted me to model for her and handed me her business card.

"Tomorrow, 1pm, the studio address is on the back,

Wear this suit and bring your bass."

For the past six weeks, I'd been told constantly how I was a rock star, a legend and monster, the free booze and food was nice but, I'd reached my limit, I wanted to get paid,

"No thank you, I am not getting out of bed for anything tomorrow unless you bloody well pay me!"

She agreed she would... within reason.

The following afternoon having no clue of a model's hourly rate, I quoted the photographer a meagre fifty bucks for my first paid employment in New York City

Being paid a pittance to look moody holding my bass while a pair of stunning Russian stick insects from one of the city's top agencies were draped over me, was... awkward.

I wasn't having very much fun at all, they hardly spoke English and I completely sucked taking direction from the photographer, screwing up several shots by looking in the wrong direction.

Embarrassed I was glad when it was over, one and done, America's next top model? more like, its next asshole.

It was my first summer in the city, having survived a foot and a half of snow, white out conditions and bone chilling temperatures over the winter.

I'd now have to endure triple digit temperatures with about a million per cent humidity and the subway, a stinking oven, nothing could have prepared me for the stench of boiled urine that blighted a lot of the system.

In July, an official looking letter arrived with my Employment Authorization Document, I could now look for paid employment.

My first interview at a local Guitar Center didn't go well, the manager told me the name of the game was hustle.

Then the interview was suddenly interrupted by an angry pair of his employees bursting into the office threatening to lay each other out if he didn't intervene.

Answering an ad in the back of the village voice, and by Parlaying my recent experience at the film festival, I landed a full-time position at a Film & TV Prop House in Harlem.

Housed over several floors in an old factory near 125th Street, it paid decently enough, although their inventory was not catalogued so locating a customer's list of requirements could turn into a lengthy treasure hunt.

A month later, I received an email from Robby the egotistical guitarist.

His words were carefully chosen, seeking to butter me up, how he had instincts about good players, dug my playing and thought I'd be a great addition.

Ending the email stating he had some Killer drummer trying out next week, If I wanted to come down, he was sure I'd dig no pressure at all, peace out, man.

With little hope but nothing to lose, I agreed to meet.

Robby, it seemed had mellowed or at least got his ego in check and to be fair, the auditioning drummer, Mitchell was indeed a killer stick smith, but more importantly grounded and fun to hang with.

And just like that, I was in a band an unnamed trio without a singer.

At each rehearsal we we'd jam, cover Led Zeppelin, Engine was one serious audiophile and relentless in recording and documenting every single note we played.

Once we had a handful of original songs worked out, Robby started placing ads for singers on Craigslist, once he had three or four potentials interested, he'd invite them down to try out.

Most of those who dubbed themselves singers turned out to be terrible but finally one guy who was buzzed having come directly from a Yankees game walked in.

His voice was incredible, after jamming on a few random covers he asked if we knew anything by The Doors

We jammed out a version of "When the Music's Over" Yankee Doodle, delivered an almost perfect vocal, when it came to the breakdown section, he let it all hang out, literally.

Maybe he was caught in the moment, feeling the need to pay tribute to the songs author, Jim Morrison, who back in 1969 attempted to whip a Miami audience into a frenzy by asking them if they wanted to see "It"

Yanking down his shorts he whipped out his knob.

With one fist brandished and his other hand grasping his tackle he roared "I want to hear the scream, the scream of the butterfly!"

Mitchell threw his sticks across the room, I tried to suppress my juvenile giggling, Robby simply told him, "Sorry man."

After that vulgar display of penis our guitarist decided screw it from now on, he would bolster his own ego by now taking on the lead vocals.

The three of us still hadn't come up with a name for our collective, I started to feel the same way as fifteen years before Commander Two Half Pints had chanced upon our name.

Many had been bandied about, I dug The Gunpowder Plot, but Robby was reluctant due to its use of the word gun, Mitchell favored, Riot house the nickname for the Hyatt House on LA's Sunset Strip.

Made infamous in the seventies, Keith Richards had thrown a ton of TV's out of a usually closed window, Led Zeppelin's drummer John Bonham had ridden a motorcycle through the restaurant and Jim Morrison had been kicked out for hanging out of window, screaming at the world.

But as a name, it made us sound like a slightly more evolved hair metal band, Mitchell shrugged he wasn't married to the idea.

As it was an unseasonably chilly night outside, Robby gave the pair of us a ride home.

Negotiating the late night gridlock of traffic on Delancey Street we hit the approach to the Williamsburg Bridge, our ever enthusiastic stick smith now had a had a tale to share about the structure "I always get a good hold on my balls whenever, I go over this span, man" Laughing I asked him why, he replied an old friend's great great grandfather had been one of the bridges designers and had revealed to him that there were many flaws in its construction,

"Hang on a minute, I said to Mitchell.

It's been standing for over a hundred years" he now bugged his eyes and gently shook his head as he turned to face me in the backseat.

"It's true, Man, any-day now, this could all collapse, even tonight we may end up unleashed in the East fucking River!"

Looking at the massive suspension cables as we passed underneath, I imagined them suddenly giving way the three of us yelling "Shit!" in unison.

Mitchell remarking "Told you so, fuck me ragged, goodbye balls!" as the section of the bridge we were traversing fell away and we were sent plummeting into the black depths.

But not tonight, pulling off the exit ramp, onto Grand Street at a red light, the whoop whoop of a cop car behind us and over the speaker the officer advised him to pull over.

"What? Mitchell exclaimed ...I think we are about to gain some more rock n roll notoriety!"

Robby had a rear taillight out and received a fine, we offered to chip in, but he waved it away as it had been out of commission for at least a year.

Now, obsessed with coining a killer band name, I would google my ideas, first ensuring they weren't taken and presented my proposals to the guys each week.

None got two thumbs up, at our next rehearsal Robby greeted me with a "Fuck Man! meaning he was about to drop some world-shattering revelation on my ass.

He had been jerking off in the shower that morning, far too much information for me but the tosser loved to over share.

"Man, suddenly I get a vision of this beautiful goddess with four breasts and ten arms, He gushed.

Anyways, she leans forward and whispers in my ear...

By embracing your past, you will move forward.

My ears popped and I busted my nut.

So, the band name is...

"The Ex-Junkies... From Queens!"

I was in disbelief, Mitch and I didn't represent that, in fact we'd never shot up or snorted anything in our lives!

After nearly a year, a couple of recording sessions and several laughs together, I said fuck it,

Quitting the band in a cowardly fashion, the way Robby and I had first connected, handing in my notice via email.

As a former addict Robby may have sobered up sober but he was still prone to a junkie's behaviors.

Wild mood swings, irrational temper tantrums whenever he felt he didn't have complete control over the band.

Secondly and more important to me that was a really fucking dumb name.

THE STACKER THE SHERRY'S & THE ANONYMOUS FIVE

WOODLEY GREEN UK 1988

Eighteen months after paying an arm and a leg for my first piece of shit bass, I'd saved enough to afford a much better one along with a 45-watt bass amplifier

My new albeit also secondhand bass was a Thunder 1A, made by Westone another budget Japanese brand.

It was black with chrome hardware, two gold control knobs and a couple of silver switches.

The A was short for Active Circuitry, which was powered by a 9-volt box battery that fitted in a hole in the back of the body behind a removable backplate.

This apparently boosted the output of the instruments treble and bass frequencies.

That technical crap was terminally dull to me, all it really meant was, flick those two switches if you want to shake the room.

Which was terrific fun whenever I felt like steamrolling over Ricks guitar but not so much if I forgot to unplug after playing as it left the battery would drain in about ten minutes flat.

The action was low which made it a lot easier to play and it sounded like a proper bass should.

Producing rich, clear, and deep notes nothing at all like my first bass's tone of a farting elephant.

Rick and I still jammed most weekends in my parent's garage, but at a more reasonable volume so as not to raise the ire of the neighbors.

However, the randy rabble of girls driven mad with desire over our collective musical prowess never did beat upon the door.

Rick had developed a crush on a shelf stacker who worked at the supermarket in our local shopping precinct.

She was short with waist length brown hair, buck teeth, and massive pair of...assets.

For a fortnight he had dragged me around the store every afternoon to gawk at her from afar.

This stalker level of admiration soon got creepy and his inability to make a move was starting to do my head in, so I told him to shit or get off the pot.

Thursday afternoon he dug deep and finally mustered his courage.

"You wait here" he commanded.

"And don't dare fucking look!"

Rick marched away.

I hid at the end of the aisle and peeked round the corner as he practically skipped towards her

The object of his desire was filling the chiller cabinet with Ski yogurts as he blurted out his punctuation free proposal.

Hey...Hello, er Hi!

My name's Rick, you're very pretty, what's your name? Would you like to go out with me?

Don't worry, I'm not a stalker, honest... I do have a job.

Now out of breath he took a deep one, and added a far more cocksure.

"Oh yeah and I play the guitar."

Her reaction was one of being completely taken aback and utter confusion.

"Oh golly, er hello Rick, I'm Gemma... she blushed.

Who's your Mate?" she pointed to where I thought I'd been undetectable.

"Oh, him? that's Steve he's my bass player, we play in a band together!""

Gemma was now a lot less flustered.

"Look, I don't date she said bluntly.

"Any road, this band of yours what's it called, then eh?"

Rick looked terrified having been called on his bullshit

"Pulling Machine!" I shouted, she laughed.

"That's a rubbish name she rightly remarked.

You should change it to something more appropriate like... The Stalking Wankers!"

Cleary she was having fun watching him squirm.

"I'll tell you what, Gemma proposed.

Why don't you and Steve meet me and my friends up at the Bull & Chequer's tomorrow night, say eight o'clock?"

Rick beamed like a Cheshire cat after snorting a kilo of cocaine.

"Ok, it's a date!" he gushed.

"It most certainly is not! she admonished.

I don't date remember."

Rick nodded frantically.

Good, that's settled then.

I'll see you two stalkers tomorrow night"

For the next twenty-four hours, Rick was insufferable.

I lost count of the number of times I reminded him that she hadn't said yes to going on a date.

"It's not like she had an opening for your stiff proposition!"

I shouted in frustration, but it all fell on cloth covered lovesick ears.

Rick was acting as if she'd batted her eyes twisted a lock of his hair and told him in a seductive growl.

You, me, big boy, tomorrow night... guaranteed shag

Rick had been preening since he got in from work at 1pm and when I knocked on his door six hours later, he still wasn't ready.

He'd already washed his hair twice, changed outfits five times and had three shaves.

Upstairs in the bathroom he was wincing as he plucked at his nasal hairs with one hand while slathering himself in way too much aftershave with the other.

At last Rick was satisfied he was as pretty as possible and began the nearly two-mile trek to the Bull & Chequers, as we walked, he left a fragrant wake.

Approaching Headley Road roundabout just a kiss away from the Pub we got our collars felt by the cops, who were parked in the bus stop.

"Good evening, gentlemen, may I ask where exactly you are headed?"

"Up the pub, Rick Replied.

"I see, when you arrive at the establishment, do you plan on consuming any alcoholic beverages?"

"Indeed, we will" Rick said.

"When you've finished your drinking do either of you plan on driving home?"

"Doubtful as neither of us can drive."

I informed the officer.

"Do either of you have any drugs about your person?"

More annoyed than angered in my mind, I started to form a response.

Why yes, officer, if you care to look inside my jacket here, I have all manner of illegal, substances for your perusal and potential purchase.

Would Thames Valley's finest care for a tab or two of Lysergic Acid Diethylamide?

How about powdering your nose with some devil's dandruff the good old Bolivian marching powder?

Its fresh as a daisy, flown in just yesterday from Brazil.

Maybe you fine upholders of law and order have a hankering for some amyl nitrate?

I'm sure you both must be bored shitless having now detained my friend and I for no reason other than the length of our hair and unconventional attire.

Nah, maybe not, the Pigs weren't renowned for their love of sarcasm, Instead I pointed toward Rick and told them.

"I'm not carrying anything officer, but my mate here is in possession of half a bottle of Drakkar Noir, as you can probably smell it's *all* over his person."

The pigs were not amused, I was deemed uncooperative given a verbal caution and the pair of us were treated to a pat down.

Between the pig's inquisition and my back chat, we had wasted thirty minutes and Rick was now seriously upset.

"Fucks sake, were gonna be late man, she's probably already bailed, thinking I've stood her up!"

Reminding him for the millionth time how she'd told him she did not date, had invited both of us and the time frame of 8pm was probably more a window than a deadline.

Rick was still hacked off and seethed.

"Yeah, but If I don't get my end away tonight, it's your fucking fault!"

Taking a left onto Church Road and the right-hand fork to Woodley Green.

There stood the destination for Ricks not a date with fate, The Bull & Chequers.

Formerly a farmhouse, it had been one of the first four public houses from a long time ago when our hometown of Woodley, had been known as just "A clearing in the wood."

The grounds housed a car park on either side, a decent sized Beer Garden with wooden benches out back and an extension built onto one side.

Gemma and company were spread over several tables in the extension, a structure of white framework and glass she called The Greenhouse

The collective referred to themselves as The Bull & Chequers formation drinking team, she wasn't sure of the total number of members but twenty or more were known to gather there most Friday and Saturday nights.

Most of the gang was a cool and fun group of misfits that didn't fit in with the mainstream tribes, just like Rick and me.

The team were united by their love of music, mainly hard rock, and heavy metal.

We made fast friends with several a few of which were musicians and began making the trip to the Bull & Chequers most every night.

As I'd suspected Rick didn't sow any wild oats with Gemma that night and over the next few weeks they went on a couple of non-dates

Then, she broke it off, her excuse being she had too many problems, needed to get her head straight and of course it wasn't him it was her.

In actuality it was entirely Rick's fault, I'd accidentally overheard her describing him as smothering and far too clingy.

His broken heart soon turned to stone as he channeled his anger and rage into words and roped me in to collaborate on our first attempts at songwriting.

I wouldn't class them as protest songs more a gentle way of Rick saying *You buck toothed bitch how could you dump me before I got to shag you!*

The first tune "2 Many Problems" made it as far as an awful chorus and tedious riff.

For the second tune I had couple of passable chord ideas and for the words I re-wrote some of Ricks more scathing thoughts on Gemma

"Hair, Lipstick, Tits and Teeth, you may be short but you sure ain't sweet."

But it was clear as a songwriting duo we sucked.

We needed some talented assistance and so decided we should join or form a band.

Most conversations up the Pub would range from bitching about the lack of hard rock on the Jukebox, dissecting Anne Rice's latest novel, or talk would turn to some Canadian band, a three piece "Power Trio" named Rush.

We'd never heard of them.

They were discussed in hushed revered tones, many thought of them as musical gods and their playing prowess peerless.

The band had already been around a while, releasing their self-titled debut album in 1974.

On the strength of this collective admiration and wanting in on the conversation, I bought their most recent album "Hold Your Fire."

Quite frankly, I was pretty disappointed It had the typical over-polished eighties hi-tech production.

None of the tunes were particularly heavy compared to the thrash metal I had been deafening myself with of late.

The songs still rocked but only occasionally and in a very different way.

Repeated listening's though uncovered memorable hooks, examples of superior musical ability and an emotional heft to the lyrics.

The bands musicianship was so far off the charts I couldn't even fathom who was playing what, marimba's, synthesizer's even a bloody orchestra was shoehorned into the grooves.

They sure knew their onions and the term power trio was apt as between them they generated a massive sound that defied their size.

Rush was a progressive rock band, Prog in shorthand, their playing impressive to most musicians, but acted as chick repellant due to the complexity of most of their songs not being that female friendly.

Bassist and lead vocalist Geddy Lee sang complex melodies in a high register while he simultaneously played incredible basslines.

He also played the Keyboards when he wasn't playing the bass or used his feet to trigger samples and swathes of sound when he was still playing four strings.

Everything he played on the album was WAY beyond my skill level but on the opening track "Force Ten" it sounded like he was playing something fairly simple for the first minute or so.

Almost chewing up my cassette copy rewinding it over and over, after a week, I had one minutes worth of Geddy's shit down, I proudly played it to Rick.

"Look, I can play like Geddy Lee!' I squealed.

Playing a steady pulse of notes on the second string of my bass, the A string, I was totally locked in with what he was playing on the cassette.

He shouted at me to stop.

"Well, yeah.... that's part of it" he said.

Then, he explained what I'd assumed was a guitar playing chords over the open A string bass part, was being played on bass at the same damn time!!

Underneath which guitarist, Alex Lifeson was playing what in a less ambitious band would have been played by the bassist, a simple, steady chugging A chord.

"How the fuck can he play the A string and chords at the same time?! I wailed, lowering my head in shame.

"He's only got four fucking strings!!

Now, I was able to join the conversation at the pub several folks told me that the new album was far from their greatest work and not the best place to start discovering the mastery of the men of Willowdale.

I should have started with their fourth album, as that was when they had hit their stride musically and honed their signature sound.

Seeking out a nice price vinyl copy of "2112" released back in 1976, at first, I thought I'd picked up the wrong album, there was clearly a different band on the back cover, they had long hair, dressed in white silk kimonos, and looked like a bunch of baked hippies.

The needle gently dropped, after a weird swirling sci-fi sounding collage of sound, a stop start instrumental track called the "Overture" kicked in, it burst into a galloping section a bit like Iron Maiden with someone wailing "Wooooaaaaahh" in a high register echoing voice, the climax of the track where I assumed the title came from as it sounded like rocked up version of The 1812 overture...

An explosion sound effect gave way to a short guitar passage, some bloke softly stating, "And the meek shall inherit the earth" and the next part of the side long "song" began,

Now, this was some heavy shit man big guitars, crashing cymbals and huge drum fills.

The singer sounded like an angry, screaming woman "she" banged on about Priests, Temples of Syrinx's and how I should come and join the Brotherhood of man

The side long epic, then moved through a few peaceful passages, at one point, a guitar was being tuned for about a minute to the sound of a waterfall in the background, what the bloody hell was I listening to?!

Then, it got even heavier, the screaming woman's voice pitched ever higher, then it became sad, melancholy, before the side long side resolved, or dissolved rather into an even more manic instrumental and some voiced that sounded like Mission Control at NASA stated, repeatedly that...

"We have assumed control."

The record was so weird that I put the needle back down and listened to the whole damn thing three more times.

This WAS the same band, back in 1976 they had been in their early twenties they had become much more reflective and mature on their latest album "Hold Your Fire" while there were always a few musical hallmarks on each record, I learnt that Rush never made the same album twice, evolved and expanding their sound constantly.

Beginning as a blues based hard rock trio with nods to Led Zeppelin, by the time they had reached 2112 their fourth album, they had taken a deep dive into the murky musical waters of classical, and progressive rock, creating side long multipart epics like their hero's Yes and Genesis.

I was hooked and spent all my extra cheddar on their back catalogue, the first listen to any of their albums was often confounding but like a musical onion, sans tears, the more you listened the more the layers fell away, and the songs made sense.

That was the magic of Rush challenging the listener while retaining just enough of their core sound to keep you resetting the needle, rewinding the cassette, or re-starting the playlist.

With our new nigh on nightly routine revolving around the Pub. You could find the two of us in The Greenhouse banging on about how we were looking to form a band.

Boring whoever was within earshot about how someday we'd be richer and maybe even a little famous, when our rock n roll band took the world, ok well maybe just Reading then by storm.

Our collective bullshit didn't catch the ears of any willing musicians, but we did recruit of a pair of roadies for our hypothetical band.

One night The Sherry Brothers, Morgan, and Ron, walked over to our table, introduced themselves and offered their services for the incredibly reasonable outlay of a couple of beers a piece per show.

They would provide transport to and from our shows and lug all the heavy shit back and forth.

The older brother Ron told us.

"The way the pair of yah never fucking shut up about it means, you're bound to have a band sooner rather than later, right?" He smiled.

Morgan was the same age as me, he wore thick glasses and had shaggy black hair.

He had a hilariously sarcastic and frequently offensive sense of humor.

Ron was in his mid-twenties and had the physique over a slightly overweight grizzly bear, he sported a huge afro and worked as a trackman for the railway.

He was more a lot more laid back and less sarcastic than Morgan but just as funny.

Morgan worshipped just one band Iron Maiden, he rarely listened to anyone else and when he did it would only be bands that sounded just like them, the German band Helloween for example.

He loved that galloping rhythm that Maiden traded in which made most of their songs sound like a heavy metal horse race. Their bassist, Steve Harris played with his fingers incredibly fast and his was always the most prominent instrument on their records.

His relentless style of playing was a highlight to fans, but it irritated me to no end plus he played one of those boring s fuck Fender Precision basses.

The truth was I dismissed him Maiden, and all that equestrian paced shit they pedaled as I was envious, and it was way beyond my current four string skills.

Ron wasn't quite as picky with his musical preferences, if pushed he may cite Black Sabbath as his number one but just long as shit was heavy enough for him bang his head, as he once said, "It's all gravy, innit?"

The Sherry's lived with their parents in a huge house on Caldbeck Drive their dad's job frequently called for him to take go overseas on business and he'd schedule his trips either side of a weekend so he could take their Mum along.

This came in handy as once a month and the boys got to throw a big house party.

The next one was this Friday, over the next week Malcom mentioned some very special guests were due to attend but wouldn't tell us who.

"You don't know them but you pair of bulimic fuck-sticks soon will" he'd teased.

Friday evening as we walked up their driveway, we passed a poorly parked black Volkswagen Van.

Sweet wheels I thought and wondered if they belonged to one of the mysterious special guests.

An already well-oiled Morgan answered the door, greeting us in his customary insulting fashion.

"Fuck my old boots" he slurred would you look at this pair of desperate dickheads!"

He shouted behind him to no one in particular.

"Oi, which one of you jokers invited sad sack Eeyore and his coked-up mate Tigger?!"

We laughed at his casual disrespect.

I asked Morgan if he'd heard the new Iron Maiden single "Can I play with Madness."

His eyes bugged, or course he had, he'd bought the picture disc, poster bag, 12" single.

"Fucking got it all, son."

Clearly thrilled I'd asked after his beloved band.

"It's a modern metal masterpiece, I trust you'll agree, Stevey?"

Nodding in mock agreement, I told him.

"You must be chuffed they finally wrote a song just for you, Morgan looked momentarily confused...

I mean "Can I Play with Myself?" I quipped.

Obviously, it's about you being a total wanker and a compulsive seed spreader, innit?

"Bastardo!" Morgan shouted, taking a mock swing at me and ushered us frantically into the kitchen.

There he presented his pride and joy on top of the fridge.

Two cases of Budweiser, the American beer wasn't freely available in the UK at the time, Morgan had procured the booze via a work mate whose dad worked on a US military base and swiped it from the squaddies storeroom.

He threw us each a can,

"Down the Beaver snatch!" he toasted. I took a gulp and tasted, insipid disappointment.

Morgan laughed at our grimaces.

"What did you pair of lanky pricks expect?

Them septic tanks ain't exactly known for their brewing skills of course it tastes like shite!"

Draining his can, he crunched it and threw it in the sink.

"Besides my darling fucktards I bought this bullshit brew by way of a celebration.

And... you two twats are about to fall at my feet and thank me profusely he laughed.

"Get to the point, you four eyed toss pot" Rick told him with a grin.

Morgan puffed out his chest in pride, vocalized a poor impression of a trumpet fanfare and made his grand statement.

"I, Morgan Sherry, Lord of everything that gallops, shreds and bangs heads have finally found you pair of dopey dipshits your new band!"

He'd got totally bored waiting for us to form one, so he had press ganged three of his friends into considering forming one with us.

In the living room he gestured to three guys talking amongst themselves.

This was the trio of special guests he'd been teasing us about all week.

First was Rod a year younger than me and possibly the happiest person I'd met in all my eighteen years.

Short, with bushy hair a huge grin, dressed in snow washed denim and sparking white hi-tech techs trainers.

I'd soon learn he had an uncanny knack of finding the funny side in the most negative of situations.

Rod hadn't been in a band before but played a bit of guitar and was lethal if left alone with a Xylophone.

For our potential band, he fancied chancing his arm at singing.

"Don't call me Rod, he told me.

No one does apart from me Mum, call me Ski mate!"

He laughed as he explained his nickname which didn't denote, he was obsessed with the sport.

"Skiing's boring, those silly fuckers are constantly on the piste mate!" he quipped.

Turned out he loved yogurt especially as a post doobie snack, His alias was derived from his favorite brand.

"Mate, you can't beat an ice-cold pot after smoking a red-hot joint."

He assured me.

What struck me the most about Ski was he was full of hope and laser focused on the possibilities of tomorrow.

He simply had no space to rent in his head for the regrets of yesterday.

Next was Clive a tall laid-back bloke with long straight red hair, he didn't say much but what he did was hilarious, being blessed with a quick bone-dry wit.

His older brother had worked for a national touring band and when they had neglected to pay him, he'd broken into their lockup and stolen a drum kit in lieu of payment for his services.

Clive convinced him not to sell it bought himself a couple of sticks and had been bashing away in his folk's garage for the past few months.

While he didn't exactly say "I'm a drummer" his rationale made perfect sense

If all he had to do was hit shit with sticks, how hard could it be?

Finally on proposed rhythm guitar was Dug a year older than me, sarcastic, intelligent, and effortless funny.

He had an evil grin and long wavy hair like Dave Mustaine from Megadeth.

I liked him immediately forming an instant bond as like Clive and myself, he was left-handed.

Dug was a clever bastard though and smart enough to play a left-handed guitar, unlike my dumbass.

Him having previously been in a band called "More Tea Vicar" made him instantly cool, doubly so as he also had a driver's license.

The VW Van, I'd admired earlier in the driveway was his

Dug called it The Bug.

Morgan now left us all to get acquainted signing off sarcastically.

"I'll leave you girls to massage each other's shoulders and discuss your feelings now play nice you butt ugly fucks, yeah?

Over the course of the night, the five of us discovered we dug most of the same bands and loved BBC2's anarchic comedy "The Young Ones."

After a couple of hours, Dug brought up the subject of our potential union.

"Alright, you bunch of total and complete bastards."

We've established that we like the same shit, all get along and seeing as tonight's been a right old laugh... I believe it would be quite rude if we didn't form a goddamn rock n roll band!!"

Much rejoicing, high fives and further inebriation ensued.

Then Dug led us out to The Bug, opening the back doors he revealed a row of five reclaimed airplane seats bolted to the left-hand side.

Ski lit up a huge spliff, my paranoia prevented me from partaking, instead I continued to slug on my can of Uncle Sam's Ass Water.

Dug slammed the doors shut and once the joint had done the rounds, he made an announcement...

"Gentlemen... we are about to create rock history and may well be in for a bumpy ride, please fasten your seatbelts as we prepare for takeoff... Man!"

THE HOBBIT, THE PONY & THE HOSEPIPE

BROOKLYN 2007

With my first band experience in New York City leaving a bad taste in my mouth and I decided to take a break from music.

The grudge I held toward Robby didn't last too long.

He held out an olive branch by putting me on the guest-list for my former band's debut show at Arlene's Grocery.

My former bandmates seemed happy to see me and Robby handed me the band's new three track CD.

When I listened later at home I was seriously upset.

Robby had used the bass tracks I'd recorded and shelved months ago.

Not only had he done so without my permission he also hadn't bothering crediting me on the sleeve.

The snake had been all smiles at the show, as he'd got what he wanted from our musical union.

This taught me a valuable lesson that in future, I'd insist on being credited in full or just hold onto my intellectual property.

It wasn't long until the itch to play wouldn't quit and I delved into the new-fangled my space to forage for a new band, which was so much easier.

Listen to a couple of songs on a bands page weed out the chaff within minutes, rather than wasting hours on the subway dealing with stoners, egos, and aging angry punks.

Liquid Crowbar was a duo made up of Guitarist/Vocalist Derek & Drummer Mac, I dug their songs and set up a meeting at their rehearsal room at Rivington Studio's on Manhattan's Lower East Side.

The pair were talented, Derek had a sloppy style to his playing, that reminded me of a drunk Jimmy Page falling down the stairs.

His voice was his long suit, he could muster a powerful roar like Chris Cornell from Soundgarden.

Mac was like every drummer should be, hilarious.

His technique was equally subtle and complex but always groovy.

Their material was a gritty AC/DC type rock n roll with a harder edge, one thing I knew, they sure weren't no vapid hair metal band as both were completely bald.

I was offered the position within an hour, and we celebrated our union in a nearby dive bar.

In the recent past, Derek had played in a band with Les Warner, former drummer for The Cult, the man who'd been behind the kit, at the first gig I attended back in '87 at Hammersmith Odeon.

Rehearsing twice a week, in a handful of months we had a tight forty-five-minute set of original material and our first show booked at a basement venue on Avenue B in Alphabet City, Manhattan.

The area had now been gentrified in the past it had gotten its official name from the lettered avenues and unofficially from the type of drug you could score on each one.

Aside from Derek's tuning issues which would become a constant bane for the band and part of Mac's kit collapsing during the second song, my debut NYC show went well, and we drew a decent sized crowd.

During next rehearsal Mac mentioned a friend had reviewed one of our shows on this music blog.

His one-line review cited our band as being... solid.

This review had led to a mysterious nameless A&R man getting in touch with Mac he wanted the band to perform a showcase for him.

I was not impressed by the news of his alleged interest, my problem being ahead of each show one of them would make an announcement that something like

"Hey man, have you heard who is coming to the show?

(Insert name of some industry person, I'd never heard of)

"They're the cousin of the sister of the guy who once had Jimi Hendrix's mailman in the back of his cab!"

Rapidly this had got old to me as they never showed up.

Following a rowdy late-night gig at Arlene's Grocery on Stanton Street, an inebriated Derek collared me to scream in my ear over the din of the band onstage.

"Guess who's here tonight?!"

I sighed...

"No fucking idea, tell me?"

"The fucking hobbit man!!!"

Amused by his liquored-up enthusiasm, I laughed and asked what the hell he was prattling on about.

"You know those Lord of the Rings flicks?

I nodded.

"Frodo, man...I mean... the actor that plays him.

He slurred.

Evan, Eric, Enrique, fuck... you know him his last name's Wood."

Yes, I said, I knew of whom he spoke and yelled back at him.

"Oh, you're talking about Elijah Wood, right?

He nodded with a shit eating grin.

Now you're picking up what I'm putting down,

Well, he's fucking here dude!" he shouted.

However, Frodo was nowhere to be found.

Later I heard from less inebriated sources that, indeed the man who'd played "The Fucking Hobbit" had been holding court in the venue's front bar.

As Arlene's space was split between a front bar and a ticketed live room, I'm sure it was sheer coincidence he'd been there meeting maybe meeting a few friends for a drink or two.

Derek maintained even after he'd sobered up that he'd specifically come to see us play, but I wasn't having it.

Liquid Crowbar's raucous rock n roll wasn't exactly Middle Earth Friendly

A week later, Mac had gotten word from the nameless A&R dude who had now taken a serious interest in the band.

The man of mystery lived in New Jersey and instead of checking out one of our shows in the city, he wanted us to go to him.

This led to us getting shoehorned onto a bill at The Stone Pony in Asbury Park, New Jersey.

A proper grown-up venue that hosted national and international touring acts and famous for being were Bruce Springsteen and Bon Jovi got their big breaks.

Having been spoiled playing local venues in NYC, for most shows all I need bring was a bass, cables, and my effects pedals.

The revenue hungry, venue managers wanted a quick change over between bands to ensure no one over ran.

All the clubs we played provided a basic drum kit and a house backline of half decent or sometimes half destroyed amplification.

The Stone Pony provided a stage, lighting, and use of the house PA.

Bands on tour travelled with their own gear so there was no need for them to provide a backline.

Derek's macho obsession with volume, dictated that for this showcase gig he simply had to use not one but two full Marshall Stacks.

This was totally unnecessary as the venues sound engineer would mic up our amps and run them through the PA.

Derek could easily have got away with using just one speaker cabinet and still have been plenty loud enough.

But nope he wanted the band or rather himself to be a "fuck ton louder and look way cooler" so along with our regular equipment we packed four 4x12 speaker cabinets and two-amp heads into our cheap rental van to satisfy one man's ego.

It was a rainy Wednesday afternoon when we set off,

Three hours, countless detours, and a total distance of sixty miles later.

We drove slowly down the overcast, windswept Ocean Avenue in Asbury Park.

This was the town Bruce Springsteen's 1973 debut album had sent greetings from, to me the place looked pretty run down and far from picture perfect.

Pulling up outside The Stone Pony our name wasn't on the marquee only the name of tonight's headliner a local Bee Gee's Tribute act named.... "Tragedy"

"Well, the names rather apt, don't you think?"

I deadpanned, peering out the window through the rain while Derek offered up some optimism.

"Springsteen made it here man, he smiled.

Why not us too?"

My thinking was Bruce had already honed his material and show playing hundreds of local dives.

Spending years, thanklessly toiling away until he reached the point where he could draw enough of a crowd to headline The Pony.

When his big break occurred, I'm sure it was on a hot August night, likely a Saturday some A&R guy happened to walk in and being impressed by the size of the crowd, stuck around to see who was playing.

Blinded by the dollar signs of Springsteen's financial potential he likely offered him a recording contract on the spot, thereby making him perceived as an overnight sensation.

To my mind, that simply wasn't going be the case for Liquid Crowbar at least not on a wet mid-winter Wednesday.

The band was granted access to the backstage caravan equipped with a battered leather sofa and fridge stocked with cheap beer.

Soon after word got around that the band hailed from NYC and from then out, the venue's hospitality turned somewhat frosty.

One of the strict policies was opening slots were for New Jersey acts only.

Which made sense financially, local bands were more likely to draw an audience, it seemed the nameless A&R bloke had enough clout to have made an exception for us.

Other than our significant others, who were on the guest list anyway we'd drawn sod all paying punters.

Come showtime, I counted less than ten people in the building, including the staff.

A local promoter took to the stage to introduce us.

"Now check this Jersey, he bellowed.

Straight outtah Rikers Island jail in New York a-cithay.

Folks, I am telling you people not since James Brown raised hell on wheels deep down in Georgia have you ever seen a band bust outta' prison and manage to pull this together...

My bandmates were laughing, while I had a non plussed expression, having no idea what he was blathering about.

"Ladies and gentlemen New Yawks loudest

The notorious threesome .... Liquid... Crowbar!"

A four count from Mac's Hi-hat and we were away feedback immediately squealed at the threshold of pain through my monitor cabinet.

After the first song the soundman had eliminated it from the monitor but now my hair was now being blown back by Derek's deafening guitar that was already woefully out of tune.

Having been blessed with a playing style devoid of any finesse his psychotic ham-fisted technique, could be summed up like so...

My guitar seems to have inexplicably burst into flames, it's not a situation I'd prepared for and I'm finding it a little traumatic.

Would you all please excuse me as I frantically attempt to extinguish it

His heavy handedness meant; he'd bash his guitar out of tune within the first couple of numbers.

Taking a pause after the second song to tune back up, he asked us Mac and me to supply some technical difficulty music, we duly obliged with a blues jam.

"You know" Derek said over Our Segway

We had a fuck of a journey getting to this place...

(Which was true)

But...Jersey you have made us feel very much welcome so I gotta tell yah, it's been worth it, every second."

(And this... was complete bullshit)

We soldiered on, it wasn't easy for me as If I moved more than two feet to my right, Derek's Mountain of Marshalls would batter me senseless.

The nail in our collective coffin came when we attempted to perform a song that had been recorded before I'd joined the band, but we had never played it live.

This was by special request as it had been this song that had piqued Mr A&R's interest in the band.

When you first perform a song in front of a crowd you learn what sections work and which fall flat.

A track that sounds great in a rehearsal room may not go over well in front of a paying audience.

It's always a good plan to perform it a live a few times, adjust accordingly, like adding Pauses....

Every audience loves a good...Pause.

It shows a band is tight enough to be able to stop on a dime and when done right, the crowd get to shout whatever random shit they like to fill the silence.

"Still Water" was a dark, dynamic ballad with a lot of light, shade, whisper and thunder and a couple of good... pauses.

However, either from nerves or it being under rehearsed our performance lacked any form of finesse and we pretty much ruined it.

A direct result was the Anonymous A&R man left the building before we'd finished our set.

Following a few days of radio silence, Mac finally received a one-line email response.

Nice Try... was all he wrote.

A few months later we decided to hit the studio, with a selection of songs that unlike "Still Water" had been tweaked and refined onstage.

The cost of Studio time was of concern, but Mac had a plan to do it on the cheap which is how I ended up back in a similar environment to where I'd first started with Rick back in 1986.

Today though, I wouldn't been jamming in one, instead I'd be recording in a bloody garage.

Jason, the producer lived with his parents on a quiet street in a commuter suburb of New Jersey.

The double garage had been partially converted for use as a Live room in order to capture drums and bass, his dad still parked his car in there, so we had to set up around it as well as the numerous tools and gardening equipment.

Built onto the side of the Garage was a small room about the size of my parents' downstairs toilet.

Here was housed the mixing desk, recording console and a minuscule vocal booth.

Jason seemed keen when we arrived and if we wanted anything for breakfast.

We didn't, he shrugged pulled out a bong and baked up his.

I wasn't sure how he was going to be able to offer us professional ear after taking hits off that baby, another slight issue to consider was one of his monitor speakers didn't work.

Mac helped Jason to mic'd up the drum kit in the garage and then running through the first couple of songs.

It was July and today was set to be quite a scorcher temperature wise and while the garage had rudimentary sound proofing, it had no air conditioning or ventilation.

Back in the tiny control room, we listened to Mac tracking take after take, unaware the increasingly heat outside was being absorbed by the garage's brick walls.

A spirited drum part sounded out over the one monitor speaker that still functioned.

It sounded killer he was half a minute away from a perfect uninterrupted take of the first song, then there was a haphazard crash followed by silence.

"Whoops, not to worry Mac, Josh said over the talkback.

Let's just have another pass at that last fill" there was no reply.

"Mac, hello" still nothing.

"The dipshit, cow tipper probably got distracted checking his Phone" Derek grumbled.

He walked outside and banged several times on the garage door to no response.

"Fuck me, it's a bit warm out there" Derek said as he came back in and opened the side door that led from the recording booth to the garage.

The wave of heat that escaped was immense.

Slumped over a partially collapsed drum kit, bald head glowing an alarming shade of red Mac was out cold.

The garage had become a makeshift oven and roasted our drummer to the point of him passing out.

"Shit, The Mac man's down, someone call fucking 911!" Derek cried, pushing open the Garage doors, allowing the heat to disperse, he then disappeared round the side of the house and returned trailing a garden hose and an evil grin.

"No sleeping on the job, Motherfucker!" he laughed as he opened the valve, hitting Mac with a blast of water forcing him back to consciousness and pinning him to the back wall.

"Aaah, the fuck, shut it off!" he spluttered between gasps.

"Sorry...man, couldn't resist!" Derek giggled nervously after he shut it off.

Mac pulled himself out from behind the soaking wet drum kit and attempt to run at Derek.

The soaking had made his clothes about twenty pounds heavier and his planed sprint after the culprit ended up being a slow squelching waddle.

I watched Mac slowly slosh down the driveway as Derek legged it off up the street.

Mac staggered back to the garage, seething, vowing that prick was gonna pay, big time.

Five minutes later Derek came back unaware Mac had hidden behind a bush, hosepipe in hand, hell bent on revenge.

"That chubby cow tipper still sulking?" he asked as

Mac leapt out, blasting him with enough water pressure to put him flat on his back as he yelled.

"Payback's a bitch, you bald Motherfucker!"

THE SPLIFF, THE TRIP & THE MUDBATH

BULL & CHEQUERS, UK 1988

My pals down the pub were divided between two distinct camps, Drinkers, and Stoners.

You picked your poison and chose to raise your glass with those about to rock or went up in smoke with those who preferred to roll.

The idea of taking drugs in particular, Weed, Wacky Baccy or Mary Jane I found terrifying, and I'd turned down any invitations to have a puff in the past.

That was before I joined a band where everyone but me smoked when I considered that my bandmates had yet to overdose or get fitted for a strait jacket I figured, its high time I joined them.

It was late on a Friday night when word got round the greenhouse of an open invitation to a house party.

When we arrived the place was packed, the vibe cool and the air thick with a heady aroma.

Spinning on the record deck was *Nocturne* by Siouxsie & The Banshees, one of my current favorites.

Its creepy exquisite bleakness was an odd choice considering the upbeat mood of the party.

While perusing the other albums in the stack by the stereo, I met the party's host, Perry.

He was thin as a rake with shoulder length dreadlocks, I told him he had great taste in tunes.

"Siouxsie? he asked with a sleepy smile.

I nodded.

Yeah...she's like the ice queen of chilled out darkness, man."

He appeared lost in thought for a second, then he asked me.

"Hey, Man, do you toke?"

It wasn't a term I was familiar with, so I replied with a lie.

"For sure man I gushed

It's the best!"

In my mind Paranoia reared its never welcome head

Liar!

Now, why would you say that?

Gone and done it now, haven't you?

Fear forced a trickle of sweat to roll down my forehead as Perry presented me with a spliff the size of a Cuban cigar... there was no turning back.

With a demented grim he invited me to

"Have a bang on this number, brother!"

My Paranoia had since been replaced by more rational thoughts.

Just take it, what's the harm?

One puff ain't gonna kill you.

It's what all the grown-up rock stars do!

Right on, best be hitting this shit, then.

Taking a massive drag on the oversized joint, I coughed my lungs up, gasped for air and fell to my knees.

As I continued to cough violently, my thoughts convinced me I'd just gone and fucked up...big time.

Yep, this was it, my number had been called, bucket kicked, and I was about to die.

"That's some good shit, innit mate?" Perry asked, laughing as I beat my fists upon the floor struggling to take what I imagined to be my last breaths.

My imminent demise wasn't unfolding quite as I'd expected, there was no light, or a tunnel leading towards it and sweet FA all was flashing before my eyes.

My head felt tight as if it was being squeezed in a vice, conversely, though it was hollow and filled with air.

My body was wrapped in what I imagined to be a spicy chicken burrito.

Once I got over my coughing fit, I got back on my feet, surprised to still be alive.

My gaze fell upon my skinny black jeans, wow they looked really cool.

Shimmering like the heat haze from a plane on a runway and sparkling as if dunked in morning dew.

Moving my legs slowly, I marveled at the traces they left in the air, my beautiful billowing bell bottoms.

They were such a glorious sight I wanted everyone in the room to check them out, so I blurted out.

"Hot Flares... look everyone, I'm wearing Hot Flares!"

My rational thinking chimed in

Such a morbid bonehead!

You ain't knock, knock, knocking on heaven's door man.

You're just bloody stoned!

Oh right, good news then, I'm not in fact dying just a little dazed and extremely confused.

The Bad news...well

My mouth feels like its full of frozen sawdust dipped in molten treacle and my hair's a mass of writhing cotton snakes.

Taking a hefty swig of my Lager, the liquid crawled down my throat languidly like electric mud.

Choking, I sprayed it over the carpet, as a soothing calm started to wash over me.

The sensation travelled from my head to my chest then it spread between my legs.

My Paranoia was back with a vengeance.

It mocked me as it whispered sweet nothings.

Oh dear, Steve, what have you done?

You've just pissed your pants,

In front of the entire party
Look around everyone's laughing at you!
Panicking I screamed aloud my breaking news.
"Hey...everyone, HEY!
Look, look... I've just pissed in my pants!"
Now everyone that hadn't been paying attention to me at all looked my way, pointed, and had a right old laugh.

Terrified, I ran upstairs in search of the bog.

After locking myself inside, I sat on the bowl with my head in my hands for a very long time.

While I hadn't died or more pressingly in fact wet myself, one thing was bloody obvious I was utterly shite at getting high.

Finally, I felt calm enough to unlock the door to a lengthy queue of pissed off guests.

Head hung low, I shuffled back down the stairs and slumped on the sofa.

Letting out a huge sigh while my paranoia sought to further torment me.

What's wrong?
You don't look very well.
Perry spiked that joint.
You've been poisoned!
Looks like death's back on the menu!
Great, bloody typical, out of the bathroom and into the graveyard.

My paranoia may have had a point as I did feel a little queasy.

In my head it twisted at my sanity.

Tap tap, Curly whirly cuckoo!
Up around the bend
That's why your head is rotating.
No, it wasn't my head that was turning, it was the turntable on Perry's Hi-Fi that was spinning me right round like a record.

Nope, now the whole room was whirling around me like fairground carousel.

Oil and water, grape with the grain, or in my case mixing a belly full of Fosters with a swede full of weed was rapidly starting to disagree with me.

Making a bolt for the kitchen, I reached the sink in time to unleash a hellish stew of hot lager laced with chunks of stomach lining all over a huge stack of dirty dishes.

Wiping my mouth on a dish towel, I tiptoed to the front door out into the night with my twinkling hot flares guiding my wobbly walk home.

Backwards in Black, Beggars Hill, UK 1988...

Perry would become a semi-regular at the Pub, he dug dark goth shit like me and introduced me to Anne Rice's Vampire Chronicles series of books.

Occasionally he'd bring a friend with him one of which was Mario, he was short with blackened teeth and tight curly hair.

The guy was a real ray of sarcastic sunshine, the life and soul of any funeral.

Best of all, Mario was even more useless at getting high than me.

Weed would have a reverse effect and make him even more depressed trigger a major mental meltdown.

Being constantly and monumentally miserable was Mario's raison d'être, sharing the same bleak worldview as Neil the depressed hippie from the BBC sitcom "The Young Ones."

Life to him, was just one big bummer.

A couple of times a week Mario would drive Perry to the Pub in his beat up old Mini.

Perry would head in and ask if any of us were interested in doing a bit of "Trainspotting"

Stoner code for who wants to take a ride with us up beggar's hill and get baked?

Tonight, the pub was less busy than usual for a Thursday, Rick was home recovering from the Flu while Clive who'd been hitting it too hard lately was staying in.

So, it was just Me, Ski and Dug who answered the call of the Mini's feeble horn when it pulled into the car park.

Mario had good news, well for us at least, which he delivered with a complete lack of enthusiasm.

"Perry couldn't make it, he grumbled.

So, he gave me a bunch of his stash to apologize.

Dug and I clambered into the backseat while Ski rode shotgun, he had his driving test in a couple of weeks and was hoping to get some practice in.

Mario started the car or at least he tried to on the fifth attempt he got lucky, and it shuddered into life.

"Hey man, is it cool, if I drive on the way back?"

Ski asked, Mario eyes widened in horror as we lurched haphazardly onto Church Road,

"Don't hassle me, when I'm driving man!" he snapped back clenching his hands tight on the wheel as he went into an irrational rant.

"Ski, look you'd best fucking forget it, coz that ain't gonna happen he barked.

"Look, it's my name on the insurance, yeah?

Ski nodded slowly.

You get us into a fender bender, my neck is in the noose, right?

Besides, I've you before how I'm a person of interest with Thames Valley Police

Ski just stared at him grinning inanely tolerating his tirade while dug and I giggled in the back seat.

"Hold on a sec. queried Dug.

How did you, Mario Brown the most boring bloke in Berkshire, suddenly become a person of interest?"

"Piss off" he shot back.

Its coz of my priors, innit?

You're having a laugh ain't yah? Dug chuckled.

Stroll on mate, you're dreaming if you think the Pigs give a shit about a minimal criminal like you!"

His sarcastic grin was met with a quick glare from Mario who now told Ski.

"Anyway, the answer's no...

Fuck no!

I'm not going to jail for your little joyride because when it inevitably goes tits up, it's me that'll get sent down and with my luck, I'll likely get life!

"Nah mate, Dug chimed in

They'll let you off lightly with the death penalty.

"Fuck you man" Mario mumbled under his breath and began to sulk.

Now, utilizing persuasion, logic and above all common sense, Ski restated his case.

"Hey chill, out brother" he placated.

"Ohm, Ohm... cool breeze, easy now, innit.

He soothed.

Thing is whenever I'm baked, my brain gets all foggy and well it makes me drive, like really... super...slow.

Mario was starting to look moderately less furious as Ski made his closing arguments.

"Look, it'll take me ages to drive us back but there's zero chance of me getting into an accident.

He stopped himself and giggled.

"That's as long as I get back before the sun comes up, otherwise I might end up colliding with a Milk Float."

Mario frowned, sighed then very reluctantly agreed.

"Fucks sake, go on then" he seethed, changing the gears noisily.

It was a minor miracle the mini ran at all considering how much Mario abused it, the exterior was pockmarked with numerous dents and scrapes.

The seat well on the passenger side had a hole in the floor large enough to put your foot through and power the car Fred Flintstone style.

On-top of that the rust bucket had an annoying tendency to stall at the most inopportune moments.

Racing down Waingel's Road we crossed the parish line past the last of the streetlights and plunged into darkness.

Flicking on the high beams, Mario accelerated as the road curved to run parallel with the railway.

He almost missed the turning for Beggars Hill and frantically swung right, skidding onto the narrow road sending Dug and me flying across the back seat.

At the dead end he made a fifteen-point U-turn and backed up to the Farm Gate.

Switching off the engine, he wound down his window and took a long sad drag on his cigarette.

Ski sparked up a joint and soon we were caught in a smog, blasting Jimi Hendrix's live at Winterland on the Cassette deck.

"Aha yes, Sealed with a spliff."

He smiled taking a huge hit, holding his nose with one hand while the other yanked at an imaginary overhead chain.

Spluttering, he finally exhaled a huge cloud.

"Fancy a sample of Spanish Castle Magic, boyo?" He grinned, passing the puff back to me.

The Hendrix tape was one of our faves, not only did we love the loose psychedelic nature of the performance but also dug Jimi's far out between song banter.

My lug holes were drawn to Bassist Noel Redding's fuzzy over-driven Fender Jazz, it was gnarly as if his amplification was about to spontaneously combust.

The sound reminded me of Lemmy from Motorhead's tinnitus inducing tone and considering Lem had worked briefly as a roadie for Jimi it made me wonder if he'd decided "I'll have some of that."

Back on the tape deck, Hendrix was having trouble explaining to an audience, likely as stoned as himself what the next song *Manic Depression* was all about.

It's about a cat who wishes he could make love to music instead of the same old regular everyday woman.

We roared with laughter at his earnest nonsense.

Ski then busted out his impression, which had Dug and me in stitches.

"Woo Shucks!

I'm talking about some real groovy cat's man!

I'm down to my last few valve tubes my drummer Mitch Mitchell's on his third pair of arms, but fuck it, hell I don't give a damn!"

Blissed out in the backseat, I pictured myself being in that audience of twenty years ago, awestruck by Jimi's godlike talent.

My mind was then led out to the nearby pasture, momentarily distracted by what I thought was the sound of sheep snoring.

"What do sheep count when they can't sleep?" I asked.

"Don't know... Knitting needles?"

Ski chuckled.

Our mirth making hadn't infected Captain Sadness in the driver's seat who'd just spotted a pair of approaching headlights.

Being duty bound to bring us down he'd got himself into a right old tizzy about it

"Oh, no, fuck man!" he cried, his bottom lip trembling as if on the verge of tears,

Ski patted him reassuringly on the shoulder.

"Nah, it's cool, probably just took a wrong turn, that's all man."

The lights got closer as Mario's inevitable meltdown began.

"Guys, Guys! I am telling you right now, it's the Pigs!

He wailed.

This is so not fair, I don't wanna go to fucking prison!!"

Stopping a few feet from us, the vehicles headlights revealed to its occupants the dead end, the gate to the farm and a battered mini filled with smoke.

The car began to reverse slowly back to the main road.

"Look, they've gone pair of dopey dipshits."

Dug piped in, passing Mario the joint.

"Relax, have another hit, s'all good, innit?"

Mario was having none of it.

"Plain clothes cops' man, unmarked vehicle

He raved lighting another ciggy.

Them sneaky undercover motherfuckers!

Dug who was now incredibly high, started laughing.

"Fuck me, what is your deal man?

You really are the Prince of Paranoia!"

Newsflash my dear, Mario and Dug spelt it out for him.

"They... were... not fucking pigs!"

His senseless paranoia soundly squashed; he reverted to his default setting of being a miserable sod.

Man, my life is just a shit sandwich, he whined.

"And every day I take a bigger bite."

"Fuck this for a game of soldiers, I wanna go home" he cried.

Ski now used his limitless enthusiasm to break through Mario's wall of negativity and in less than five minutes he'd convinced him to drive us to another secluded spot off the old Bath Road called Toker's Corner.

"I thought only Perry knew where that was?

Dug asked.

"Yeah, Ski sniggered.

He drew me a map the other night.

Dude's got loose Lager lips."

Twenty minutes later Mario hit the brakes too hard and screeched to a halt, his high beams illuminating an unmarked turning to the left.

"It's down their man!" exclaimed Ski excitedly to Mario, who gingerly took the turning.

"Y'ur there ain't nuthin but sheep shaggers, pig pokers and carrot crunchers round these parts my lovers!"

Ski assured us in a mock west country accent as we bumped and bounced along the narrow unfinished road.

Crossing a humpbacked bridge, on the other side the road widened with a passing lay-by on either side.

Mario used the one on the right to turn around, pulled into the left and switched off the engine.

We got out to stretch our legs and take a deep breath of the country air laced with a subtle hint of cow shit.

On either side was darkened fields and above a canopy of black pinpricked with tiny stars.

Half an hour later, we were listening to Dark side of the Moon, and I was feeling comfortably dumb.

This time, it was me who noticed a distant pair of headlights pierce the darkness.

My proximity to Mario's negativity must have cancelled out my usual paranoia as I wasn't concerned in the slightest by the fast-approaching vehicle...

But it might be a good idea to at least mention it...

"Hey guys...

Ski interrupted me, sniggering.

"Yes, Steve we all know you've got Hot Flares man!"

I gestured toward the headlights.

"No, not tonight I've got my Levi's on, over there, look...

Mario stuck his head out the window and freaked the fuck out...

"Shit shitty shit, shit, SHIT!

The Pigs, they've been tracking us!

He squealed.

No, no NO!

He cried...

This is so fucking heavy man!

"Nah," Ski, replied, expelling a fragrant fog

"I bet its some randy couple looking to do a bit of shagging, maybe we'll get a free show, right lads?"

The headlights had now stopped on the other side of the bridge, the vehicle idled for a couple of minutes then it began to cross the span... slowly.

The approaching blinding high beams were joined by the flashing lights on the roof which bathed the Mini's interior in a chilling, alternating red...and blue.

Mario's paranoia had, for once been on point.

Realizing there was zero chance of escape, he put his head between his knees and burst into tears.

Leaving the stupid sod to sob uncontrollably we wound down the windows, waved our arms frantically, in a futile attempt to disperse the smoke.

Dug passed around a can of lager which we splashed our faces with then we all sat very still trying to look as sober as possible while reeking like a brewery.

On the tape deck the cash register intro to Pink Floyd's "Money" began, Its cheerful nature an ill-fitting soundtrack to our impending doom.

Turning around the same way Mario had, the cop car pulled up alongside the passenger door.

Dug whispered to Ski.

"You do the talking matey, being a singer, you rule at bullshitting strangers."

With a confident grin Ski whispered

"Don't worry lads, I'll get us out of this!"

He wound down his window as a torch was shone in his face.

"Good Evening gentlemen,

The Pig began.

Do you mind telling me exactly what you lot are doing out here?"

"Hey, oh nothing really, replied Ski.

Just talking, listening to music...er how you doing, man?"

Piggy waved the torch around the interior scanning us each in turn, I sat motionless, silent, and scared shitless.

"Just listening to music?" the Pig scoffed.

Ski nodded grinning like an imbecile.

"Yeah, mellowing out to some Floyd man we can move on if you want us to"

"Well, you can't park here, this is a private road and... The Pig stopped himself as he waved his torch back over to illuminate Mario, who was still sobbing.

What's up with him?" he asked.

"Er...um..not sure.." Ski panicked.

Dug interjected.

"It's his bird, Innit...

"She just dumped him, bloody women, eh?

He grinned.

The Pig snorted then sighed.

"Look lads, we know what you've been up to, the car reeks of it.

Now, we could nick you for being in possession of illegal substances, which would likely lead to you being charged with intent to supply.

But...

That involves a lot of paperwork and seeing as your mate here is already having a shitty night...

"Let this be your first and final warning.

The Pig pointed his torch at each of us in turn

We find any of you out here, again...

We'll arrest the lot of you, got it?"

We nodded in unison.

"Oh and you'd better drive

The Pig told Ski as he pointed to Mario.

"Your mate, he's in no fit state."

The cops pulled slowly away none of us spoke, moved, or even seemed to even breathe for a very long time...

Finally, the silence was broken by Mario noisily blowing his nose.

"Fuck fuck fuck fuck!!!"

He cried drying his red rimmed eyes on his sleeve.

In a total state of panic, he twisted the ignition key after a handful of attempts the temperamental Mini spluttered reluctantly into life.

Mario shifted into reverse gear and floored it the three of us thrown back by the sheer G-force of his flight of insanity.

"Wrong fucking way man!" Dug yelled as we barreled down the pitch-black narrow road... backwards.

"They set up a roadblock for us on the main road, we gotta find another way out!"

Mario shouted as he struggled to drive in a straight line navigating the oncoming darkness over his shoulder via the back window.

Silently I began to panic at this speed we may end up wrapped round a tree, upside down in a ditch or backing into a wayward cow.

Dug had pressed himself against the back window trying to make out and announce any potential obstacles before Mario reversed into them.

"There's a fork, coming up!" He shouted.

"Make a right, no, I mean...

Fucking hard left, now!

Bouncing up onto an inclined driveway, the Mini decided to choose that moment to dramatically stall.

The engine died, Mario screamed and slammed on the anchors as we skidded through a neat line of fir trees.

Scattering several flowerpots and some garden furniture in our wake we rolled to a creaking halt in the middle of a well-tended lawn.

From the rear window, in the near distance, I saw a light come on inside the farmhouse.

And then, I finally lost it...

"Mario, What in the fuck?!

I snapped.

"Why are we parked in the middle of someone's fucking garden?!"

"I know, I know, I know!"

He cried, twisting the ignition key frantically over and over through gritted teeth, spit and fresh tears to a terrifying clicking sound.

Over at the house a door had opened from which a shadowy figure now emerged.

It moved towards us, shouting angrily, brandishing something long and shotgun shaped.

By some miracle we must have qualified under the drunks and idiots' protection clause as the car finally, started.

Mario flattened the accelerator effectively dodging our second, in this case likely literal bullet of the night.

Spraying grass and dirt behind it the Mini ripped back through the line of trees, down the driveway and swerved onto the dirt track.

On we sped toward what I hoped was a fictional roadblock.

Racing over the humpbacked bridge we neared the turning for the Old Bath Road

"Fuck it" Mario said,

"Hold onto your love spuds lads, I'm gonna go straight through."

The streetlights on the main road came into view but there were no cops, flashing lights or any form of roadblock,

Mario shook his head.

"No, no this ain't right. Where, are they?"

Next, he let his paranoia take the wheel so instead of heading right and back to the Pub, we went left.

For the next two hours Mario's Paranoia drove us all over Berkshire he was constantly convinced we were just within the grasp of the long arm of the law

"Re-renforcements, he ranted "That's why they didn't bother with a roadblock.

"They called in air support; he yelled as he glanced up out the window

"Whirly Birds Helicopters, man, tooled up as fuck with machine guns to shoot out our tires.

Dug who was now, no longer high, and therefore extremely annoyed weighed in.

"Look the local cop shop...they've got like one helicopter and it ain't even armed, even if they were prepared to waste their resources and dispatch it, how are they gonna stop us, with a voice gun and harsh fucking language?

He rationalized.

"So, Mario how in the fuck are they going to scramble a squadron of gunned up military choppers to engage us in a high-speed pursuit?!

Mario shook his head as Dug continued to eviscerate his bullshit

"Anyway, it's not as if they'd be running down a Bloody drug cartel, even you, Mario with a rap sheet you'd have us believe is a mile long, you aren't worth it, man none of us are.

We aren't villains, like I said earlier at our worst we are all, minimal criminals.

Finally, it was the ever-upbeat Ski who managed to break through Mario's paranoia.

"Hey man, chin up, yeah?

He beamed.

"Between you shitting bricks, bawling your eyes out and Dug telling the Pigs your non-existent girlfriend had blown you out...Well...

In a roundabout way, you saved us all,

You're a fucking hero man!

Mario's face twitched awkwardly as if he was trying to smile but his nerve endings wouldn't allow it.

Instead, he exhaled, let out a huge sigh and at last drove us back to the Pub.

It was 2am and raining heavily when we pulled into the empty pub car park.

Nobody said anything as the three of us watched Mario skid off up the road, the mini's exhaust belching black smoke. I was just glad to take a piss in the bushes and see the back of the barmy bastard.

Walking home through the pour we reflected on the night's events, dug proclaimed Mario a National Treasure and one we should bury pretty sharpish, for future generations to discover.

"They'll have his bones exhibited in a museum he laughed.

And here Children we have the missing link between sanity and total batshittery

The Miserablist....Bastardio Paranoidonicus"

We all laughed as Ski added.

"Yeah, Mario Brown, he's always down!"

The Boat Trip, River Thames, UK 1988...

Late one night, over a smoke in the park, Perry told us that local psychedelic band Ozric Tentacles were playing a show that Friday at The Boathouse, an Illegal venue on the bank of the River Thames.

The old wooden barn had been abandoned for years, until a group of enterprising stoners had used it as a squat, setting up a drop in, lunch out type of residence.

To fund their lifestyle of leisure, they'd converted the space into a makeshift venue.

Building a small stage using a stack of half rotten planks installing a stolen PA, and stringing up a few borrowed spotlights.

Bands from the new age jam scene would play on weekends and the stoners charged a fiver to get in.

The Boathouse was on the Pigs radar, so there was a risk of the place getting raided.

The stoners didn't want any undercover cops infiltrating their little clubhouse, so you had to give a password to get in, which was changed every night.

Perry had an inside source on the passwords from which he'd also scored a bunch of acid tabs, the plan being to take them and add a little shock and awe to Friday night's show.

Rick and I met the rest of the band and Perry at the pub, we had a couple beers, a quick smoke and hopped on a bus into town.

Perry also brought along his best friend, Alan who was back from college for the summer.

Four years older than me, he wore studious glasses which made him look like a Math's Teacher

Sporting lank, greasy hair he spoke with self-assured authority when it came to anything drug related.

The bus dropped us at Cemetery Junction, which wasn't quite the dead center of town rather it was on the fringes where Wokingham and London Road met after skirting the graveyard.

Into the humid night we traipsed down Cumberland Road

Taking a left onto a darkened Sun Street and toward the river kennet.

Alan stopped us at the steps that led down to the tow path.

"Listen up guys, his face was stern.

The pigs have been casing the joint for a while, its likely a couple of undercover mothers are watching the tow path tonight, as it's the only way in and out."

Alan informed us we would have to walk the path one at a time,

He set off first while we waited for his signal to follow.

Taking a right at the bottom of the stairs onto the tow path he disappeared under the railway bridge.

Not long after a stone hit the water his signal and my cue to start walking.

The air grew cold as I walked under the viaduct and my mind started to entertain dark thoughts.

Once we'd all made the trip we re-grouped in the shadows on the other side of the bridge and into the marshland that led to the banks of the river thames.

A bowl of scattered stars guided us toward the looming outline of the Boathouse.

Alan stopped and produced an envelope.

Passing around the tabs, he pulled out a can of lager from his satchel to wash them down.

As we walked, I asked how long it would take to feel the effects, Alan guesstimated that in about half an hour our trips would begin.

Ski was also curious if we dug the experience could he take another trip tomorrow.

"It won't work, Alan said fixing him with a glare.

"Can't take LSD two days in a row, man."

Ski smiled back, totally unfazed.

"Better make tonight's trip a full-on psychedelic funk out then lads!" he chortled.

Once we reached the boathouse the place looked deserted

Only a muffled hypnotic beat from within gave any indication it was occupied.

Perry made a series of knocks on a battered looking door.

Slowly it cracked open and dreadlocked stoner peered out.

"Password and how many?" he asked.

"Steve Hillage" Perry replied handing him thirty quid.

The doped-up doorman then allowed us to enter, one at a time.

Inside as advertised a wild and crazy time was being had by all.

The Boathouse was filled with a dense fog bank of dry ice.

We waded through the fake mist to a wooden table surrounded by tree stumps, my nostrils chockfull of the pungent stench of patchouli and hash.

Alan handed out beers.

We sat, drank, and bopped our heads to the bands psychedelic beat.

Sooner than I'd expected, reality began to buffer, and my surroundings started to shimmer.

Everything improbable seemed sort of possible, was this it then?

The trip, the best part as Jim Morrison had once slurred, was I about to have an audience with the holy and the divine?

There was a blinding flash as the fog cleared,

Man, this was as weird as it was confusing.

Somehow, I was now floating inside the belly of a giant, blue whale.

"Bloody Hell!" I said aloud.

"Who parks a fucking whale in a boathouse?"

I was struck by a flash of enlightenment maybe the whale had swallowed the vessel that was usually kept in the boathouse.

Floating down now from its open mouth, the table and all my friends had vanished.

A pair of dogs walked up to me on their hind legs, both the color of rainbows, one smiled and the other growled.

This caused the whale above me to freak out, explode and fill the boathouse with balloons of shiny blubber.

The table now reappeared with my friends dancing frantically on-top of it.

Gasping for air, I began to retch and ran outside where I puked a hot mess over myself.

Back inside, everything had vanished once more behind the wall of dry ice.

From the fog, two figures emerged.

The two became four, then six all of them wore the same, distinctive flat hats.

"*FUCKING PIGS!!*" a disembodied voice screamed,

I fled for the door and out across the marshland.

Having put a few hundred feet between me and the now busted boathouse.

I glanced behind me, tripped on a muddy tree root, and tumbled into a bush.

Frigid with Fear, I rolled onto my back and gazed at the stars above, they twinkled and winked at me, I was transfixed.

Steve do not fall under their spell.

I thought.

Let's focus on our current predicament, shall we?

The little chat I'd had with myself hadn't helped one bit as my mind's eye flew at light speed towards their heavenly bodies.

The night sky. it was one great big sodding time machine.

Tonight's display was how they had looked, thousands of millions of billions of years ago!

What if aeon's ago they'd got bored with all that twinkle, twinkle bullshit and reverse big banged themselves into nothingness?

Ground Control to Major Arsehole, the boathouse is painted blue and there's fuck all you can do.

Except...pray the law never find you

Back at the barn, the cops were leading people out in handcuffs to a couple of police vans parked on the tow path.

By means unknown my brain had tuned into their radio frequency

Control...

Long haired male, sighted in bushes by riverbank,

Appears to be covered in own vomit, over...

(TMI, whiskey tango, foxtrot, over...)

Control...

Suspect may be having bad trip,

likely borderline psychotic,

Request authorization for use of deadly force, over....

(Go ahead whiskey, tango, foxtrot,

Light that hippie up, over...)

My tiny mind had lost any sense of rhyme, reason, or reality.

After lying in wait for what felt like half the night until at last the boathouse looked abandoned once more.

Making a muddy break for the tow path, I ran across the marsh, back under the bridge and reached the bottom of the stairs.

Behind me, a stone hit the water as Alan, Perry, and my bandmates emerged from behind a line of trees.

"Fuck me Steve, Dug exclaimed.

We were about to split, figured you'd been caught by the fuzz for sure!" he smiled and slapped me happily on the back.

Alan immediately shushed him telling us how we had to scatter and head home in different directions as the pigs were probably still actively looking for us.

This seemed extreme, it must have been hours now since the raid but whatever, I paired off with Rick.

Deciding on the route for our long walk home that we knew like the back of our hands.

Most of it was via the same roads and streets as our daily commute to Love rock only in reverse.

Earlier thar week Rick, Dug and I had been listening to the in-concert album by Black Sabbath "Live Evil" featuring their second singer Ronnie James Dio,

Dio's take on the bands self-titled track and musical calling card was far more satanic than the version recorded by original vocalist, Ozzy Osbourne.

Now in my head the creepy riff churned over and over.

Made up of a tri-tone a sequence of three notes that sounded discordant and unsettling.

Dug told us that it had been banned in medieval times when it was known as "the devil's interval."

Folks back in the dark ages considered it so evil that who so ever played it was likely to conjure up old nick himself.

Sabbath had used it to kick off their self-titled 1970 debut album completely changing the musical landscape and pretty much inventing heavy metal.

In my altered state, the sticky night air poked angrily at my flesh, streets Rick and I had traversed for years now looked darker, unfamiliar, and disturbingly sinister.

They twisted at odd angles and harbored terrifying whispering shadows.

Walking under the railway bridge the curving brickwork above heaved and pulsated.

Shafts of visible dread filled the air, our echoing footsteps enveloped and enhanced by a passing freight train, I held my hands to my head as its rumbling battered my brain.

Rick thought it would be quicker if we double backed to cut through Palmer Park rather than continuing past Suttons industrial estate and up Shepherds Hill.

We spun around and approached the park gates the railings swayed in the gentle breeze.

The tips of the fence morphed into pitchforks, they poked at my fear as the wind whispered the creepy lyrics to Black Sabbath

"Is it the end my friend?

Satan's coming round the bend."

"Fucking no way, the park's evil man" I protested.

Rick laughed, called me a paranoid twat but ok fine we'd take the long way home instead.

The long steady rise of Shepherds Hill was tough going in the hot soup of the night, Rick's face shone with sweat from the effort bleached ivory by the light of the full moon.

His pale features started to shift he looked...more evil, cruel, and unusual.

The LSD had super charged my hearing causing Ricks breathing to rise dramatically in volume.

A deep raspy croak as if his throat were blistered.

Then he began whispering,

Strange words, curses, incantations, maybe he had a sore throat as he was due breathing... hellfire?

My paranoia wasted no time convincing me, I was walking alongside something that was just pretending to be him, a demon in Ricks clothing,

"What is this, that stands before me?"

Another lyric from Black Sabbath echoed in my head as I stole a glance at the thing mimicking my friend.

Satan...wasn't he supposed to get behind me, not walk beside me?

Perhaps dropping acid opened a portal between dimensions, with my negativity and paranoia manifesting a six-lane satanic superhighway.

Upon which the devil had rode his pale horse into town.

Then the evil entity had cloaked itself as Rick to freak me out and steal my soul

My rational thoughts sought to calm me...

Steve, stop it, that's the acid talking.

Time to breathe and focus on something more positive and fantastical, yes, that's it, my faithful Hot Flares!

Look at them flow, I smiled to myself, they were very warm and looking particularly impressive tonight in the moonlight.

Finally, we reached my home, I turned to bid Rick, or rather the thing good night.

It chuckled, flashed a pair of fangs as it revealed to me, it's true, horrific form.

The big, black shape looked down at me, its red eyes afire.

With an oily snarl it croaked

"I'll see you in a few hours" and with a vile grin, it unfurled, black, tattered wings and scuttled away, hooves clopping as it vanished into the night.

My throat was frozen in fear, only a little "eek" came out when all I wanted to do was scream for my mother.

Unlocking the back door, I crept upstairs into bed.

Shaking under the covers, sleep was slow to take me each time I started to doze off, I was shocked awake by the sound of talons scratching the windowpane.

At dawn the light seemed to banish it back to hell and at last I managed grab a couple hours of shut eye.

The Mudbath, Donnington, UK 1988...

The alarm went off at 6am, I felt groggy, the fog cleared from my mind as I pieced together the events of the night before,

Blinded by ignorance and the promise of a chemically enhanced adventure.

My acid trip had rapidly jackknifed onto a highway to hell, leaving me in a puddle of fear and anxiety,

I needed to pick up the pieces and fast.

This morning I faced a four-hour coach ride to the day long alcohol-soaked Monsters of Rock festival.

Feeling chemically unbalanced, I picked up my bass for a noodle, hoping it would settle my mind.

After a few minutes, my fingers began to pick out a weird, unsettling riff, it burrowed its way into my brain, hypnotic like some kind of incantation,

My paranoia relayed a message for me.

The gateway has opened.

Now, you're playing our tune.

Next time I'll bring friends,

See you real soon!

Unholy shit, now my four string's a conduit to the underworld

An hour later, I knocked on Ricks door who was thankfully now free of wing, hoof and fang and we made our way to the rendezvous point at the Pub's car park.

For today's monumental excursion, the vast majority of the Drinking Team would be in attendance, the rock n roll tribe looked magnificent assembled in the in the morning mist.

A legion of rock soldiers, dressed in battle scarred denim and full metal leather jackets, and an assortment of band T-shirts.

A quick glance told you who had indulged in what the night before, Dilated Pupils or Bloodshot Eyes, I still felt awful and so took to drink, slugging from a 2-liter plastic bottle of cheap ale.

The coach arrived, we piled onboard, two hours into the journey I had reached bursting point and hobbled down the aisle.

Asking the driver when we were scheduled to stop, he gruffly replied it would be at least another hour providing we didn't hit any traffic.

He clearly wasn't exactly chuffed at being burdened with ferrying a bunch of no-good drunk, drug taking long hairs to and from some devil worshiping music festival

Rick told me to just piss in an empty bottle, no way, not in front of an audience, first it was gross and two I would instantly die from shame.

Legs tightly crossed, I ground my teeth, feeling each pebble and imperfection the coach rolled over as if a needle gun was tattooing my bladder.

After an hour that felt like a week, we hit a tailback of traffic.

Clenching, sweating for a months' worth of twenty minutes until we slowly began to move forward.

Half an hour later the coach took the exit for the service area, the driver pitied me, stopping to let me off before we reached the parking area.

He shooed me out the door, I sprinted as fast as a man can with crossed legs to the nearest bush.

My victory hobble was accompanied by cheers and shouts from the coach of

"Go on my son, drain that main vein man!"

Arriving at the Festival Site as we disembarked the driver gave us instructions for departure, no quarter for stragglers and zero allowance for latecomers.

"I'm leaving 11pm on the dot, if your late you long haired layabouts can bloody well walk home."

It was far from a gorgeous late August day for the ninth annual Monsters of Rock festival at Donnington Park racetrack, Overcast, windy and likely to piss down at any minute.

For me and many among the group it was our first visit to the festival, today Iron Maiden were headlining with David Lee Roth, Kiss, Megadeth, Guns N Roses and Helloween rounding out the bill.

As seemed to be the norm for any hard rock or metal focused festival the day would be blighted with inclement weather, Mother Nature obviously wasn't much of a headbanger.

The stage stood in the middle of the racetrack at the bottom of a gradual slope.

The site had been drenched with consistent rain for the past week, so little grass remained, replaced by mini lakes and endless mud.

Today's attendance was up significantly from previous years, one of the biggest draws being Guns N Roses who had outgrown their early afternoon, second on the bill slot due to the massive success of their debut album, Appetite for Destruction, by the time they hit the stage the audience had swollen to a record breaking 107,000 punters.

German pumpkin fixated Maiden soundalikes Helloween opened the show, instantly I was unimpressed unlike Morgan Sherry who loved every second.

A manic one man mosh pit, head banging, yelling along and creating his own exclusion zone.

Bored I sipped on my overpriced watered-down beer, anxiously awaiting the next act.

The band exited the stage, a pair of massive video screens powered up on either side of the stage and twenty minutes later, Guns N Roses the most dangerous band in the land kicked off with the cocky swagger of "It's So Easy."

"What's my name, Donnington?" Axl asked and a hundred thousand plus voices screamed it to him.

"No, he roared back...its Mr. Fucking Brownstone!"

The band delivered the goods in abundance, giving us what we all wanted.

Dirt under the fingernails kick ass rock n roll.

From my vantage point behind the mixing tower, I could see the violent, constant crowd surges.

The band had to pause several times, Axl asking people to move back a couple of steps to prevent those at the front being crushed against the barrier.

Before they closed with *Sweet Child of Mine* Axl signed off with "Hey, don't you guys kill each other out there"!

As it sure looked like some were trying to, having spent most of Guns set avoiding the customary festival projectile.

A Two-liter plastic bottle drained of its alcoholic contents, refilled with the consumers piss and thrown as far as possible.

Frantic Bottle Battles would sporadically break out, drunken fans having built up an arsenal of ammo,

Lobbing them back and forth in brief skirmishes, I got hit once in the head and twice in the chest in rapid succession not long after the band left the stage.

Next to play was one of Rick and my faves, the mighty Megadeth, we had seen them decimate Hammersmith Odeon back in May from the back of the balcony.

Both of us experienced that night a severe case of whiplash which we preferred to call "Neck-Fuck" brought on by constant head banging.

Our necks started seizing up almost as soon as we left the Odeon the pain lasted almost a week but for us it was invisible badge of honor and excruciating reminder of a fucking great show.

Today was our chance to see the band more up close, trudging through the mud we jostled and barged our way closer to the stage.

The PA started to blast the intro tape and suddenly we were swept up in a muddy tsunami of bodies.

The wave was impossible to escape, before we knew it, we were right against the barriers, virtually looking up Dave Mustaine's nostrils as the band kicked into "Wake Up Dead"

As the show progressed the surges and mosh pits grew ever more intense and watching the band became impossible

In the mire it was a case of survival, grabbing onto bodies trying to stay upright.

Anyone who started to go down, was hoisted back up.

One in trouble all in trouble, an all-out dirty war of man vs mud.

Mustaine yelled "We are gonna give you one more tune which features Mr. David Ellefson on the bass guitar" and the crowds recognition to the memorable opening bass riff to "Peace Sells" started another violent surge.

The force of the crowd bearing down on me started to become too much.

With everyone around me covered in a slimy layer of muck, I was unable to gain purchase and pull myself out of the muck.

The weight of the crowd causing me to drown in a surging sea of bodies.

This was it for me going out to the sound of one of my favorite bands as a squirming muddy mass closed in from all directions to block out the overcast sky.

Darkness, then...pain

As I was yanked violently out of the human sea, pulled back into the daylight by a huge figure dressed in more mud than black.

"Yah all-roight there mate?" my lanky savior asked me in a chirpy Birmingham accent,

"Cheers, I think so" I gasped, he laughed, gave me a thumbs up and was swept away in another surge of bodies.

Staggering back after Megadeth we waded through the filth to our group home base, marked by a Union Jack Flag.

Both covered in rapidly drying mud we sat and regaling those in our group not as stupid as us of our dirty dance with death.

Taking a swig of lager, a high-speed bottle of piss collided with my face, treating me to a gross splash of backwash.

I lined up for a greasy hot dog as Kiss took to the stage, the band wisely stuck to their makeup era crowd pleasers which sat awkwardly with the bands new look of Skintight spandex, bubble perms and hi-tech pointy guitars.

Next, David Lee Roth's brought his perma tanned brand of Californian fun to the stage.

His arrival was accompanied by a steady downpour not that he gave a shit that mama nature mother fucker was not gonna piss on his parade.

The heavier the rain got the more over the top Roth's between song banter became.

After a stray bottle of piss broke free from one of the frantic battles and landed onstage next to his day glow yellow boxing boots he yelled in mock anger

Who just threw that?

Oh yeah, I see you!

I'm gonna come down there and fuck your girlfriend!"

Then he attempted to educate us, with a dubious history lesson on the origin of the towns name of Donnington

"You see folks, it's in two parts, "Donning" as in a place where something cool is about to happen and "A Ton" as in lets fucking kick some serious ass!"

This cocaine fueled motormouth sure wasn't talking bout love but me, my gang and a hundred thousand soaking wet bought his bullshit and duly responded with a roar.

Our now soaking wet enthusiasm was now rewarded with a rendition of the Beach Boys "California Girls."

A song so ridiculously inappropriate and brazenly cheesy to dump on a drenched Hard Rock audience, I couldn't help but smile and join in the mass singalong despite the torrential downpour.

The weather cleared up almost as soon as Roth left the stage, and the Sun came out to bake dry the mud.

Finally, the mighty Iron Maiden unleashed their headlining set of anthemic equestrian metal as the light faded,

The masses chanted and the bonfires raged as vocalist Bruce Dickinson demanded far too often that the drunk, muddy masses.

"Scream for me Donnington!"

Once Maiden left the stage to and their signature send off, Monty Python's "Always look on the bright side of life" Played over the PA.

The cheery ditty was cut short by a solum announcement from the local police that two fans had tragically lost their lives in the violent crowd surges during Guns N Roses set and they urged us all to get home safely.

I thought back to when Axl had told the crowd to stop trying to kill each other what he can't have known then was it was already too late for two young fans.

One of the surges had caused a group of about fifty people to collapse against the barrier.

After security had removed the injured, they found Alan Dick, and Landon Siggers, aged just 18 and 20, buried under four inches of mud, the pair were pronounced dead on arrival at a local Hospital.

The shock, sadness and surreal sense of disbelief hung like a black veil over me as we navigated the departing masses.

What had been a memorable day now tarnished by tragedy.

Rick and I were silent until he turned to me and mentioned how it could just have easily been us who'd fallen and never got up again, during our frantic Man Vs Mud Vs Megadeth battle.

Back onboard the coach, it was close to 11pm and Everyone was on board except for one empty seat,

Dammit, where the hell was Ski? I thought.

Then I heard a banging on the side of the coach, "Let me in!" A muffled voice cried, the pounding becoming more frantic...

"Where's the door man, hey bussy bus take me to your driver!" the voice giggled.

Running outside there, halfway down the coach was Ski clearly chemically altered beating on the side of the coach asking the metal wall to open sesame and take him back home sweet home.

After giving him a big hug and leading him to his seat, I asked "What are you on Ski?"

He smiled sleepily his pupils fully dilated.

The silly pilchard had only gone and dropped acid again to which I questioned.

"Hang on didn't Alan tell us it wouldn't work if you took it two days in a row?" he began to giggle.

"Yeah, I remembered, got around it by staking two tabs though."

Apparently, him doubling the dosage, broke the rule.

After watching Guns N Roses set, Ski had dropped the acid got lost wandering in the nearby woods and ended up dancing round a bonfire with a friendly pack of Werewolves who only spoke French.

"Hey man, I miss anything?" Ski grinned his pupils fully dilated.

This was not the time to bring my ever-cheerful friend down so, I told a white lie.

"Not much Mate, bit muddy for Megadeth, pissed it down for Roth as for Kiss and Maiden boring as fuck, man."

The coach rumbled into life Ski turned to gaze sleepily out the window, smiling he howled a fond farewell to his Lycanthropic amigos.

THE GENERAL & THE DRAG SHOW

WEST 49TH STREET
MANHATTAN 2012

"Now, Lemme tell yah sumthin" his deep, Brooklyn drawl was menacing, almost threatening.

He paused for effect as my thoughts raced to fetch my paranoia.

Boy, you sure can pick em can't you?"

"Wonderful, you've discovered yet another six-string psycho.

He's probably connected and your about to get whacked.

Soon you'll soon be safe, sound and sleeping with the fishes!

Outside my head in the harsh reality of the squalid rehearsal room he finally answered my question.

"I work for the Metropolitan Transit Authority, deep in dem tunnels, in the dark with the rats and the filth.

Down there I'm a King, the Don, boss of an eight-man crew, my soldiers don't even move until I allow it to happen.

Now when I answer dat radio, HQ telling me an express train is headed our way at fifty miles per hour"

Them nine cars of screaming steel is passing two feet from my face, I taste the sparks, my teeth shake and my heart pounds like a goddamn jack hammer.

"Now DAT is what yah gotta give me!"

For fucks sake all I'd asked was

"Could you please tell me exactly what the band is looking for in a bass player?"

A couple of months before, Mac and his wife had a baby Derek didn't like the fact that he could no longer commit to Liquid Crowbar's routine of two rehearsals a week.

Derek would then get falling down drunk for the sessions that Mac was able to attend and become belligerent, questioning his commitment to the band.

While I tried to stay out of it, I couldn't help thinking that Derek was being a dick.

Mac soon quit the band, telling me he'd much preferred playing Dad to his new arrival than playing with a bitter old lush.

The band had lasted a mostly fun eighteen months and for me it was now back to My Space and Craigslist.

Which is where I found Dino, band capo and lead guitarist for Devils Backbone

A towering six foot seven inches of testosterone and Sicilian machismo, with a mane of jet black hair and jaw hewn from granite.

Dino's deep baritone Bensonhurst accent made everything he uttered equal parts menacing and hilarious.

His bands name was totally fucking ridiculous, but I no longer cared about such a triviality.

They had a good set of songs, a record deal, and a new album to promote.

Their over-the-top ad on Craigslist had proclaimed once they recruited the right bassist, who I just learnt would be expected to generate sufficient subsonic seismic activity to give Dino a coronary event.

Well then, they would wage Rock N Roll war on a global scale.

Devils Backbone had a producer/manager, not only would I have to impressive the band, but I'd also have to blow his hair back.

Backbone was made up of Dino on guitar, Julius Caesar complex and foot fetishes.

Taylor on drums, political rants and being dull as a dial tone. Lastly, Freddy on lead vocals, casual anarchism, and questionable performance art.

Impressed that their ad stated they had a record deal, I was a bit let down when it turned out that the record label was a one man show run by their producer/manager, Jake who had made his name in the industry crafting obscure dance remixes.

Deciding he wanted a pet rock band, he'd forked out for the recording and manufacturing of the band's debut album and was now looking for a return on his investment via the band's income from live shows, merchandise, and CD sales.

After an excruciating showcase rehearsal, where Jake kept stopping m the band to inspect exactly what I was doing with my fingers he gave the band the nod and I got the gig.

We began rehearsals for my debut show in Atlantic City, New Jersey's seedier seaside answer to Las Vegas.

Like Liquid Crowbars bust of a showcase at The Stone Pony, the venue didn't provide any backline.

Embarking on a four-hour drive with all my equipment, I had hoped we were at least playing a decent sized venue.

Le Grand Fromage was well hidden on a darken side street, a good ten-minute walk from The Hotels and Casino's lining the boardwalk that faced the Atlantic Ocean.

The venue was a restaurant, more specifically it was a Pizza parlor.

Upstairs, between the circular tables and the checkered napkin dispensers was a small, circular stage that hosted bands on Friday and Saturday nights.

Years ago, I'd played a show at the Purple Turtle with Empire State, where we got paid for performing in Pizza, I suspected tonight's payment would also be made in dough.

The band had a security guard as part of their entourage. Dino had bragged, beforehand how he could have easily handled any issues personally, but he wanted to stay focused on "taking heads off" with his lethal six string axe attack.

"I'll leave dah crowd control and chin music to Archibald."

He'd told me.

Our security officer was shitfaced when he arrived having polished off a bottle of whiskey on the bus ride down and soon made a hinderance of himself, hitting on some of the more attractive patrons.

Jake had told us, that the venue had a built-in audience, but it wasn't exactly packed for a Friday night, I guessed most of the weekend revelers were gambling in the strip of casino's a few blocks away.

Still, we gave it some heft and put on an energetic show, that was until Freddy decided he wasn't satisfied with the crowd's response.

Grabbing a garbage can from behind the stage, he emptied the contents and sang with it on his head for a couple of songs.

This garnered more laughs than wows from the sparse crowd which pissed him off even more.

Now, that he'd presumably grown tired of the stench he removed it and hurled it into the audience.

It sailed into a table occupied by two couples and knocked over their drinks.

This got Freddy a reaction and they were not happy with him at all, telling him in no uncertain terms to fuck right off.

He glanced over at Archibald, who instantly steamed in, throwing the table aside and securing one of the unhappy customers in a headlock.

Deciding the best move was to ignore the unfolding fracas, we carried on playing.

Finishing our set to no applause, as most of the crowd were now busy brawling with Archibald.

Quite how his pugilistic approach would win us new fans, I wasn't sure, maybe his thought process was to beat them senseless into adoring submission.

For his sins, the band were banned for life from playing the venue.

Next up was Tammany Hall on Orchard Street back in the city.

A Hall in name only, a night club with several levels and an awkwardly placed stage close to the main entrance.

Paying guests had to walk past the band to get to the bar, we drew over sixty paying people despite dealing with a bonehead of a doorman and rude staff in general.

Dino declared this a total victory over the Lower East Side of Manhattan.

Stating his loyal troops had "Tore the place apart" which I scaled back to a more realistic "yeah, we did ok."

At the following rehearsal Freddy told the band of an opportunity to get in at the ground level.

In fact, it was slightly lower than that, by performing at a brand-new venue in Bushwick, Brooklyn called Rock Bottom.

He talked it up a storm, a couple of his friends ran the place, who had told him at least fifty people could be found playing pool there on any weeknight even without the draw of a band playing

Bushwick had still not been swept up in wave of gentrification that had transformed many parts of Brooklyn.

The neighborhood was still, fairly rundown and not particularly safe after dark.

Dino didn't share in my fears when I brought it up with him if it all went to shit and the band got wiped out by some gangbangers in a drive by shooting.

His contact at the Village Voice would write a tribute piece on the band, hailing us as fearless hero's.

On the Night of the show, Freddy called me as I was about to leave, telling me to press the buzzer on the front of the building marked "#175" to gain access.

"Hang on, this place is, in an Apartment?"

"Sort of" he unhelpfully replied.

Loading my car with my cabinet, bass, and a pocket a flask full of whiskey.

Freddy had also mentioned that while the venue had a bar well *kind of...* they only sold cans of beer.

Rock Bottom or the Apartment where it was located was in a particularly. dangerous section of Bushwick.

Fortunately, I found a parking spot right outside, it might come in handy for when I was chased by a bunch of rooting shooting thugs post show and needed a quick getaway.

Unloading the gear, I wheeled my cabinet up to the building and pushed the buzzer.

Telling the answering voice, who I was they released the lock.

Lugging my bass cabinet down a long hallway to a front door, a stoned looking hipster answered.

Wheeling the cabinet into someone's actual occupied apartment, down a narrow wooden set of steps to this alleged hip, upcoming and happening venue.

A half-finished concrete basement.

There's was a homemade, unpainted makeshift "Bar" to one side, a wooden, two-inch drum riser near the back wall, next to it a beat-up pool table and the only places to sit three sets of car seats in various states of decay.

This place was a damn tomb,

This was no legit venue more a speakeasy, or a squat.

A really terrible band, played before us by the name of Bonez.

But, with no venue staff or stage manager to enforce a schedule they set up and started playing whenever they felt like it.

They hit, the stage, sorry the concrete floor, just after 10:00pm, two hours after Freddy told us they were due to perform.

We had no choice but hurry up, wait, and suck it up while they did an excellent job of nearly emptying the place.

We finally go on about 11.30pm and play in front of a massive audience of three people.

Dino is having to play in an awkward stooped fashion, due to his six-foot seven frame being a few inches taller than the low ceiling, he frequently forgets and throws his head back a few times when going into a solo, banging his swede on the ceiling leaving him with a dumbass dazed expression,

We only play about forty minutes, it's fun, sort of and we play well seeing as we haven't rehearsed since the last show.

We would have played longer if Dino's "Weapon of Mass Noise Pollution" his Matchless all tube head hadn't blown half the speakers in his cabinet, frustrated by his sudden drop in volume he climbed onto the tiny drum riser, which he used to launch himself into the air expecting to land super hero style and bask in the crowds adulation, but the low ceiling wins once again and he smashes his head into it, falls forward and lands face down on-top of his guitar, The resulting casualties are two guitar strings, a cut forehead and a mild case of concussion.

A true triumph in the face of absurdity.

Now that Rock Bottom had been demolished and Bushwick in general according to Dino been.

"Fucking Decimated"

He laid out his next campaign.

To the Garden State of New Jersey, he would lead us to wage all out-rock n roll war, saving those we converted to our cause from the mid-life crisis mediocrity of Bon Jovi.

The gig was outdoors and an afternoon performance at yet another unconventional venue.

A Racetrack, an hour's drive from the city.

The organizers of an annual classic car show needed a band to provide the musical entertainment for potentially thousands of fast driving, hard drinking hot rocking punters.

Dino's approach to this show was the same any other, for weeks beforehand he'd pontificate at length as if he were some expert in Military Strategy.

General Dino would lead, us his glorious troops from the rear to divide and conquer the audience.

We would take them by storm, reduce the venue to rubble and leave those that didn't kneel before us to eat our dust.

I had to chuckle at the tactical asshole.

Dino declared that a mere racetrack would be no challenge, they didn't have a hope in hell.

The stage was set up inside the Centre of the track and faced the overflow car park, which meant the car show with its potential audience of "thousands" was a good three hundred feet behind the band.

To the right on Dino's side about the same distance away was the empty racetrack flanked by stadium style seating.

Dino didn't seem too concerned when we took to the stage to an audience of the sound crew and a couple of confused lost looking car enthusiasts.

He was convinced our opening sonic salvo, would cause the distant masses to cease admiring the vehicles and come running to witness us weave our rock symphonies.

Two songs in and we were drowned out by the PA crackling into life over at the racetrack

"Good afternoon, folks and welcome to Dragmania!"

The announcer boomed.

A line of hot rods appeared in the distance and started to line up directly behind the stage whilst we continued to play.

They revved their engines in unison it seemed in a bid to drown us out.

Before the next song, Dino maxed the controls on his Amp and turned it around to face the rumbling line of Dragsters.

"Lemme tell yah something!

He yelled over the mic as they revved in response.

"You no dick fucks can't drown out dah Devil!"

Taylor counted us in, and we played the next two songs back-to-back.

Glancing over at the track, I could see the first dragster was now in position on the starting grid.

With a massive roar that shook the stage it blasted off with the force and volume of a Jet Engine.

Its short blast up the track completely drowning out us and pretty much everything else within a square mile radius.

Dino was frothing at the mouth in pure rock fury as he turned to face the line of Hot Rods,

"You dirty Jersey sons of bitches, can suck my big Marshall dick!" he went to perform a Pete Townsend stye Windmill, hitting an E chord which fizzled out with a loud pop as Dino's amp blew its speakers.

Freddy had surprisingly been tolerant of this dragsters noise pollution thus far, but with his Commander now silenced.

He exploded with rage...

"FAAHHHUUKK!" he threw the microphone aside, kicked a monitor speaker over then turned to face Taylor and the drum kit.

Our dial tone of a drummer recognized the red mist of rage in Freddy's eyes and for once showed some emotion, his face went white, a mask of utter terror.

Grabbing each side of the bass drum Freddy yanked at it, scattering stands, cymbals, and Taylor in four directions.

Ending the song in an explosive cacophony of chaos.

Dragging the bass drum and what was still attached to the lip of the stage, he threw his weight behind it.

It teetered for a second before landing on the concrete of the car park, missing its target audience by a good ten feet, the clatter and crash it made was answered by the line of dragsters dixie horns and deafening revving engines.

Ending the brief skirmish that had been the New Jersey Volume War.

The following week, the producer, Jake told the band he'd landed the us a showcase set at some industry event on the upper east side of Manhattan.

Dino told me how it was for charity, ergo no pay but it was the place for the band to be seen.

"All the big dick industry suits will be there, yah know all the money men"

Fucks sake not this again I thought having been through this crap with Liquid Crowbar, I knew too well the drill, Blah blah it's a loss leader of a show and if the celebrities or big boys even show up, they will likely arrive just in time to miss our set.

Only this time, they didn't.

After our set which was met with muted applause, the special guests were announced, Ex Rainbow & Sabbath drummer Bobby Rondinelli, took over the drum kit and Testament guitarist Alex Skolnick stepped up on second guitar.

Using us minus Taylor as their backing band we played an unrehearsed version of "War Pigs"

Bobby bashed the kit behind me with an insane amount of power.

I tried to keep up whilst trying to look cool, but I was utterly terrified, the last time I had been in the same room as Rondinelli, I had been watching from the balcony at Hammersmith Odeon when he occupied the drum stool for the mighty Black Sabbath in 1994.

When it came to Skolnick, I was getting a good kicking a few feet below him in the mosh pit when he was on lead guitar for Testaments show at London's Astoria in 1988.

Somehow, I got through our impromptu performance which went down way better than our set.

Locational Logistics were starting to cause problems within the ranks, Freddy had moved to Ocean City in Jersey a three hour drive away, he'd only make the trip to Manhattan to play shows with us, writing new songs was just an exchange of files and emails back and forth, and I got a little miffed that the first time the band played a brand new song in the same room together was when it made its onstage debut.

I continued to bite my tongue, even when we travelled down his place to record a new song one Sunday.

He and his wife rented the apartment above his wife's gallery, it was a great open space to use a portable recording console to lay down the track.

But Sunday was a big business day for the Gallery, nobody thought to shut up shop while we hit record so several takes also captured the cheerful chime of the front door as another potential patron dropped by.

Come the next show at a bar and grill/club near Times Square I'd had enough and played the last song, sitting on the back of the raised stage with my back to the audience.

At the band discussion in the restaurant afterwards without Freddy as he had a train to catch, I argued that I couldn't see the point in us sticking with a singer that lived three hours away when we could surely find someone suitable who lived in the city

Dino, Taylor, and producer Jake didn't agree.

Keeping typically tight lipped I seethed while I supped my beer.

Later, I sent the band.

A lengthy email re-stating my point.

Dino was the first to respond.

"Lemme tell yah sumthin, while it was typed grammatically correct, I read it in his voice as I did the next line which was...

"Now, just relax and cool your jets."

After five minutes of ruminating, I fired off a one-line reply... "That's fine, I quit"

MILK MUSHROOMS & CUSTARD

VAUXHALL DRIVE UK 1988

In the sobering aftermath of the festival, I swore off drugs. Henceforth my sole source of alteration would be in golden liquid form... mine's a pint of Fosters, please.

My drug free existence would soon be derailed by Dug who made a beeline for me up the Pub a few days later.

His wide-eyed expression clearly that of a man on a mission

"Stevey Boy, he said excitedly.

A word in your shell-like ear, me old son"

Walking me to an empty table in the beer garden, he unveiled his dastardly plan.

The band should once again drop acid and real soon.

"Saturday to be exact... he informed me with a crooked grin,

Aghast I asked.

"What in the fuck?!"

"Look man, he replied.

I ain't talking about going back to the boathouse, besides the joint's been abandoned since the raid.

What I'm saying is I've secured a safe, controlled environment where there's no danger of the Pigs kicking in the front door man."

After making sure he wasn't being overheard he revealed the location.

"My folks have gone to Marbella for the week so we can trip at their gaff"

"NOPE!'

I exclaimed.

"Dug...You can fuck that idea sky high!"

Had he already forgotten my disastrous experience not even a week ago,

How I'd evaded arrest by the narrowest of margins or my terrifying stroll home with Rick's demonic doppler ganger?

Seriously, man" I shouted, angrily.

You've got the memory of a bloody goldfish!"

Dug shushed me and supped on his pint.

"Nah mate, he smirked,

I ain't forgot none of that but this time...

He winked, then whispered...

Got you totally covered son."

"The second you start to get paranoid, or Satan rears his horny little head, you just gotta remember one thing...

Milk...

He let the word hang, while I sat there incredulous.

"Milk brings you down, man" he smiled.

"Milk?" I scoffed,

He gave me a look of genuine concern.

"Yes, indeed mate its density absorbs and blocks mental negativity.

You just got to knock back a big old glass of it and it'll chill you the fuck out.

Taking a large gulp of Fosters, I was no longer pissed off but, still not convinced.

"Cows, for example he explained.

Did you ever wonder why they're so mellow?"

"Don't know"

I shrugged.

"Think about it, man...

Grazing away all day not a care in the world, you know why...

They're all fucking high on their own supply!"

We laughed.

While that was total bullshit, the fact Dug had gone to the trouble of uncovering a potential magic bullet to murder my paranoia was quite touching.

But...there was a one slight snag he hadn't considered, and I'd completely forgotten.

Whilst under the influence of LSD it's virtually impossible to eat or drink anything for the duration of the trip, which lasts an average of twelve hours.

With none of that in mind, I said.

"Fuck it, I'm in"!

Dug chuckled, raising his glass in a toast.

Here's to you giving old nick the elbow and getting drunk on the fruit of the udders!

Saturday morning, Rick and I walked through the misty drizzle to Vauxhall Drive.

Dug answered the door of his parents' house in a dressing gown and Megadeth baseball cap, he was halfway through demolishing a bowl of Frosties.

"Wise move to line the stomach before a trip."

He advised leading us into the kitchen, where Ski and Clive were already sat at the table chowing down.

After fixing us a couple of bowls, we headed to the living room, which Dug had decked out like a sleazy opium den.

The curtains drawn, candles lit and sleeping bags covering the floor.

Three lava lamps and a ton of joss sticks provided the swirling, fragrant ambience.

For visual stimulation a VHS copy of Empire Strikes Back played on the TV, with the sound muted.

As for the soundtrack, a double tape deck played a loop of albums by Floyd and Hawkwind

Dug handed out cans of Fosters we sat in a circle raised them to our band, having a right old laugh and dropped the tabs.

Laying on my back, I clung to the hope that what was about transpire wouldn't be any worse than last week's demonic nightmare.

My gaze flitted between the fish-tank and the Imperial Walkers on screen silent assault on the rebel base.

I still felt hungry and returned to the kitchen to make some toast.

Laying back down, I took a large bite the crunching sound it made rose in volume to the threshold of pain and caused the room to vibrate.

The butter had smeared in my palm where it now slithered and bubbled in slo-motion.

I was mesmerized as it cascaded in rivulets from my fingertips, a golden, greasy waterfall ending in a shimmering pool on the carpet.

Meanwhile, things had got seriously fucked up between the Fish Tank and the TV, the fish were now part of the Star Wars franchise having experienced a massive growth spurt and attaining the power of flight.

Their open mouths spewed vivid green laser beams all over the screen while a battalion of tiny Imperial Walkers marched through the sediment of the Fish Tank silently blowing tiny bubbles.

After closing my eyes for a few seconds, when I opened them again, I was alone in an empty white room.

A shape started to form in the distance, it was hard to make out as the snow-white horse's hue was identical to the room,

As it trotted closer, I could make out its rider, a horned figure in black figure brandishing a pitchfork.

Shit, I thought, the horse began to gallop toward me.

Coming to a halt a few feet from me the rider dismounted as it cheerfully whistled Slayer's "Angel of Death."

The thing flashed its pristine white fangs as it skipped merrily toward me.

"Well, Hello again...

It said in a voice ancient and evil.

For this week's exciting episode, the dirty demon had half inched Dug's face, it smiled as I shook in my sneakers and Paranoia placed thoughts of sheer terror in my head.

Oh fuck no...

Now, Dug's the devil in disguise

It's happening...AGAIN!

The demon, held a taloned finger to its blackened blistered lips and shushed me...

"For fucks sake, man" It snarled.

You really need to chill out!"

And snapped its fingers sending me back to the living room only now the walls and the floor were throbbing, like the room was alive...

Freaking out I beat my fists upon the floor.

"Help! Dug, dug...DUG" I shouted.

Milk, Man, I need MILK!"

My desperate words formed a hot air balloon of orange, which rose to the ceiling, burst, then violently shot up one of my nostrils.

The shock of the illusion knocked me flat on my ass. Determined to beat this fresh hell, on my hands and knees, I crawled to the kitchen, where the other guys were sat at the table, arguing.

Only these weren't my bandmates, they had their faces, but the demonic quartet also had horns, white fangs and pitchforks.

"Fucking Hell Steve!" they roared in unison,

Paranoia burst back into my brain...

Welcome to Hell Bitch!

Your inner demons are currently on tea break.

But soon enough...

They'll be back and...

You'll be toast!!

The demon that wasn't Dug peered at me, his look almost one of concern.

"Oh, fuck no, fuck man, no!"

It howled at me, spitting soot as it shooed its demonic disciples aside.

The blackened being sat me at the kitchen table and slammed an ice-cold glass of milk in front of me.

The thing that wasn't Dug now leaned in and whispered in my ear, its breath was hot and stank of Sulphur.

"Instant comedown in a glass son"

It snorted.

"Also...a great source of calcium

All you gotta do is...Drink.

And that devil, he damn well made me do it.

Taking a tentative sip, then a slurp and finally a huge gulp.

Oh, yuk it felt like a yogurt covered breeze block as it slid awkwardly down my throat,

I must have spent over an hour trying to finish the glass, the distraction of the task at least did bring me down little by little.

The demons put their pitchforks away and retracted their fangs until they became my beloved bandmates once more.

Back in the living room Rick was now laid on his back, transfixed on the ceiling, legs outstretched frantically pedaling an invisible bicycle.

Shaking him, I tried to break him from his trance, Unblinking he whispered a mantra, over and over...

"Not the fucking Ohmriff, again, again, again again"

Clearly, he was a lost case at least for a few more hours.

Having had enough of this acid bullshit for not just mine but the entire bands lifetimes I decided to leave.

Mooing to myself to keep the demons at bay all the way home.

Sunday afternoon, Dug called my home phone.

Once he'd established, I was alive and still sane, somewhat.

He told me how he was sorry, wanted to make it up to me and went straight to the hard sell on a fun new way of tripping yet another day and night away.

I almost hung up the phone in disgust.

"No, man wait a second... He pleaded.

No more Acid, I promise, I'm talking about Shrooms man,

Ingesting or imbibing this simple, humble vegetable creates a magical state of chemical alteration.

Well, technical it isn't a veggie it's a fungus but...

I interrupted him.

"Dug, hang on, run that by me again...

You now want me to eat a fucking fungus?"

"I do, Magic Mushrooms man, they're totally natural! he enthused.

You see acid gets cut with all sorts of shit so you're always rolling the dice as to whether they end up doing your head in as well you know."

Fuck no man, I am not doing them!" I said adamantly.

Steve, I swear on Lemmy's grave this will be totally different" he pleaded.

I pointed out that Lem wasn't dead... yet.

"On Hendrix's Valve Tubes then!

They give you a clean paranoia free high."

What Dug was in fact banging on about Psilocybin a hallucinogenic property found in some wild growing mushrooms and eating them raw or drinking their distilled essence should, theoretically give me a cool, trippy experience free from freaking out or invoking any demons with pitchforks.

The fear of missing out, being easily led and pretty fucking stupid, meant it wasn't much longer until I took the bait and dug reeled me in.

Sunday had been a blisteringly hot day and the evening hadn't offered much in the way of relief, as I sat on a bench in the beer garden with my bandmates.

Sweating profusely, we wiped our brows periodically with our pint glasses.

Dug's Mushroom caper had been in the works for a while, Alan and Perry had harvested a crop of the freaky fungus a week ago from a top-secret location.

Keen to know where anything I ingested came from, I pressed Dug as to where they'd found them.

"Not sure man, he frowned.

I mean just go two, three miles in any direction from where were sitting right now and all grass and cow shit, so pick a field any field man"

For the past week the batch had been dried, pressed, and distilled into a potent liquid.

The two Harvesters of Psychedelics now approached our table with their heady brew.

Pulling a thermos flask from his satchel, Alan asked if anyone would care to join them for a Cuppa

Dug had already briefed us on the stupidly obvious code word and now the pair of them headed to the far side of the car park and hid behind the tree line.

Taking turns to have a dose of shrooms mixed with our lagers we then sat back at the bench and had a sip.

"Pfft!" Rick coughed and sprayed a mouthful over the table "Now that... is fucking gross!" he spat.

As all our lagers now tasted utterly disgusting, we resorted to necking them as swiftly as possible.

Twenty minutes passed and I was now bored.

"Well, that was pretty horrible, now what?"

I asked as a welcome cool breeze pierced the stifling night, above the stars had become obscured by clouds.

I could have sworn one of them made a belching sound as a hot, dense snow begin to fall.

The rest of my bandmates seemed unaware of this impossible change in the weather and just sat there laughing like baby hyenas.

The breeze increased to gale force and whipped the snowflakes into a humid blizzard.

Stupefied, by its hypnotic swirl, I asked the hyenas,

"How can it be snowing when it's still fucking hot man?"

My inquiry was even funnier than whatever they'd been laughing about in the first place especially to Ski.

Who now beat his fists upon the table

"Hot Snow, man, look out man it's a Boiling Blizzard a Temperature Tornado."

Tears of mirth ran up and down his cheeks and sparkled like diamonds.

Suddenly he stopped, his face serious as a heart-attack and rose from his seat to announce.

"From clearing to copse to forest they call to me, their bite is no worse than their bark, I must take my leaf's and join them.

He laughed to himself.

Word up my woody brothers,

Ski hears you rustling!"

He wobbled through the blizzard, to the line of trees at the back of the garden.

Forcing himself between the branches and trunks he fixed me with an unhinged stare, twisting himself into a shape mimicking the surrounding foliage.

He smiled and then the great Tree-Ski declared.

"Look at me, I'm a fucking tree!

I'm gonna grow forever man."

While he looked peaceful, green, and rustic, I'd become fearful of the red-hot blizzard that now raged all around us, it looked like we may end up getting buried in it.

Trapped deep beneath a white-hot blanket of snow and slowly burning to death.

"How are we going to get home?" I shouted Alan gestured to Dug's Bug over in the car park, which had magically transformed into a Tugboat and was bobbing up and down, on a sea of oily tarmac.

The beer garden wasn't the safest of places for us right now considering our altered states and the impossible weather.

Also, the long holiday weekend meant the pub was busier than usual and host to more of the ilk that after a few jars were prone to casual violence.

A bunch of babbling stoners, especially one telling all and sundry he was a fucking tree would be liable to receive a damn good hiding.

Alan's parents like Dugs were also out of town, so it was time to retreat and ride out of the rest of the summer snowstorm at their place.

The only obstacle that stood in our way was how to uproot Tree-Ski, Alan managed to soon convince him that soil in his parent's garden was much richer in nutrients.

"Pick up your roots, man he smiled.

We'll plant you out by the patio, you'll grow much quicker and a lot taller up there!"

We all squeezed into the Dug's Tug Bug.

With a roar and belch of black smoke, Dug sounded the foghorn, and we chugged off through the white-hot death toward safety and inevitable insanity of the Fairwater Estate.

Alan's Parents lived in a large, detached house on Old Bath Road not far from suicide bridge where Rick and I had diced with death on the railway tracks two summers back.

Dug dropped anchor and we headed inside; the joint was still filled with guests from a party Alan had thrown two days beforehand.

I found an empty chair and laid back in it, watching the stippling on the ceiling slowly drip onto the carpet and dozed off.

Two hours later I'd come down from the shrooms and felt stable enough to join the party.

From the conservatory I heard instruments being tuned.

Oh boy, this was about to get ugly, I mused and grabbed a Foster's from the fridge.

Alan, Perry, Clive, and their new friend Rusty, were setting up their gear for one freaky Weed Whacker of a Jam.

Rusty had been hanging out with the group a couple of weeks, he was Australian and staying in the UK illegally.

To call him a bassist was a stretch, after finding a discarded bass in a dumpster on a building site, Rusty had ripped out all the frets and painted it multiple colors with oil paint.

While it looked truly hideous, he was regardless proud of his four-string technicolor nightmare and named it Rainbow Deep

A Fretless bass is a lot more difficult to play than a regular one, without metal frets you have no markers to indicate where to place your fingers for each note.

It's pretty tricky to play in tune without the frets as a map, so the player has to feel where the notes are like a violin or cello.

When fretless is played with a modicum of skill, it can produce a warm and expressive sound,

None of which applied in Rusty's approach to the instrument.

He hadn't bothered to learn how to tune his bass and the extent of his skills was he knew how to play two basslines... badly.

The first was a simple four note reggae riff, the second was the same lick played in reverse.

Rusty's amp had its controls superglued to max as he wanted to shift serious air with his good vibrations.

The four-man jam now began it wasn't as such a performance more a gradual unravelling of tune-free weirdness.

Alan and Paddy were both proficient guitarists, using various effects pedals to create parts that merged, fought against, and occasionally complimented each other.

They echoed and swirled like a stoned orchestra tuning up backwards... underwater.

Clive would with start a simple rhythm, leading into a repetitive, hypnotic beat which was usually the most listenable part of the madness.

Meantime, Rusty who had no sense of timing, tempo or song structure would start playing whenever he felt like it.

His overpowering, monotonous bass line looped over and over until he got bored and switched to the reverse version.

His out of tune boom, destroyed anything vaguely interesting the others were jamming.

Rusty wasn't the only party guilty of repeating himself, like most of us that whenever we learnt a new chord or riff, we'd proudly play the damn thing to death.

Perry had recently mastered the magical "Hendrix" Chord, Jimi had used it frequently and most famously on "Purple Haze."

Technically it was known as an E7 with an added sharp 9th but fuck me that was boring.

Perry had now been playing that same bloody chord using several rhythms for nearly half an hour.

Alan, began to vocalize, warbling like a didgeridoo.... Dug shouted in my ear.

"Nah Digeridon't fucking do it man!"

Perry now started chanting some Scottish sounding bollocks

Along with Clive's beat, Rusty's monotonous tune free bass line, it was the sonic stuff of nightmares.

Alan, now launched into a horrible feedback filled solo as Perrys chanting morphed into a cleansing "Ohm...OHM"

Meanwhile I began to wonder if my ears would ever recover.

Taking a took a couple of hits from the doobie Dug handed me, didn't make them sound any better but it prevented me caring.

Alan and Perry went back to chanting, in my altered state, the crap they were babbling became clearer.

Eyes closed, greasy hair plastered to his sweating face, I heard Alan's chant as...

"I'm an undercover policeman, I've tumbled your gang man, this is a bust!"

Perry's highland yodeling became "We are the pig's man and you lot are all going down!"

Once more, Paranoia had me in its icy irrational grip

So, I locked myself in the bathroom and rinsed out my ears.

Ten minutes later, I wandered into the kitchen.

Sat at the table having uprooted himself from where he'd been planted by the patio.

Ski was back to his jovial self and hatching plans with Dug and Rick to secure sustenance for the household.

"Rick, what does this say?" Ski flicked a twig from his hair trying to make sense of the massive handwritten list of munchies...

"Two tins of Ambrosia" he replied.

"Oh, cool you mean the Custard, yeah?"

Rick nodded, once we'd cross checked and confirmed the list, I volunteered to assist Ski on The Food Run,

Outside there wasn't a single flake of evidence of the Red-Hot Snowstorm but the heat and humidity remained

Jumping into the passenger side of the Mini that Mario its former owner had almost reversed to death, I forgot about the Fred Flintstone friendly hole in the floor and my foot hit the driveway.

"Fucking ouch!"

I yelped pulling out of the hole and it started to throb.

Ski was now street legal but couldn't currently afford a car.

Mario had inadvertently provided him with a set of wheels after disappearing mysteriously two weeks ago.

We guessed he had gone back to Spain from whence he once came, personally I was glad to be shot of the moron.

Before vanishing, he'd dumped the Mini in the pub car park.

After a week, the landlord walked into the greenhouse and told us we could either get rid of our mate's car or he'd charge us for it to be towed to the scrapyard.

Late the next night after closing closed Dug broke into the Mini made a mold of the lock and somehow got a set of keys cut, which he handed to Ski.

He loved the unreliable rust bucket and was a damn fine driver if he didn't get too high.

After coming down from Alan's Mushroom Tea, he'd topped himself up with a few slugs on Perry's Elephant Bong.

We sat in the car; he sparked up a joint and offered me a hit.

"Ready to go man?" he asked, I nodded, the car started on the seventh attempt and for the next ten minutes we sat doing nothing with the engine running.

Ski's thought process, sense of time and perception slowed to a crawl whenever he got too high and right now, he was baked as fuck.

"Ok" he giggled another five-minute passed as his brain told his hands that maybe putting the car into gear just might, make it move.

"Well, alright, you'd better hold on tight mate!"

We lurched out of the driveway, took a right onto Old Bath Road, and headed east at a whiplash inducing 15 mph.

"Where did you get your license? in a fucking Christmas Cracker?!" some miffed motorist shouted from his open window as he angrily overtook us.

"Man, that dude is mental Ski chuckled.

he's gonna cause a pile up, going that fast."

He took a last pull on the roach and tossed it out the window.

"Well, he was only doing about thirty and you know you could go just a tad faster, Ski" I encouraged.

"Yeah, your right this is taking ages, why is the garage SO far away? Fuck it, let's floor it!"

Our destination, The Wee Waif filling station was a ten-minute drive each way from Alan's.

Dug held the record at six minutes, tonight's outward journey would take us over half an hour.

Twenty minutes in I nodded off for a handful of minutes, When I awoke, I checked the speedo, bloody steady on I thought, Ski was now pushing twenty-two miles an hour.

"Goddam Man, I am SO hungry, he giggled.

I could eat a horse, a pig and two goats!

Fuck it, I'd even eat the farmer that grew them too!"

I was starting to feel dizzy.

"Hang on, Ski, where the fuck are we?!" I asked three times until he finally heard me.

"Oh yeah...I took a detour, some negative vibe merchant overtook us, and told me to speed up or get off the fucking road.

Dude sounded important, man, probably a pig or something so, I figured, I'd best do what he told me."

Ski had taken a random insult yelled from a window as an enforceable demand.

During my micro nap he'd turned off the road onto a Rugby Pitch and been slowly driving in circles ever since.

Turning to me with a look of utter bewilderment he asked if I thought the dude had been taking the piss.

"Yes, Ski I believe he was ever so gently yanking your chain, now you see that flood light over there, drive towards it, make a left then take a right and we'll be at the garage before you can say Boomshanka, ok man?

Fifteen minutes later we trundled onto the wee waif's forecourt.

Twenty-four-hour garages would lock their doors at 10pm and only the attendant in the shielded glass booth would have access to all the goodies.

Most normal folk would fill up with petrol, pay the dude behind the glass and maybe sheepishly ask for a snack or two.

Not us, being powered by the puff, we didn't need no stinking gasoline we had come for the snacks, pretty much ALL of them.

Approaching the glass encased attendant, Ski pulled out the crumpled list.

His befuddled mind ensured he took his sweet time to methodically flatten out the piece of paper on the glass before he was satisfied it looked presentable enough.

It was now very late, or rather extremely early as the sun would soon be on the rise and the attendant didn't seem exactly thrilled to see us.

"Evening Mate" Ski offered; the attendant grunted as he corrected him.

"It's almost dawn actually."

"Oh right, sorry good morning then man!"

Ski beamed.

The attendant's shift was nearly over but he still had to deal with us, two of the most infuriating customers ever.

"No, I want four pot noodles, one of each flavor, not all the same"!

He sighed at Ski's request, tutted, and wandered back to the shelf to switch them out.

"Nice one, smiled Ski.

Next were gotta take a deep dive into the chiller cabinet.

Ok? Cool, now grab us five Pork Pies, one Melton Mowbray three cheese and pickle and one normal one, you know with that yucky jelly in it"

"Like this?" the now infuriated attendant held up the wrong brand for the third time,

No, man that's still not it, its Bowyers that makes it

Finally, he found the correct one and piled with the other pies on the counter tray then paused to ask.

"Ere, you pair of Jokers got enough cash to pay for all this?"

I shut him down by slapping three ten-pound notes on the counter as Ski went back to the list.

"Well alright dude... halfway there already

Ski grinned while the Attendant frowned.

Now we all got sweet teeth and I want candy man, now be a boss and bust open the chocolate box!"

"Six Twix, four Mars Bars, two Bounty's, no not the same, one needs to be plain chocolate."

The attendant dropped the confectionary on the counter and swept them into a second nearly full plastic bag,

Ski still wasn't done.

"Now we need some refreshment to wash that shit down man,

Grab us six cans of coke, two cherry the rest fat coke I mean normal coke, no, put those back none of us are on a diet man!"

The attendant dropped the six cans into a third bag.

Oh yeah and one Iron Bru and four Quattro's"

He shuffled back to the fridge cursing under his breath.

By the time The Garage grump had picked, packed, and tallied all our shit up.

We had driven the poor bloke to the brink of madness and almost forgot the most important item...

"Fuck, Shit... Custard!

I shouted.

"We can't forget Ricks custard.

Ski, he'll having a fucking fit!

"NO, we ain't got no custard not in the cans anyway"

The attendant barked at me.

"Now, you look here, mate he growled.

I've had just about enough of the pair of you, I've got the packet mix, you can have that it or bloody well lump it!""

Ski smiled...

"Good enough, lay six sacks of that shit on me, my man!"

He shuffled off grumbling at having to travel all the way to the back of the store to fetch them.

"Thirty-two pounds and seventy-three pence" he demanded we paid with the three notes and a ton of change, which he was totally over the moon about.

"Wow, we totally bummed that bloke out, man!"

Ski laughed as we pulled out of the Forecourt and hit the Bath Road at a law flouting 24mph.

The sun had risen by the time we returned to Alan's kitchen and emptied the spoils of our snail's paced escapade onto the table. And like ravenous vultures our friends fell upon the feast.

"Fuck me Ski its tomorrow already!" Dug exclaimed.

"You dodgy fuckers take the scenic route?

"Well, somehow this rugby pitch got involved... I laughed and told him I'd fill him in later.

"Hang on, where's mine...

Rick asked.

Don't tell me you fuckers forgot. Again!

He complained.

Fucking hell man, I'm always getting fleeced!

"No mate, I got em, Ski smiled.

Just in a far more portable, transportable form!"

He fished the packets from the bottom of the bag and flung them on the table.

Rick sighed.

"Oh, well you tried I suppose."

Tearing open a sachet he shook its contents down his throat.

"Ugh, ewww!" He spluttered and sprayed white powder all over the table.

Fucking yuk...pfft, tastes like shit man!"

"Bloody Brilliant!" Ski exclaimed as he emptied the rest of the packets onto the table and neatly shaped the powder into lines.

Coke...Custard, same shit, innit? He giggled.

"Anyone got a straw?"

DRAMA QUEENS & CYMBAL MONKEYS

MARCH 2013, LOWER MANHATTAN

⧜

Ten days after giving Devils Backbone the single finger salute,

I had auditioned for and landed the bass position in a new band called Vertical Smile.

The line comprised of an unhinged blonde tomboy on lead vocals and guitar named Trick.

A ex heroin addict on lead guitar called Caine.

And on drums, Jeff who informed me almost immediately that he was the bands third drummer in eighteen months.

A week after I'd joined Trick scheduled a photo shoot to introduce the new line up.

Jeff, AKA drummer number three had better things to do and didn't show up.

Following a heated phone call with Trick, number three was fired.

With my debut show a month away, after much groveling I enlisted Mac from two bands back Liquid Crowbar as the bands fourth albeit temporary drummer.

A week before the show, Caine decided to quit, breaking the news to Facebook, instead of letting the band know, first.

The next day, he sent a group text.

Sorry... think I lost my mother-fucking mind yesterday,
Please can I re-join the band?

I'd kept Mac updated on the drama but by the time I told him that Caine wasn't in fact quitting.

Drummer number four decided to remove himself from the situation and his text to me read...

Well, Steve lots of luck with that drama, see yah later!

Vertical Smile wasn't destined to be the most stable of my musical endeavors, due to Caines's diva like online tantrum we were now a trio and so debut show didn't go on.

It was now onto the grind of auditions and weeks of enduring some truly awful cymbal monkeys until we finally found a suitable fit for the drum kit.

Number Five was well groomed nice guy, who worked on wall street.

A competent drummer who's playing style was safe and solid, his recruitment was a compromise as what Trick really wanted was a animal behind the kit.

However, he was reliable and for the next year no one was fired or threatened to quit the band.

Mahwah, New Jersey, Summer 2014...

Running my hand slowly over the massive recording console, I asked Trick

"Do you think we can dust for his DNA?"

Exported from Barnes Studio in London the prestigious recording desk had been built by Rupert Neve.

On the other side of the pond, it had been used to create hit records by Queen, Phil Collins and... Culture Club.

I'd thought maybe, Freddy Mercury had left some of his mojo on the desk while recording Queen's soundtrack to the movie "Flash" and if I found a sprinkling of it, it would enable my band to record something equally majestic.

It has been a mission and a half to get this far mind and since joining the band we have gone through three producers.

Today is our second session tracking a new album, which has already been downsized to an EP and will soon end up being just a single.

Some might have said the band was not fully prepared, while others may have thought that trick our increasingly demanding lead singer/guitarist is expecting champagne level perfection while paying her collaborators peanuts.

Greenpoint, Brooklyn, April 2013...

Two weeks after joining Vertical Smile

The three of us gathered in a basement studio in Brooklyn the plan being to track two songs for a proposed single.

The producer is some local big shot whose credits include several successful NYC bands.

He was rude with a short fuse and didn't see eye to eye with the session drummer Trick had hired for the recording as the band was still looking for a permanent fifth stick-smith, for what she's paying the so-called session ace, it ends up taking him hours to lay a decent rhythm track.

A couple of months later, I was in the basement of a townhouse in Upstate New York.

With money tight, I recorded my bass parts playing along to a drum machine.

The machine was efficient, but progress was slow as the producer was more interested in taking hits off his bong rather than assisting the band in potentially making one.

Later that year we spent a frigid couple of evenings in a studio in Astoria, Queens.

We at least got one song out of the session with a producer that our new drummer, number five had previously worked with.

Only there was one slight...or I should say, *Sight* issue.

The man behind the board had a fantastic set of ears but he was legally blind!

His magic recording console was equipped with software that talked to him like a giant Speak & Spell.

This called for complete silence whenever we were in the room, in case the built in hypersensitive microphone picked up some flippant remark that it didn't recognize.

Which would cause the console to then crash as a robotic voice announced.

"Re-Booting, resetting...please stand...by."

Then we'd wait anxiously as it went through its startup sequence, hoping we hadn't just erased what we'd spent the last few hours working on.

Not long afterwards Caine decided once more to quit the band.

His timing was perfect, just before a string of three closely grouped shows only this time I insisted his decision should stick.

In two weeks, we re-worked our songs to suit a trio of vocals/guitar, bass, and drums.

We got through the shows by the skin of our teeth, but Trick still wasn't happy with drummer number five who she still felt wasn't dangerous enough, with another recording studio booked, she decided to bide her time and sharpen her axe.

Back to Mahwah, NJ, Summer 2014...

The studio's live room was wood lined which apparently made it great for acoustics, I certainly hoped so as the space was the size of a small cathedral.

The time-honored way to record a song is in layers, like sponge cake or Lasagna, drums first then bass, guitars, keyboards etc., vocals being the pretty frosting.

To save time and dollar bills, Trick wanted to use guitar tracks she had kept from a previous session in another studio.

Our new producer connected the hard drive and pulled her tracks up in Pro-Tools, he looked confused, tutted a handful of times and then slowly shook his head,

"We can't use these" he said.

One of the tracks was tuned slightly differently to so it couldn't be layered, plus the tempo of each individual track wasn't identical.

"They're not all in time or in tune" he sighed, pushed the talk back button, and told Number Five who was set up and ready to record in the live room.

"Hold fire in there, we need to have a bit of a conflab."

Trick didn't agree with the producer's critique of her recordings and told Five to start tracking to them regardless.

After struggling for hours through multiple aborted takes,

Trick asked Five angrily what his problem was, this was the final straw, and it wasn't no nice guy who kicked open the door to the control room thirty seconds later.

Furious, he stood in the doorway with his personal fan under his arm "I don't have a problem!" he shouted.

"The fucking problem is you princess!' and he threw the fan at Trick.

She tried to duck but instead of the shit hitting the fan, the fan hit the shit.

Looking at me red faced he said.

"I don't know how you put up with her."

And five then quit.

I once quipped that after their bassist John Entwistle died in 2002 and the band, The Who was down to just Pete Townsend and Roger Daltrey, they should have renamed themselves "The Two."

Maybe that's what me and Trick should have called ourselves now that Vertical Smile was also a double act.

Foolishly I still believed in the songs we have written and Tricks talent which often enabled me to ignore her incessant inability to not be able to get out of her own way.

At this point, there really was no option but to pull the plug and I fully blame MTV for what happened next.

The concept for the networks successful "Unplugged" show was to take an established platinum selling band or singer/songwriter, especially those who'd normally play Arena's, Festivals or Stadiums and have them perform in a far more intimate setting.

Leaving the towering Marshall stacks, gargantuan drum kits and pyrotechnics in the storage lock up.

Strip the songs down to their bare bones and perform them on acoustic instruments while sat on bar stools.

Playing a show within these limitations is a challenge.

Sat across from each other playing acoustic guitars is how most musicians collaborate and create songs in the first place.

For me, putting our material under such scrutiny was, unnerving.

Also, I had to consider performing with a Marshall Stack Security blanket not only covers up a multitude of mistakes but doubles as an instant conversation killer.

When you play unplugged, you can hear the audience and I mean really hear them.

Not just the cheers between songs, you can follow entire conversations your audience is having while you're playing.

Now, the silence is up for grabs

"Play a song you know!" the crowd would cry.

"You first" I'd retort.

One of our first acoustic duo shows was playing a fancy club that was hosting a Sirius XM DJ's record release party.

Across the street from the glamorous venue stood a glistening high rise apartment building of glass and steel in which I was informed Tom Cruise owned a penthouse.

For tonight's show, a rumor was doing the rounds that Lady Gaga may show up.

Having gone through similar speculative shit in the past, I paid it no mind.

Word had spread like a forest fire on the anti-social networks and the venue was packed, most of whom had no interest in the event itself.

Their sole reason for showing up was likely along the lines of...

Where the fuck is Gaga?

I want a selfie...

Then, I can be insta-famous by association.

The bar was to my side of the stage and was rammed by the time we went on.

The stool on which I was positioned far too close to the line waiting to be served, mid song, playing and "singing" one guy decided he'd waited long enough, and squeezed his behind onto the stool, I was already sat on.

It all went downhill from there.

Back to the search for another Cymbal Monkey, what would become drummer number six.

After a month we had narrowed it down to two candidates, one was the talented young son of an established drummer who played in several local successful bands the other was two years older than me and struck me as being a bit off.

Eventually we went with the latter figuring he'd be a bit more loyal.

Famous venues like the Bitter End in NYC had capitalized on being the venue where the likes of Lady Gaga were first "discovered" which is usually a white lie, what they should say is she played the place a few times, several years ago to a handful of regulars when nobody knew who she was.

Even some bands believe this simply playing the venue will afford them an opportunity for overnight success.

My two deluded band mates for example who decided that Six's debut show with Vertical Smile should be at The Bitter End.

The challenge here, being to layer the lies thick and fool them into booking us, pretty much an unknown band.

A couple of weeks of emails, phone calls and a metric ton of bullshit and we snagged ourselves a Friday night slot at 11pm in... February.

The more famous the venue, the more money they want to make and the practice of double dipping and flipping the venue is commonplace.

A typical evening at The Bitter End would begin with five bands playing a forty-five-minute set each piece from 7-11pm.

Then the venue becomes a night club with a DJ and a higher cover charge until 4AM.

That Friday in February was frigid and in the early evening snow began to fall,

When I headed out from home to the venue around nine it was close to being a blizzard.

When we arrived at the venue, two more bands had been added to the bill, which meant our slot had been pushed to one o'clock in the morning.

Meaning the band would now be playing early enough to go toe to toast with the local all-night diner's Breakfast special.

The long night rolled on and we hit the stage around 1:30am playing to a handful of people most probably drunk enough to not even remember where they were let alone the name of our band.

Commerce won out in the end, the manager banned us from playing there for life as we'd failed to draw enough people and left us us out in the cold.

With Vertical Smile not drawing particularly well in the city we decided to play a few neighboring states.

Theory being feed them folks starved of rock n roll, create a buzz around the band and word would get back to the city which would bump up the attendance for our hometown shows.

Easy on paper rent a van, grab these sleepier states by their lapels, assault their ear drums with a massive concussion of rock n roll and break America.

New Jersey was closest so first on our hit list.

Crafting a template email to send to venues, which was so full of utter bullshit, bragging how well we could draw in the city, that we had a ton of fans who travelled from Jersey to the City for our shows and we would for sure pack their place out.

We didn't get a single response from our digital cold calling until two weeks later a venue replied with a list of dates.

We booked a Friday night slot at The Rocking Roadhouse about an hour's drive into the Garden State.

The venue didn't provide backline and the other bands scheduled to play on the bill weren't prepared to share with a band from New York they'd never heard of.

Six took care of renting a van to get us and the gear there, only he totally fucked it up.

When we arrived to pick it up, the rental office had no record of his reservation after much pleading the clerk offered us all she had left.

In the corner of the vast warehouse was a huge filthy refrigerated truck, you could have fitted a flash frozen a couple of Orcas in the back, but the tiny cab only had two seats.

I thought it would be just and fair punishment if we had Six ride in the back and accidentally engage the refrigeration.

Instead, a milk crate was procured for him to perch on between me and Trick in the cab.

Trick navigated the unwieldy truck through gridlocked traffic to the Holland Tunnel and our first Escape From New York while a massive storm hit the city.

Under the river and into Jersey, the squalls increased intensity of the downpour looked more like a Hurricane with visibility on the Garden State parkway down to almost zero.

Then the directions provided by Six proved to be as useless as his skills at negotiating the rental.

Pulling into the Roadhouse's parking lot two hours later, the Hurricane had since moved on to batter another state leaving a gentle drizzle and localized flooding,

Jumping from the cab and landing in a mini lake, got my night of on the right foot as it soaked right through my boots.

Inside, it seemed empty for Friday night, only a few regulars propped up the bar all of whom gave us three New Yorker's the stink eye.

Topping the bill Tonight was Roadkill, a veteran local band, their lead singer/guitarist Karma Crash swaggered into the venue not long after we had.

She acted like she was Jersey answer to Joan Jett, only she looked more like Alice Cooper after he'd got a bubble perm and spent too much time at the tanning salon.

The sunburnt nightmare, thought of us as a no-good female fronted novelty act.

Until we played our set that is and blew her off the stage before she got a chance to put a boot on it.

Roadkill was at best average, I almost felt for her guitarist who's pained expression made him look as if he wanted to be anywhere but here.

Later I found out that Karma Crash had been a child star, her career reaching its peak when she was 15.

Still, though she trading on long forgotten glories she wasn't going to win or break many more hearts, now she looked a grizzled, washed up 55.

She stalked the band on social media for a while pleading to get her band on a bill in the city, I told her it wasn't up to us then she asked me to join her band so she got blocked and sent back to obscurity.

The following month a trip to Connecticut for a show in a town called Reading.

Midway through the set, I felt compelled to educate the audience on the proper pronunciation of their hometown, they were in luck tonight, seeing as I hailed from the original Reading in Berkshire England.

"It's not supposed to sound like something you do to with book, I chided

"Its pronounced, *REDDIN*, Innit?"

Which went down about as well as a turd in a punchbowl.

One again we'd been blessed with a sparse audience, what hadn't helped was Bon Jovi's drummer Tico Torres's son's band was playing a free show in the bandstand across the street and swiped most of our potential audience.

Onward then to the city of Brotherly Love, Philadelphia and to The Legendary Dobb's a bar/venue in the Centre of town, like the equally legendary Stone Pony in New Jersey a bunch of bands had got their break at the venue, Tool for example back in '92 who now sold-out Arena's the world over.

For a destination venue with a built-in audience and our prime slot on a Friday night we drew next to no-one, still there was a great Pizza place across the street.

Famous for their oversized pies, just one slice was the length of my arm, and it was so delicious, it made the two-hour drive to play to a nearly empty room worthwhile...almost.

Next in our campaign to smash the states into submission was a much longer trek, but worth the drive as we had been offered our biggest pay day to date, the band having been selected to play at a Festival in Fairfax, Virginia.

The amount the organizers were offering just about covered the cost of gas and hotel rooms.

The multipage contract agreement was filled with all sorts or legalize and restrictions, for example we couldn't in any way use any form of profanity as part of our performance including gestures and the band would also not imply, incite, or encourage that the audience instead use profanity.

We would keep our set to a precise forty-three minutes and we would not play any shows for two weeks before the performance within a two hundred mile radius of the Festival site, Sheesh, I guess ok then...

The stage was opposite the candy floss stand and Ferris wheel, so we drew a few passers who hadn't been expecting to see a rock band let alone one fronted by a girl with long blonde hair and a Les Paul, some teens and a few families stayed to watch us.

The youngest of the kids were intimidated by the band at first but soon started dancing in a little line, which was encouraging to see.

My little rock n roll trio corrupting the youth of Fairfax.

REHEARSAL INFERNO & THE TALE OF TWO HALVES

CEMETERY JUNCTION UK 1988

Since the band's formation, the five of us had become fast friends but as a musical unit we were pretty much, well... naff.

As we'd yet to come up with a name, out of frustration I started referring to us as The Anonymous Five

Tasking myself with coming up with the music the few original song's we had cobbled together so far were borderline juvenile in their simplicity.

For reasons I couldn't fathom, I'd was unable to string more than two riff or chord sequences together.

All the bands I listened too had songs with multiple parts even simple punk tunes by The Misfits sounded epically well-crafted when held up against my toddler friendly codswallop.

Establishing a riff, verse structure, chorus, a middle eight.

And the knack of knowing which parts went best together was a skill that for now would elude me.

At least the band had a decent lyricist in Dug, who was on a gap year from university where he'd been studying philosophy.

Far more accomplished at his assigned task than me, his well worded outlaw poetry targeted immoral multi-national companies, celebrated his fave band, Hawkwind and extolled the benefits of his preferred breakfast cereal, Frosties.

Our little band had some tough competition in the form of the biggest rock act in town... Empire State.

The band members were often far too aloof to grant The Greenhouse with their presence and if they ever did show up it would usually be after 10pm when they'd either just got back from a gig, rehearsing, or been embroiled in a writing frenzy for their new album.

The problem was that even if I was starting to love to hate the band, an Empire State show was an unmissable outing for most of the Drinking Team.

The Anonymous five went along to the next one curious to see if they could back up what I felt like was their self-generated hype.

Painful as it was to admit, I couldn't deny they were a damn good rock n roll band.

The four of them could all play well, their songs didn't suck, and their gigs attracted a significant number of females.

We would continue to attend their shows regularly,

Not that we were becoming fans, it's just that was where all the best-looking girls were at.

Empire States lead singer, Seth, looked a bit like Led Zeppelin vocalist Robert Plant, but he sounded nothing like him.

Blissfully arrogant he'd attempt to emulate Plants' signature banshee howls regardless. dramatically arching his back, he began to wail his face and neck gradually glowing bright red as he went way off key and swiftly ran out of air.

A legend in his own mind Seth was roaring a challenge to the Gods of Rock n Roll, but in reality, all his red-faced squawking did was dislodge some dust from the ceiling fan.

DC was their baby-faced wizard of a lead guitarist.

He was only seventeen, handsome with a lengthy well-conditioned mane of hair and blessed with a set of cheekbones you could ski down.

He also had the musical prowess to back up his good looks with a six-string skill level on a par with Eddie Van Halen.

And he certainly knew about it.

His over confidence, I perceived as arrogance, was just a part of his Rock Star persona and the jammy git's girlfriend was a dead ringer for Belinda Carlisle only she had bigger knockers.

On bass was Jacob, a better player than I was, he could be a little aloof, but he tolerated me, well he had no choice as he was often asking to borrow my bass amp.

Finally, there was Adam, their boffin of a drummer and the oldest member of the band he didn't drink and could be a bit of a motormouth but was pretty much an oracle when it came to his knowledge of music.

Empire State frequently played at Hatton's, in Cemetery Junction on the outskirts of town.

The main reason they played there so often was that management turned a blind eye to the fact half the band and most of their audience were not yet of legal drinking age.

The band had the whole performance thing down, DC would start the first song by dragging out the guitar riff, throw a few dramatic poses and whip his long hair around.

Milking the crowd's reaction to a feverish pitch before finally sliding into the song proper, which sounded a lot, maybe too much like The Kinks "You really got me"

Only Seth's lyrics weren't about being got by a girl or anyone else for that matter, instead he sang about the moon, being in its light but there was no cause for concern because everything was gonna be alright.

The band would then play a more up-tempo tune that dealt with matters of the heart mixed with some sort of potion that related to an emotion and a bit of a commotion

The band would then pause for a breather and a swig of lager.

Seth would shake his bottle blonde perm and make his first address to the audience or more specifically...the Ladies.

Leaning on the microphone in what I'm sure he felt was an irresistibly seductive manner, he began...

"I said ah woohoo, well alright Reading, how y'all doing this evening?" Seth boomed.

Predictably this got some whoops, cheers, and a fair few fuck yeah's

"I said LAWD have mercy, it is HOT...in here tonight.

Seth roared, shaking his blonde locks.

I said Reading are you people out there HOT...tonight?!"

Tonight, it was a bit nippy out and with most of the crowd still wearing their jackets, their reaction was one of confusion.

Inclement elements be damned, Seth pressed on anyway...

"Lemme say it one more time...I said, oh lord would you sanctify me when I ask these good people, my faithful rock n roll flock, are you HOT tonight, my people are you burning up?!

And only then after allowing a pregnant pause for effect would Seth drop his southern fired preacher act and add in matter-of-fact fashion...

'Well, people...you may be HOT but, hey man, yah know...

"I'M COOL!"

The girls, or rather the ones young enough to buy into such corny bollocks would coo and cheer while we would holler from the cheap seats.

"You...Fucking Wanker!"

Being the late eighties, Empire State were duty bound to have a show stopping power ballad in their repertoire.

The more successful rock bands of the day had found incorporating an arm waving tear jerking anthem in the set would attract more females to their shows and wherever fair maidens gathered their would-be suitors were sure to follow.

Curtail creativity put more bums on seats, sell the place out and go platinum man.

Empire's cigarette lighter in the air was a clinically crafted tearjerker, an epic ballad engineered to show that not only can we rock you like a hurricane, man, but we are supersensitive, and you know, totally in touch with our feminine sides...Baby.

Now, would you mind awfully if after the show we took you home sweet home for a quick shag?

The song itself was pretty good musically, going from whisper to thunder with the right amount of dynamic light and shade and even the lyrics weren't especially cheesy.

Once Seth got to the repeated closing refrain, his poor diction made it sound like he was singing "You're leaving me, you're leaving me, SOLO!"

This had led my ever dry witted drummer Clive to assume the song was Star Wars related.

Seth's words channeling the anguish, the turmoil that poor Chewbacca went through after his pal Han Solo got flash frozen and turned into a table in The Empire Strikes Back.

Thanks to this brilliant misinterpretation, Empire States emotional showstopper became for me a comedic highlight.

Back to the issue of coming up with a name for my band by which I'd no become obsessed.

It's been over explained and frequently embellished upon how famous bands had come across their names, Black Sabbath?

From a poster affixed to a bus stop across the street from the band's rehearsal room advertising a horror film.

Led Zeppelin? derived from the phrase that the band would probably be unsuccessful and go over like a Lead Balloon,

My first band eventually got its name by accident in a turn of events not worth documenting in the annals of rock history, it didn't stop me daydreaming though.

That one day the tale might be painstakingly inked with feather and nib onto a scroll of parchment for future generations to dig up and after poring over the text think...really?

Well, that was bloody stupid!

It might have read something like this...

The Anonymous Five & The Tale of Two Halves
A Clearing in the wood, The Land of the Angles in the year of our Dio
MCMLXXXVIII

Across the way from a bridle path stood an old Public House, named The Bull & Chequers.

The establishment's main function was to serve alcoholic refreshment to those of legal drinking age or any that dared hoodwink the publican into believing they were with their fake ID.

Many that darkened its doors were seeking to get seriously sauced.

Tie one down they would overindulge and get royally rogered up.

Bingeing on the heady brews dispensed by the spiritual advisers that manned the bar.

Any thoughts of disporting themselves in an orderly fashion were replaced by a single purpose, a race to the finish.

The race to reach as advanced a state of incompetence as possible before the toll of the bell and the publican's grim announcement of

"Time at the bar, gentlemen, please"

Thick with prickly humidity, was the evening air in the beer garden that night, where no flowers grew, and our tipsy tale begins...

A quintet of youthful wastrels who call themselves The Anonymous Five have gathered upon a wooden bench.

In the glare of the security light, their sweat glistens as they sup on their ales and bask in a shared state of mild intoxication.

While four of them grin like demented jesters not all are merry from mead.

IT'S ONLY GOT FOUR STRINGS 193

The youngest of the groups three southpaws, named Steve is sad, downhearted they have yet to come across a moniker for their freshly forged rock n roll band, the morose wretch doth whine.

Without a name, they lack identity and as a musical concern surely, they have no purpose.

The other four shrug, many times before this night has, he brought the matter to light, so they choose to ignore his whining and resume their giggly imbibing.

Late was the hour and close it was to the call for last orders, when by means of magic or pure coincidence,

Commander William Horatio arrived, a man whose arrogance is boundless, the Anonymous five despise him and think him a pretentious cock snot.

He is employed by the military and in a highly classified capacity, so it is out of mockery the five call him Commander.

The thirst of many who have drank before on this night has led to the bar exhausting its stock of manly pint glasses.

With a condescending grin, The Commander approached the quintets table and bids them good evening.

The group look up from their ales, what meets their eyes, shocks, outrage's disgusts them even.

For the smarmy squaddie holds his drink in both hands!

His request for a pint of ale has been shamefully served divided between two humiliating half pint glasses.

"Woah, lock up yer beer, the Commander's here!" the oldest and wisest southpaw named Dug exclaims.

Suddenly he leaps to his feet to address his fellow inebriates.

"My dear Rock Lords, Thrashers and Motorheadbangers, lend me your beers and join me in raising your *PINT* glasses!"

The five stand united before the confused and eternally uncool Commander.

Glasses held high, they rejoice, namelessly anonymous the five are no more as Dug senior declares "I hereby name this rock n roll vessel... Commander Two Half Pints!

May the horns of Mephistopheles guide us and strike down all that seek to sink us!"

I was overjoyed Dug had finally given the band a name, it may well have been an utterly ridiculous one but at least there was a story behind it.

Now that the anonymous five had a collective identity, we could focus on the task of becoming a better band.

To achieve this, we would first have to start shelling out for a decent practice room and the best place in town was, The Cell.

A rehearsal complex just two doors down from Hatton's housing four studios the biggest and best equipped of which was studio two.

For Commander to nab a slot there was nigh on impossible as it was always fully booked and usually by Empire State.

The other three rooms were incrementally smaller with less fancy equipment.

Occasionally we got lucky with a cancellation, managing to book a three-hour slot in studio one or three.

Still, I'd dream, if we ever got to play in studio two like Empire State did, then just maybe some of their rock star juju would rub off on us.

One evening a strong storm system had kept most people away from the Pub.

The Greenhouse was barren except for me, Rick, Dug and Ron Sherry our roadie extraordinaire.

Supping our Lagers in silence I gazed at the pour outside.

The weather suited Ron's mood, one of his tasks as a track-worker for British Rail was to lead the clean-up crew that recovered the remains of The Jumpers or as Ron referred to them as

"Them poor sad sacks, that's chosen to end it all by throwing themselves in front of an Intercity 125"

Ron would go on the lash if he'd had a particularly messy day on the old permanent way.

Today had been especially grim and when the three of us arrived he'd already been in deep in his cups for hours.

In an advanced level of inebriation, he now mused on his gruesome workday.

"A fucking, eyeball" he exclaimed as he scratched at his freshly unevenly shaved head

"Oh yeah... and a shoe!"

Supping on his pint he looked out the window, addressing no one in particular

"When it hit him, the train was doing 'bout a hundred... vaporized the poor bastard."

Ron then fell silent and looked distressed after taking a hefty swig of his lager he continued.

"Fucking easy day though, he smiled.

The gaffer let us knock off early, said the rest of him's probably stuck to the front of the train... briefly he looked grim once more.

Still... gotta a free ride though, didn't he?"

He grinned.

Turning back to Rick, I continued my argument about Pink Floyd's new bass player Guy Pratt.

Floyd was currently on tour in support of "A Momentary Lapse of Reason" their first album since original bassist Roger Waters had left the band.

For the tour, the three principal band members, David Gilmour, Rick Wright and Nick Mason had been augmented by a second drummer, keyboard player and guitarist, three female backing singers, a saxophonist and on four strings Guy Pratt.

I'd played Rick my VHS copy of their live show, "A Delicate Sound of Thunder" and Mr. Pratt's playing style had immediately got right on his tits.

"The prick would be better off calling himself Guy Twat" He scoffed.

"As he acts like a proper one onstage, playing that Mark King slap happy crap, that you love."

Rick's last statement was true, I did love slap bass, an advanced style of playing made famous in the UK by Level 42's bassist Mark King even if it was beyond my current skill set.

The tricky technique was executed using the thumb instead of fingers or a pick.

Hitting the lower E and A strings with your thumb, then plucking or snapping on the higher D and G string with four fingers in a claw type position.

When it was played with proficiency it created a rhythmic, funky sound, like drumming on the bass.

Slapping the bottom strings subbed for the bass and snare drum while snapping and popping the higher strings provided cymbal hits and accents.

Guy Pratt had employed it a briefly a few times during the Floyd Video, having been all the rage for most of the eighties with the decade winding down, its style was fast falling out of favor.

I wasn't going to admit it to Rick, but I'd become an avid student of Pratt's playing even though most of his tricks and fancy licks were too tough for me.

Not that this stopped me rewinding the tape over and over trying to decipher what the hell he was doing.

Rick had got my goat.

"Fuck off, he's a great player" I shot back.

"And he only slaps a couple of times during the show."

Rick readied himself to rip into him further, but he was interrupted by a soaking wet Ski bursting through the side door,

"Lads, Lads!" he pleaded, gasping for breath, and helping himself to a hefty swig of Ricks Pint.

"What is it now?!"

Rick growled, clearly in no mood for his gerbil faced enthusiasm and more than a bit miffed he'd just drunk half his lager

"It's a good job you dodgy fuckers are all sitting down!"

Ski began.

He paused to beat a dramatic drum roll on the table.

Dug was getting impatient.

"Come on, Spit it out, Ski.

Ron's had a shitty day, and I could really use a break from these two women bitching about slap happy twat.

Ski's face glowed with pride as he shared his news.

"Friday night, 7 till 10, The Cell, Commander Two Half Pints, Live and Outrageous in Studio...

Ski paused to bow theatrically.

Fucking TWO!"

There was a brief silence as our collective jaws dropped until Dug finally said.

"I'll be dipped in dog shit, nice one Ski!"

Friday night, we pulled up outside The Cell in Dug's bug my head had been in the clouds for days.

Tonight, live at last in studio bloody two, Commander Two Half Pints.

Equipped with the best amps, plush carpeting and a brand-new PA system that didn't sound like overcooked popcorn after half an hour, I simply couldn't wait to breathe the room's rarefied air.

The Cell was run by a laid-back hippy named Sammy who was also partner in a bar in town called The Purple Turtle that occasionally put on live bands.

Bursting in the door, the room was enveloped in a thick and pungent cloud.

Sammy was slumped in a chair, behind his desk, eyes closed with an enormous spliff in his hand.

"Shit! exclaimed Clive

He's smoked himself to death!"

While he hadn't expired, he was however completely out to lunch with the psychedelic fairies.

Waving my hand to disperse the smoke, revealed his girlfriend Beth underneath the desk on her knees.

The poor lass must have dropped something, but it looked like she'd found it between Sammy's legs.

Noisily, I cleared my throat.

"Oh...shit, Sammy panicked as he was snapped out of his blow job bliss and sat bolt upright.

Fuck...crap, shit...er, all-right lads!"

His rapid movement had caused Beth to smash her head on the underside of the desk, who swore like a profanity loaded machine gun as she scrambled to her feet.

"What's going on fellas?" she asked trying to regain her composure.

"Nuthin much Bethenny " Ski said, his face about to crack as the rest of us looked around the room desperately trying not to piss ourselves laughing.

That would have been a bad idea because Beth scared the shit out of us.

Four foot nothing with dreadlocks to her knees and a body like a Marshall Stack, she sang in a death metal band called Beth & The Bollocks.

They sounded a bit like Motorhead having a bar fight with Slayer and their gigs were notorious for being violent,

Random fights would frequently break out in the audience, the instigator of which was usually Beth.

Sammy asked Ski with a smile.

"I forgot to make a note, which room are you boys in again?"

"TWO!" we said in unison, far too loudly.

"Oh, man, I'm real sorry DC just called he sighed.

Yah know, last minute session, some kind of emergency"

Empire State or rather DC were afforded preferential treatment when it came to booking Studio Two, Sammy would tell him no worries and just scrub out whomever had already booked the room.

Sammy shrugged his shoulders.

"Sorry lads he said taking a huge drag on the spliff.

However...he expelled a cloud and pointed toward the ceiling Studio Four's free" he spluttered.

The five of us sighed.

It's an oft told rock n roll tale that honing your craft in a crappy and dingy rehearsal room can be inspiring as if being mired in squalor and filth will magically lead you to create your best work.

Not so with my band there's simply no way a multi-platinum record was ever birthed in The Cells dreaded Studio Four.

"Of course, four is free... it always fucking is!"

I whined under my breath as we trudged miserably up the rickety wooden staircase to the hotbox from hell

Studio Four wasn't much bigger than the average garden shed and so the four of us would have to huddle facing Clive as the rickety old drum kit took up half the room.

The equipment was ancient and most of the speakers needed replacing, there were no windows or wall coverings and the sticky, threadbare carpet was stained with who knows whose fluids.

At least, the room had a ceiling fan, which was equipped with two speeds, category five or off and if you left it on while the PA was still running, it would short out the power.

Playing as many songs as we could, until the heat was unbearable Ski would then flip off the PA and we'd bask briefly in the cooling breeze of a miniature hurricane.

After a few swigs of beer, he'd forget to switch it off, Ski would flick the PA back on we'd start playing and be instantly plunged into a sweltering, silent darkness.

After a couple more attempts and getting bumped from Studio Two, we reluctantly accepted, the only way for us to rehearse with any regularity at The Cell was to become Studio Fours bitchy house band.

A month later the ceiling fan died, Sammy said he'd have to put up our hourly rate to offset the cost of replacing it, we settled for keeping the lights on and got on with sweating out the poison.

During a break one night we staggered down the stairs and collapsed in a sweaty mess on the leather sofa opposite Sammy's desk, the five of us sticking fast to it.

Ski painfully peeled himself from the leather and told us he had to go out and see a man about a dog.

Fifteen minutes later back up in Rehearsal Inferno, he burst back in.

"Sorry, it took longer than I thought, he began.

But...you'd better brace yourselves boy's coz... I got us a gig!

Ski had twisted a few arms, called in several favors, and booked the us our debut show as support for Empire State's Xmas Eve show at Hatton's.

It's fair to say he probably expected us to go utterly ape-shit holler, hug and high five each other.

Personally, I just felt an extreme state of fear and a sense of utter dread as I told him...

"Ski... we can't I mean, we ain't got enough songs.

I whined.

Fuck... we just ain't ready man!"

I hated to harsh his mellow Dug agreed.

"Yeah man Dug agreed.

Even when we manage to get through the set without fucking up, we've probably got a nice... cozy thirteen minutes."

Ski was utterly immune to our negativity and smiled as he explained how we should all think of the gig as something to aim for and it being a kick up the ass.

"Lads, it's the middle of August he smiled

We've only been a band three months, the gig's four months away, so worst case scenario we'll be twice as good by then!"

His logic was flawless and over the course of the rest of the summer and into the autumn we improved... a bit.

Still our set was a bit too short, until dug hatched a fiendishly cunning plan, in fact it wasn't particularly cunning but fiendish in its simplicity.

All we had to do he said was learn a few parts of Empire States popular songs, mash them into a Medley and re-write the lyrics to rip this piss out of the band,

"They've got it coming man, he laughed.

"We'll knock them down a peg or two, question their sexual prowess and shop them as being underage drinkers!"

Part of me felt guilty that what Dug proposed was a fist to the face of the hand that had fed us the show... but fuck it, I'm sure it they'd see the funny side.

After months shedding pounds in sweat equity in the rehearsal room from hell from Christmas Eve was now just a week away.

Commander had cobbled together a thirty-minute set of ramshackle originals, a couple of questionable covers and our epic six minute "Tribute" to Empire State.

Dug bought cheap white t-shirts and emblazoned them with the band's logo stenciled with felt tip pen.

He had personalized each one with a slogan on the back, "Lock Up Your Beer" "Show Us Your Beaver" and for mine...

"Crap bass player"

Dug's, girlfriend went to town as our makeup artist, plastering us in blusher, eyeliner and crimping our hair.

She finished off our look with a generous frosting of fake snow.

No matter how bad we ended up sounding onstage at least we'd look absolutely fucking fabulous up there.

Our two-man Road crew, the Sherry Brothers were thrilled to be of use in their self-appointed positions, Ron as transport specialist and refreshment procurer, having borrowed the van from work in which he'd stashed a couple of cases of Lager for the post show piss up.

Morgan as Mr. Marshall Stacker and Master Packer to "Mate, I'll carry the heavy shit and make sure it all fits in the van, he said cheerfully.

"I mean, can't have you limp pansies chipping your nail polish, can I?

The week flew by and my long-dreaded day of reckoning finally dawned.

December 24th 1988...

Hatton's 120 London Road Reading, United Kingdom unlike the Electric Banana in NYC's Greenwich Village a venue that never existed where a fictional band Spinal Tap didn't once play.

Hatton's did but. don't go looking for it as its not there anymore.

At 8pm sharpish, Ski grabbed the microphone.

"Hey Kids, Happy Christmas, he beamed

"I hope you dodgy fuckers have locked up your beer, coz the Commanders here!!"

Clive counted us in, and we lurched violently our thrash metal paced cover of Eddie Cochran's "Come on Everybody."

The extreme sense of fear and dread I'd been feeling in varying degrees since Ski first told us about the show, within seconds had inexplicably disappeared.

All that remained was the band, lights, and the audience.

Somehow, I was inside the music and man it was utter bliss, absolute euphoria, I was astonishingly high and amazingly paranoia free.

Each time we paused for the vocal cue of "C'mon Everybody" Ski would hold the microphone in front of whoever was close in our only bit of scripted stage schtick.

We'd each blurt out "Get fucked everybody...Get pissed, get stoned, etc. depending on how the mood struck us.

Having made his rounds, Ski then turned toward the drum kit and thrust it in Clive's face, who looked terrified and responded with a confused.

"Er...WHAT?"

The song became even more of a musical mess as I turned to catch Clive's eye.

"Fuck it" he mouthed and gave us a four count into the first of our original songs "Life's a Beach."

Just as ramshackle and only fractionally less rapid in its pace, afterwards the crowd was kind with their applause as if to say, "aww, look at those brave young boys, they may be fucking awful but at least they are giving it a go, bless them!"

We served up a messy version of Dug's signature ode to his fave cereal "Frosties (They're Great)" and then it was onto my big moment, "The Munster Mosh" a mash up of the Munster's theme and Anthrax's "Caught in A Mosh" we started with the theme tune went into a section of "Mosh" then back to the Munster's.

The speedy bass riff for "Mosh" had been tough for me to master and Rick & Dug had flat out refused to learn it, I'd told them, I'll play it the riff four times on my Jack Jones, then you two come in playing an E minor chord only you gotta play as fast as you fucking can!!

Munster's section over, I moved closer to the front of the stage for my brief moment in the spotlight the rest of the band came to a feedback drenched halt, and I started to play the frantic bass riff.

Bah, bah, click...oh, shit.

In my head, I imagined a ringside announcer appearing stage left, grabbing his dangling microphone to announce...

"Ladies and Gentlemen, boys and girls may I present to you in his four-string onstage debut Mr. Steve Steele playing, absolutely...Nothing!

Because for the first and only time in my life I had broken a string live. Onstage.

And it wasn't just any string, but the lowest tuned, thickest string on a bass guitar, the E string.

The brief riff, I had been about to perform solo, only required me to use one string and it was this string, the great big bottom E string, that now dangled useless and limp from the neck of my bass.

The heady feeling of euphoria took a swift nosedive towards shame and total humiliation.

I looked down at my feet, behind me and back at the string...

Then, it hit me, just play the same riff on the next string up, that's the A string, Steve, that is simply brilliant!

Playing the riff, the required number of times, Dug and Rick came back in, playing what I'd told them, to the letter.

The pair of them bashed away on an E chord just as fast as they could, while I blasted away in A,

Mere words cannot convey how hideously awful it sounded.

Even by our own low musical standards, playing in two different keys simultaneously was an unforgivable aural sin and a fairly sick joke to pull on an unsuspecting audience who'd so far been quite flattering of our incompetence.

Shrugging off the shame of my personal disaster I jumped offstage and begged Jacob to lend me his bass for our grand finale, something he'd never have agreed to had he'd know what was about to occur.

Dug stepped up to the mic...

"Hey there people, we'd like to say thank you to all of you and the lovely ladies from Empire State, for allowing us to come out and play."

I heard DC shout from the bar.

"You're welcome...Wankers!"

"This is our gift to you Dug continued

But more so to. Them

Have a happy Christmas this is our last song...

Rock N Roll, Baby, I'm an Animal!"

The tribute began with the riff from the song Empire State opened their show with, which caused the crowd to go nuts.

Six minutes later we train-wrecked into feedback filled finale, the Sherry Brothers stormed the stage and cleared our gear offstage as rapidly as possible.

To me it had been a blissful blur up there, the experience giving me a high like nothing else.

Once everything had been loaded in the van and Empire State had started their set, we snuck back in looking for a round of celebratory Lagers.

The barmaid had just served a furious DC his pre-show beer told us.

"You lads were a laugh, but you might want to make yourselves scarce as he was not a happy fucking camper!

YYZ...WTF?!

LOS ANGELES, 2015

The view from the hotel room window was simply breath taking...

Six lanes of bumper-to-bumper traffic in both directions at a complete standstill on the 405 expressways.

It was the middle of a weekday afternoon.

Out in LA, rush hour was around the clock, no wonder distances here were measured in time rather than miles.

Hitting the local store for a quart of milk might take up half the day in LA LA Land.

The hotel was in Inglewood a seriously sketchy neighborhood and it was entirely my fault we were here.

Having dropped the ball securing tickets for the Madison Square Garden show on Rush's R40 tour.

They'll be back, I thought, add more dates in the fall for a victory lap through the Tri-State Area.

As the tour went on rumors abounded, while the band were evasive and remained tight lipped it was an open secret that this was it, the unofficial final tour.

Two miles from where I stood was The Forum, a 17,500-capacity arena, built in 1967, Rush's had played and sold out the venue several times before during their lengthy career.

My wife and I shared a love for the band, she had discovered them in the early eighties and attended her first show with her best friend in 1983 at the Syracuse Carrier Dome.

My first Rush gig had been nearly a decade later several thousand miles and an ocean away in 1992 at Birmingham's NEC arena with my bestie, DC.

Despite growing up on different continents Rush had been a constant, soundtrack to our very different lives.

Inside the cavernous interior of the LA Forum the atmosphere was one of bittersweet excitement

A sold-out crowd lit up with anticipation, gathered from all over the country and the globe to witness one last live celebration.

A few minutes before showtime, I felt a keen sense of melancholy at this being a farewell to my three kings.

The lights went down, the show began and right away...

I felt it.

This was going to be one of those uncommon shows where both band and audience are perfectly in synch.

A shared connection where they feed and feed on each other's energy.

When Geddy Lee sang "I wish I could live it all again" during a monstrous version of their latter-day classic "Headlong Flight" a felt a tear roll down my cheek.

The visual presentation of the show was one of reverse chronology, beginning with their most recent material and staging, slowly turning back the clock via the lighting, choice of amplification, even switching Neil Peart's entire drum kit as the band took the audience further and further back in time.

The second set closed with a twelve-minute excerpt from my beloved epic "2112" here comes that screaming woman again...

Only he's now a much calmer, softly spoken 62-year-old man, but still able to able to jump back to 1976 summon his wild and crazy 23-year former self to deliver a jaw dropping rendition.

After the twenty-minute encore stuffed with their very earliest material we reflected on the experience walked to the car, on the way running into couple of longtime fans we'd previously met at our hotel.

The pair had ridden their Harley's all the way down from remote part of Canada to see the show and seen the band numerous shows since 1974.

We gave them a ride back, sharing stories and a sad sense that our long journeys with the band were now over.

The tribute show, it seems to be a poor choice of terminology for what's essentially a group of musicians doffing their cap to an established band with a performance of their best-known songs.

Beyond drawing attention to the band, the original authors of the tunes aren't getting a penny, no tribute in the monetary sense while most of these copycat acts can make out like bandits.

In all my bands while the primary focus was to play original material, we would pepper the sets with cover versions

It's a hard sell trying to get a room of strangers to pay attention to songs they've never heard before.

The method my bands had employed was to knock the crowd over the head with a couple of our originals then throw them a musical bone for sticking with us, in the form of a song from a band they'd probably know.

There's two ways to approach a cover version, deliver a carbon copy or make it your own.

A band can get away with the latter, providing they've already developed their own successful sonic signature.

This isn't the best approach if the first time an audience heard of your little beat combo was ten minutes ago.

In Commander Two Half Pints, we'd half arsed our covers, cheating our way through any sections of songs we couldn't play by mashing up different parts of unrelated songs into medleys.

Playing longer sets with Empire State meant incorporating many covers and learning the big rock hits of the day to keep the audience happy.

Our shows included songs by Guns N Roses, AC/DC and as DC was a big fan, I loathe to confess, Poison.

Ski had us do a rocked-up version of Tone Loc's rap smash "Funky Cold Medina" which went over really well as did our show closer care of the Beastie Boys "Fight for Your Right to Party."

More recently I had been house bassist for a couple of fun tribute shows dedicated to the music of Janes Addiction and The Police.

For The Police show all the musicians taking part refused to perform "Every Breath You Take"

The collective opinion was they were sick to death of it being played on the radio, I didn't disagree, and breathed a sigh of relief as I was still haunted by the experience of Incognito's disastrous rendition of the song.

January 2017, NYC...

I really had made a rod for my own back this time, signing up my four strings for the ultimate tribute show.

Playing a set of ten songs dedicated to the Men of Willowdale, Rush and challenging myself to replicate the intricate bass lines of my low-end hero, Geddy Lee's.

There was a final dress rehearsal tomorrow night.

Mulling it over a glass of wine, I was distracted by my phone ringing.

The name on the screen caused me to roll my eyes, for once I didn't let it go to voice mail and picked up.

"Hey Steve...the caller chuckled.

Feel free to tell me to go fuck myself if you like but..."

As I was pretty sure what Dexter the organizer of the Tribute show was about to ask me, I was sorely tempted to tell him to do exactly what he'd asked.

The skinny was the bassist he'd recruited for the first part of the Rush show that focused on their material from the seventies had dropped out, I had only been signed up to play bass in the second set.

The unnamed bassist had either come down with flu or been in a car accident, maybe both, Dexter wasn't exactly sure.

The show was Saturday night and the dress rehearsal for both sets was tomorrow night.

And its Thursday and fast approaching 9pm.

Waving away his offers to pay me in either cash or weed, foolishly I told him I'd do it and frantically wrote down the ten songs to learn.

"Look, we can sort that shit out later, I told him.

But right now, I really must be going because I have less than 24 hours to memorize ten more fucking songs!"

We laughed as I signed off with "Thanks a lot buddy!"

Staying up most of the night I attempted to get the songs down, exhausted and running out of time, I called in sick for work.

Friday night, after a final rehearsal of the second set the one I had signed up for at Rivington Studios,

I headed upstairs to another studio where the guitarist and drummer for the first set were waiting along with the guest vocalists assigned a song each.

None of them looked particularly happy.

Instantly I felt the tension

Both guitarist and drummer had been drinking, they assumption was this was gonna be a bust, it simply wasn't possible for me to learn ten songs worth of complex bass parts in less than twenty-four hours.

As I set up, they didn't say much.

Any reservations they had I couldn't be concerned with.

My task at hand was to play the ten tracks with two complete strangers, attempt to gel musically and make it sound as if we had been playing together for years.

Guitarist, Marc, and Drummer Joel were diehard Rush fans, a pair of Rushians if you will.

The pair had been listening to and playing the band's music for decades and this was my in...

An instant connection bonded by our rapid fandom, we gelled just fine and after a couple of hours.

Marc offered me the rest of his quart of Makers Mark

"Fuck me... he slurred.

You... ARE... the man!" he gave me a hug; faith was restored and now the show could go on.

Arlene's Grocery on Manhattan's Lower East Side had always been my favorite place to play in the city.

It had a decent sized stage, great back line cool staff and a badass soundman, named Hugh.

Even my worst shows there where better than the best I played anywhere else.

At 10.00pm, I took to the stage with Marc and Joel for the instrumental opening section from 2112, "Overture."

The place was rammed, and the audience was with us from the very first note as we continued to blast through a well-received selection of the band's early classics.

Dexter took time to introduce the band near the end of the first set, when it came to me, he announced me as being.

"Such a badass that he's also playing bass for the second set as well!"

It was nice to be thanked publicly.

Bookending the set as it had begun with an extract from 2112, the frantic feedback and wah pedal drenched "Grand Finale"

Then to the bar for a much-needed beer or three.

The second set started off well the crowd seemed even more energized.

A running gag I'd shared with Dexter who was tackling vocals for a song in each set was a play on letters based around Rush's challenging instrumental "YYZ."

The complex piece was next up.

"YYZ-WTF?!" we'd say as in Why, Why Zee the Fuck, are we trying to play this?!

For the intro which was played originally on a triangle, both Dexter and the DJ Mick came out with one each and tapped out the morse code rhythm for YYZ, the code for Rush's hometown airport of Toronto, they were so hilarious out of time with each other that it almost derailed the entire piece.

Any minor mistakes I'd made during the show faded away when held against, the musicians as a collective performance.

Playing twenty songs by one of my all-time fave bands to a full house where the crowd was so into it, that, Mick, told me their stomping up and down was literally shaking his DJ booth.

One hell of a night and one little victory for this little four stringer

They say you should never meet your hero's, right?

Theory being that years spent admiring them from afar in your mind has elevated them to the level of a deity.

Should you ever happened to run into them, their actual persona cannot possibly meet how you've built them up to be.

Cliche's they're repetitive for a reason and as celebrities usually a lot shorter in the cold light of reality.

Maybe that phrase should read...

Don't look up to your hero's as they are often vertically challenged?

The few times I've been lucky enough to be a few feet from greatness, the very air had changed.

Tony Iommi from Black Sabbath for example, he smiled when I introduced myself as a fellow south paw and it didn't bother me in the slightest that he seemed more interested in checking out my wife's rack, I was honored in fact, and I thought...

"The bloke that invented heavy metal and every single great guitar riff ever is checking out my bird's boobs, Marvelous!

Union Square, NYC, December 2019...

Time suddenly stood still...

Just a few feet from me he shuffled past accompanied by a handler and the bookstores burly security detail.

And, duh of course he was a lot shorter than I'd been expecting.

The man was dressed in black, trademark converse sneakers and John Lennon style spectacles, his shaggy long hair looked like it had recently been dyed.

Here he was, in the same room as me, my hero.

A legend of the low end, one beast of a bassist and a master of the four strings.

A book signing isn't the ideal place to meet your hero's or in my case my all-time bass idol.

The pressure's immense, like a job interview, but compressed into thirty seconds.

A tiny time frame, in which I must get across what his band's music and playing has meant to me for the past thirty odd years.

Hours later, it was finally my turn to climb the stairs to my hero's makeshift throne and have my copy signed.

Scared shitless, I was determined to make a minor impression on the man.

Maybe I should ask for a selfie together?

Like nearly everyone else before me, but what if it came out blurred or I was cut out of it?

No thank you, Instead, I handed his assistant my phone and asked her to shoot a video of our exchange.

Ok, deep breath, Steve, now GO!

Stepping forward, his aide took my book and placed it before him he looked up at me and smiled,

"Hi Geddy, I'm Steve Steele, I blurted out nervously,

How are you?"

"Hi Steve!" he replied cheerfully busying himself with signing the book...

" I just wanted to say thank you" I began nervously.

You know, for being such a huge inspiration in my playing and for providing the soundtrack to my life well, well apart from one song...er, Tai Shan, cos that one well... it's a bit shit."

He chuckled, at my critique of an unpopular Rush song one he, himself had once described as being "An error."

We exchanged a fist bump; smiles and it was over.

Rush had disbanded after the last show in LA in August 2015, the three-o had been a constant presence to me for decades and a shared love of their music had help me to forge decades spanning friendships and a strong marriage.

Now, I could add a fifteen second cringe inducing video of when Steele met Lee along with a copy of his beautiful book of bass inscribed with...

"Hi Steve Steele!

Geddy Lee"

THE DISASTER PLAN

HATTONS UK 1989

Commanders debut show had been musically atrocious but a ton of fun for both the band and audience.

On the strength of it, we got another booking supporting Empire State at Hatton's in March of 1989.

Playing our second gig, fairly straight without the make-up, crimped hair or half a can of fake snow to hide behind, made for a more unnerving experience.

However, our original songs were a little tighter and we'd added a solid cover song by Hawkwind.

"Quark, Strangeness & Charm's" original lyrics were bollocks so Ski & Dug re-wrote them and retitled the song.

"Drugs, Hawkwind & Beer" summing up the band's lifestyle in four minutes.

To close the show, we dragged DC & Seth from Empire State onstage to jam an unrehearsed cover of Black Sabbath's, "Paranoid."

This wasn't the best idea as aside from the main riff, none of us knew how to play the rest of the song.

When it came to the words, Ski and Seth only knew the first verse and just kept trading off on the same four lines.

Fed up with the pair of them sounding like broken records and seeing as I at least knew all the words.

I attempted to take over the vocals, having never really sung into a microphone in public, my voice was pitiful and nothing close to Ozzy's Osbourne's whiny register.

Overall, it was a total sonic shit show and for no reason other than the crowd recognizing at least the first riff it went down remarkably well

Afterwards once Morgan had removed his fingers from his ears, he gave me one of his brutally honest performance reviews

"Delightful load of bollocks that was Mate" he beamed.

"Paranoid? now that I certainly was not expecting, its inclusion seemed to take you dopey twats on stage by complete surprise as well."

Yep, Matey" he summed up.

Rotten cherry on top of the shit cake son,

Tony Iommi would have been looping the loop in his coffin if he'd been dead."

After what I felt had been a lackluster gig and my feeling that despite maximum effort the band seeming to be making minimal progress.

I decided to dedicate more time to practicing, inspired by my latest four string hero Cliff Burton from Metallica who some scribes had been moved to cite him as the Jimi Hendrix of bass.

He certainly had a unique approach to the instrument.

Playing with his fingers at blistering speed and performing an impressive distortion, wah pedal drenched bass solo at each of Metallica's live show.

Sadly, though Cliff had already joined Jimi Hendrix and so many others in that great band in the sky,

Having been tragically killed when Metallica's crashed after hitting a patch of black ice in Sweden in September 1986, He was only 24.

Like many musical talents taken too soon, since Cliff's passing, he'd became an inspiration to thousands redefining in his short time on earth what could be achieved with only four strings.

On Metallica's first two albums Cliff played a Rickenbacker 4001 inspired by Geddy Lee's from Rush's use of one.

The basses were handmade in America and way beyond my price range, even so, if I had the cash, I felt I wasn't a decent enough player to justify owning one.

On the back cover of Metallica's third album "Master of Puppets" Cliff's last, was a shot of him playing a badass looking black bass, an Aria SB1000 which was made in Japan and significantly cheaper than a Rickenbacker.

And so, help me Dio, I was gonna bloody well get one.

Meantime, Rick was frustrated with his Flying V it rarely stayed in tune, he was obsessed with Ozzy Osbourne's former guitarist Randy Rhodes who had also been killed in in his early twenties in a plane crash.

Rick now lusted after his Jackson Signature model.

It was ludicrously expensive more than $3,000 adjusted which was way higher than a Rickenbacker's already lofty price tag.

His thinking was the opposite of mine, if he bought a superior instrument, it would magically make him a much better player and he persuaded his father to co-sign on a bank loan to put purchase one.

To me that was like Rick blowing a hundred grand on a Ferrari before taking a single driving lesson.

I was also fed up with my temperamental Calsboro amplifier and wanted a more reliable one made by Trace Elliot an expensive UK made brand.

After saving for months, I now had enough to spring for one of their cheapest models.

That weekend Rick and I took the train down to London, then a Tube to The Bass Centre in Wapping the nearest Trace Elliot dealership.

I'd always been intimidated by music stores, whenever I'd went into one to try out a potential new bass, in my mind, I had a few fancy licks to put it through its paces.

As soon as the assistant plugged the instrument in, I'd be stricken with chronic case of stage fright.

Frozen in the critical spotlight of the loitering, commission seeking salesman I was unable to recall how to play pretty much anything other than the most basic of parts.

Inside the Bass Center's cavernous showroom was more basses, amps, and accessories than I'd seen under one roof in my entire life.

The rumbling racket was unbelievable, a booming cacophony of four string chaos.

A plethora of bassists playing boutique priced basses most could never hope to afford with varying levels of skill.

Over in the Trace Elliot section was a tall thin man dressed in tight blue jeans an expensive looking leather jacket and cowboy boots.

He stood with his back to us playing an odd, shaped bass at ear splitting volume.

His percussive technique was drowning out all the other four string abusers in the vicinity it sounded to me as if he was plugged into every amp in the store.

Rick's jaw visibly dropped, he knew who he was and now enlightened me as to his identity.

"Fuck me, Steve!" he shouted in my ear over the deafening rumble.

"That's, The Ox...man!

I wasn't sure what he was talking about.

"Huh? Who's that then?

"John...Fucking, Entwistle, man!"

He gushed.

Rick was right, the skinny giant in the posh clobber was the legendary bassist from The Who and bearer of the nicknames The Ox and the far more inappropriate The Quiet One.

With his swept back grey hair almost dusting the ceiling he stood stock still like a rock star statue, meanwhile his hands and fingers were a blur, playing impossible licks with lightning precision and speed, just a few feet from us.

Everything he played sounded amazing.

My Paranoia now helpfully interjected...

You could never hope to play like that.

You should just quit right now!

My inner enemy was right, I could never hope to attain a fraction of his skill or even reach the level of most of the other players in the store that The Ox was currently wiping the floor with.

I was living a four-string pipe dream.

Time to jack it in go home, sell my shit and chop off my hands.

My gaze then fell upon a black Aria bass on a stand plugged into a small Trace Elliot Amplifier.

It was the same model Cliff Burton had played.

The instrument was second hand but aside from a few tiny dings and scratches it looked almost new.

The amp it was plugged into was marked Reduced for Clearance; I checked the price tags of each.

There was some divine Rock n Roll intervention going on, maybe Cliff had seen to it as I had enough dosh to buy both amp and bass along with enough change to buy Rick and I a round of celebratory pints.

Armed with my fabulous new bass I was keen to put it through its paces with the band, but after the mediocre second gig, rehearsals were no longer much fun for me.

Giving up getting high, had been great to clear my mind and focus on becoming a better bassist.

But my abstinence was causing a rift in the band and slowly we started to drift apart.

My bandmates were into free form bands like Ozric Tentacles and local dub reggae lunch outs, Radical Dance Factor.

During the last few rehearsals those influences had started to seep in, and I simply wasn't into it.

It was time for a change and very hard for me to tell my friends I no longer wanted to play with them.

Rick had stopped washing his long hair, letting it form into dreadlocks, Morgan Sherry had done the same and would become my replacement, having bought himself a cheap bass and taught himself to play.

The band continued as a quartet, taking a more psychedelic mainly instrumental approach, the new line up lasted for a couple of shows before they spilt up.

Meantime Empire State had caused a firestorm of Gossip in the Greenhouse after controversially sacking their lead singer, Seth.

The spilt had been far from amicable and Seth had decided to form a new band to compete, he asked me to join, with nothing on my musical horizons and the guy striking me as being a lot humbler since his dismissal, I signed up.

On lead guitar we recruited Carl unlike me and Seth he had short hair, not that it was a dealbreaker, the dude was cool.

Straight as an arrow while shamelessly camp, he could pull off pairing a shocking pink wife beater with a white denim jacket and make it look totally rock n roll.

Joining us on the drums was baby faced Gary.

Aged just sixteen he was already an incredible gifted drummer and had already mastered several of Neil Peart from Rush's challenging parts.

He drove a white triumph TR7 sports car which great for impressing the girls but not exactly practical for a drummer as Gary could only fit half his kit in it.

Our songs re-used lyrics and titles Seth had written with Empire State all Carl, Gary and I had to do was come up with some new music.

Seth wanted the band up, running and onstage before Empire State could stage their comeback with a new singer.

They beat us to it by a month and managed to keep the identity of their new singer under wraps until the night of the show.

Carl, Gary, and I attended the band's return to Hatton's stage.

Seth decided to stay home having mentioned something about having to hot oil his hair.

A few minutes before showtime, Ski stepped onto the stage and adjusted the mic stand, I simply assumed he was there to making some extra cash as a roadie for the band.

Adam then started a simple beat, DC and Jacob picked up their instruments and delivered a bulldozer of a groovy riff.

Ski was back at the microphone, and he now began to to sing...

"I never thought we'd have a problem I thought I love would always last."

Hang on a minute, I thought as the penny dropped and it sunk in that my old lead singer was Empire States new front man!

Ski was a huge hit with the established crowd, his between song banter wasn't geared toward making himself look cool it was about making people laugh and frequently at his own expense.

Coming across as relatable to the audience was his true star quality, if he could get up there and sing into a microphone, then anyone out there could too.

Having nailed the comeback, Empire started playing all over town.

One show was at the Purple Turtle Bar, that Sammy who ran the Cell was also a partner in.

The band gained more notoriety from their faulty dry ice machine than their performance, when huge clouds of the stuff billowed out of the open front door alarming a few passing motorists, one of whom called 999 causing the Fire Brigade to pay the venue a visit.

My new band fronted by their former singer,

The Moonlight Babies made our debut a month after Empires re-birth with Ski.

Musically we were better than Commander, but our shows didn't go over as well as Empires.

Essentially, we were competing for the same audience and dawdling in the slow lane while Empire State with my former lead singer, raced ahead.

A few more mediocre shows, Seth decided a re-think was in order, electing to knock it on the head and break up the band.

Back in The Greenhouse word had gotten out that DC had been paid to play on an actual proper record as a six-string gun for hire.

It wasn't a full album, just a seven-inch single, but it was still a big deal especially to me.

The 45 was being sold at the coolest independent record store in town, Listen Records.

That weekend, I went out and bought a copy of "Split Personality."

The band was called Shy, comprising of singer/songwriter Alfie Shy and DC on guitar.

For the single the drums and bass had been handled by the producer.

It sounded a bit like Kiss, but more poppy and cheesier.

On the cover was a filtered black and white shot of The Jack the Ripper Pub on the outskirts of town.

In the foreground stood DC, dressed in a business suit Alfie was seated in front, looking up at the sky.

DC looked cool but Alfie's gormless expression and the camera angle made it look like he was confined to a wheelchair and DC had pushed him up the Pub for a swift pint.

DC had since forgiven me and the rest of the members of Commander for ripping the piss out of his band the previous Xmas Eve.

The aloof attitude that had pervaded Empire State had been swept away since Ski joined the band and DC, and I would soon become good friends

After congratulating DC on his recording debut, he mentioned Alfie had just booked Shy's first show, some massive open-air festival in June and he was looking for a bassist, second guitarist and drummer for the performance.

DC had already dropped my name to Alfie, who'd asked him to pass along the message, if I was interested or if not at least available

"Well, I am available I told DC.

Got a couple of gripes though, one the song's rubbish and secondly the vocals suck"

DC didn't disagree "Innit? he laughed.

"Thing is, Squire, Alfie pays for everything, rehearsals, food, beers in the pub both before and after. he beamed.

Bottom line, at the very least it should be a right old laugh."

Within a couple of days, I'd set up a meeting with Alfie.

Venturing to the far side of town, to uncharted Tilehurst and even further afield than Love rock Road where I'd worked as a Postal Cadet.

Over a curry at his local Indian Restaurant Alfie lightly grilled me, a huge fan of The Beatles and Rush who originally hailed from Liverpool he spoke with a thick Liverpudlian accent.

His long hair looked awkward against his stiff business suit and novelty Kiss tie.

"The single" he said between scoops of steaming madras "Is not an accurate representation of how the band is gonna sound on the fooking stage" he informed me.

Alfie seemed clued up on how the music game was played, garnering record company interest with a couple of poppy singles which once the deal was inked, the band would disown, electing to play much heavier and less commercial material.

"Once we are on their roster we can do what we want, Alfie stated.

"The suits sell the shite out of the singles, and we become bigger than Def Fookin Leppard.

Nodding in mock agreement, his master plan already had me thinking it had little chance of success.

Alfie picked up the tab, I got the gig, and he'd told me he'd be back in touch once he'd recruited the rest of the lineup.

Two weeks later the live band had been finalized with Aslan on second guitar and T-Bone on drums.

Like Alfie both were from Tilehurst and had played together in a thrash metal band called Futile, who I'd seen them play a few months back supporting Empire State.

I thought they were total bollocks loudly voicing my displeasure when they covered or rather murdered my fave Metallica song "Welcome Home."

Alfie set up a meet, greet and drink up at Hatton's for the new band to get to know each other.

Aslan was cool, laid back quick with a quip and an enviable lengthy blonde mane.

His Barnet coupled with a pasty complexion made him look like a man lion hybrid, hence his nickname derived from the novel the Lion the Witch and The Wardrobe.

He didn't act high and mighty like the King of the Jungle, but Aslan was a wizard when it came to women and was constantly juggling several lady friends.

T-Bone was obsessed with Motley Crue especially their drummer Tommy Lee, he'd not only stolen his nickname but also Lee's stick twirling, show boating moves.

His looked a little like Michael J Fox, only in this universe, Marty McFly had let his hair grow out, got addicted to booze and been too pissed up to drive the De-Lorean Back to The Future

T-Bones gloriously sarcastic sense of humor made up for his unfortunate looking face and I began I hate to love you man friend/ foe ship with him.

Swiftly reaching a drunken state care of Alfie's credit card, the four of us were having a blast while our stone-cold sober singer tried to wrangle us, to outline his Disaster plan.

"Lads, he declared raising his coke in a toast.

Tonight, we stand at the precipice of success, the opportunity of a lifetime"

He went on to elaborate on how there was tons of record companies looking to get rich off a band like us.

He just needed to get a few ducks in a row, and they'd soon be chucking hundreds of thousands of quid at us.

Alife set up a photo shoot to re-brand and re-launch the band formerly known as Shy as Incognito

He'd been forced to change the name as there was a band in America with the same name that owned the copyright.

Having retained the services of a high-profile legal team, Alfie was currently preparing up for a "Transatlantic Lawsuit" as the US version of Shy had already filed a restraining order against him.

DC asked how that was even possible seeing as Alfie and the band were already "restrained" by the presence of a few thousand miles and the Atlantic Ocean.

Alfie replied that what with the mountainous paperwork and legalize, his team may have misinformed him, and the notice served might have been an order to cease and desist, either way, he was adamant...

"Them septic tanks are welcome to the poxy name" he said soberly.

"And they ain't gonna be shaking us down for a single fookin penny."

How a band in America could possibly be aware of Alfie or the band's existence, in 1991 with the internet donkeys' years away from being a part of every household

Add to that there was no record company and the 45 was only being sold in one local independent record store.

The lawsuit was great for publicity, Alfie had told us, re-launching the band with an international headline grabbing scandal, of course every word was likely utter bullshit but at least it was entertaining

"Anyway, Lads" Alfie concluded.

"I need to get home to make a vital, international phone call."

DC insisted before he left to supply the table with four more pitchers of fosters so that, yah know the four of us could discuss more band shit.

Alfie didn't seem so happy about this but reluctantly obliged.

First thing the four of us established once he'd gone was how we hated the new name, secondly, we were unanimous none of us gave a shit as long as Alfie kept the booze coming, we were all up for the crack.

The following week we met for the photo shoot.

Everyone insisted on being as pretty as possible smothering themselves in greasepaint and eyeliner while I was adamant to go au natural.

Which explained why my face was exceptionally shiny on the finished glossy black and white poster that got fly postered all over town, plugging the single announcing the name change and the date of the band's debut show.

We got into a routine, once a week meeting for beers on Alfie's dime followed by a half arsed boozy three-hour rehearsal and within six weeks, we had a forty-five-minute set.

The four of us being several years younger than our sober lead singer, we had zero interest in defeating the demon alcohol and still fully embraced several forms of substance abuse with each rehearsal a thinly veiled attempt to bankrupt Alfie before the band could even play its first show.

Alfie's picked a few cover songs to bolster the sets handful of original songs.

The covers been selected to maximize the audience's reaction no consideration had been given to whether he could actually sing them.

And so, onto the band's debut performance the much touted by Alfie "Huge" Festival.

It wasn't anything of the sort, just a small biker rally in a muddy field ten miles outside of town.

A couple of hundred people had so far shown up but due to the bad weather most had elected to stay inside their tents in the surrounding campsite and only a handful of bothering to attend our late afternoon set.

The band was paid in drink tickets, for once Alfie seemed chuffed, he wasn't going to have to shell out for our booze, that is until we got through the lot of them well before showtime.

Dressed in tight black jeans, loud shirts with our luxurious long hair, conditioned and perfectly groomed.

Our front man, opted to dress in filthy sneakers and pristine, white velour leisure suit,

Alfie certainly stood out and for all the wrong reasons.

Halfway through the set, he took off his white pants to reveal Union Jack boxer shorts, his strip tease had been met with giggles, Alfie had been expecting screaming Beatlemania and then everything had gone to complete shit following the fall out generated by our truly awful version of Every Breath You Take.

The four of us had zero sense of shame following our disastrous debut show, our thinking being it wasn't our band, we were just a gang of unpaid hired hands being plied with alcohol.

We were still laughing about it a week later when we met a still fuming Alfie for an emergency band meeting to discuss what had gone wrong and brainstorm a new approach.

As he laid our "payment" for our attendance, six pitchers of Fosters he revealed some shocking numbers.

Out of the initial pressing of a thousand singles, just twelve had been sold the day before the show and not a single copy since.

The posters featuring the band photo advertising the show and single that Alfie had plastered all over town had either been defaced or simply torn down.

His theory was the song had been too poppy to sell a put us on the map, so he'd booked us into a recording studio to track a new song that was a lot heavier.

Alfie laid out his new approach that if we could get down on tape how the band had been borderline heavy metal on that stage then we'd be inking a deal in no time.

A week later we hit Alley cat Recording Studio.

The plan was to record "A Girl I used to Know" a more up-tempo track alongside abysmal bubble gum pop sounding B-side "She's Not My Wife."

While the engineer was taking ages to get a decent sound out of T-Bones drums that met with Alfie's satisfaction, the band had abused his American Express card up in the studio bar.

All of us were in advanced stages of mental incompetence when it was time for T-Bone to start tracking drums.

He wobbled into the studio, sat behind the kit and fluffed take after take.

It may have only been 4pm but he had proved himself vital assisting us, in drinking the studio bar dry of Foster's.

"What the fuck is wrong with you?" Alfie asked T-Bone over the talkback mic.

" Fuck this bollocks, I needs some whiskey!" he slurred

"You shit faced slag, Alfie retorted.

Look at yah, can't even keep hold of yer fucking sticks, how the fuck is Whiskey gonna help?

Alfie's didn't bother waiting for T-Bone to reply his face started to redden as he beat his fists and then his head slowly on the recording console in frustration.

"Trust me Alf, I can still do this, T-Bone staggered to his feet behind the kit raising a shaking hand.

"Whiskey keeps me steady as a big old rock son."

Go send Aslan out for me Fire Water and everything will be sorted, yeah?"

Alfie was furious, gave a huge sigh, turned to Aslan, and handed him another credit card.

He returned half an hour later with the largest bottle of Jack Daniels the liquor store had, the three of us took a few slugs while T-Bone poured himself a large glass which he necked in a single gulp.

His face went ash white.

"Boyz, time to lay down the Thunder sticks" T-Bone spluttered as he walked into the closed glass door to the studio and fell flat on his arse.

"Good Grief" exclaimed Aslan.

After Alfie poured an ice-cold pint of water over T-Bone's head, he was angry enough to lay down some usable drum tracks.

My first-time recording bass in a proper studio was unremarkable and instantly forgettable.

Despite being pretty lit, I tracked the two songs, fairly swiftly with no incidents.

My motivation was to get my parts down as soon as possible as it was cutting into drinking time.

Aslan was next, setting up his amp and effects pedals to lay down the rhythm guitar.

After listening to Aslan's competent takes both the engineer and Alfie began scratching their heads as each pass was marred with either white noise, popping or a high-pitched whistling.

First, they switched out Aslan's amp for one of DC's Marshalls.

It didn't cure the problem, so Aslan then used one of DC's guitars, still the issues persisted.

Alfie seethed at the console said fuck about ten times and began to bang his head once more on the desk.

"I've got it!" T-Bone sprayed a mouthful of Fosters over the desk "The sloppy prick is still using his own pick!"

No-one had thought that something so small and seemingly insignificant could have been the cause or in fact, considered replacing the real culprit Aslan's ancient and almost burnt-out instrument cable.

Once Aslan had finished his tracks, the engineer was teetering on the edge of a nervous breakdown.

Rubbing his temples, he advised us to go home, sleep of the booze and come back as late as possible the next day.

"Fucking sober if at all possible" he seethed.

On Sunday, we found him drooling in his sleep under the desk, surrounded by empty beer cans.

Alfie kicked him "Come on slag, times wasting, me vocals is next."

He then spectacularly delivered take after tune free take while we mocked him mercilessly from the other side of the glass.

The engineer sipped on what was left of the Bottle of jack Daniels and told him, grimly "We got it" having given up trying to get a complete performance of either of the songs.

He was now faced with the lengthy task or piecing together a listenable vocal track by chopping and splicing together Alfie's multiple takes.

Now it was onto the final stretch, time to train wreck the backing vocals.

Between the four of us, we'd make sure two of us actually sang the line correctly while two didn't so the poor engineer had to unravel who was singing what before he could piece together the takes that were right.

Beer cans were popped once the red light came on and usually into the mics.

We also thought it would help Aslan sing in tune if we held him upside down while he tracked his vocals, it didn't but it was hilarious trying to see him try, go bright red and almost pass out.

Back at the desk T-Bone pointed at the telephone next to the Engineer.

"Ere mate can I call up to the bar on this?" he asked.

"Well, technically yes, the engineer replied.

But it's probably not a good idea though."

His advice was immediately ignored by T-Bone who now asked.

"Fucking choice, what's the number then mate?"

He then dialed the number and put it on speaker phone.

"Hello?" a stressed-out female voice answered.

"Alright my lovely, this is T-Bone from the band, Incognito, I need four pitchers of Fosters and eight shots of Tequila delivered to Studio two forthwith... that means immediately...ok, I thank you very much."

The female voice was not amused.

"You want what? I'm not a waitress, I'm run off my bloody feet up here.

T-Bone began to laugh "Now listen here, I don't mean no disrespect."

She cut him off.

"No, you boys listen up, you can bloody well come upstairs and wait to be served like everyone else" and hung up.

"Sake's man, who shat in her Cornflakes this morning?" T-Bone laughed as he dialed the bar again.

"Hello...this better not be you again" she asked fuming "Yes love, its big old T-Bone again, now look here making records is thirsty work.

Me and my boys are pissing away thousands of quid in your shitty studio and we deserve to be treated like the rock stars we like to think we are, ok?

I'd like me booze delivered in ten minutes with a smile, yeah? choice, T-Bone out.

After he'd hung up the engineer was laughing even harder than the rest of us, "Now you've gone and done it!" he warned.

T-Bone asked why, He explained that wasn't just a bartender he had been talking to, but the wife of the studio owner, she'd fill in on the weekends when she wasn't on tour as a low rent wannabe Bonnie Tyler.

Big whoop said T-Bone, the engineer elaborated that she was notoriously hot headed and prone to fits of violence.

T-Bone went white.

As requested, ten minutes later Bonnie the Barmaid burst though the studio door, but she hadn't brought any booze, instead she was baying for T-Bone's blood as her aqua-net assisted shock of blonde hair scraped the low ceiling.

"Alright, which one of you wankers here calls himself T-Bone?" she asked, livid with rage.

We all pointed helpfully to where he was curled up in a ball shaking underneath the recording desk.

To build a buzz for the upcoming single and meet what Alfie called extreme demand from everyone who had missed our catastrophic debut performance, he booked the band a second gig, at Hatton's.

The venue had recently been remodeled, renamed The Granby Tavern and a new larger stage had been built on the opposite side of the building.

"Were on the cusp of greatness lads, we just need to keep ourselves in people's minds"

Alfie had told us during his pep talk, in the car park before the show,

Some "fan" of the band well, to call him that would be a lie had come up with the genius idea of getting Incognito T shirts made but with a twist,

The T-shirts were printed with the promo shot from the phot shoot added in magic marker above the band name was "I Hate..."

We took to the stage with our up-tempo recently recorded single.

Alfie seemed happy or as happy as he ever got to see ten people lined up right in front of him and dancing.

Soon he had a perplexed look on his face as they had with their backs to him, then as he sang the song's opening line, they turned to face him their custom t-shirt silently stating how they really felt about the band...

We HATE...Incognito.

Alfie's jaw dropped, he missed a verse, went bright red and huffed, puffed, and seethed his way through the rest of the set.

He berated the audience before the final song,

"I wanted to say a sincere fuck you" he glared towards the ones in the offending T-Shirts.

We don't care if you hate us, it's too fucking late as you already paid us!"

Afterwards while Alfie was still furious, he was still, inexplicably optimistic, after all he reasoned, playing to an audience that despised the band meant we were seriously starting to make waves.

If we stayed with him, we would start going places, he turned to address DC.

"Especially you, sim, coz that band of yours, Empire State is going fucking nowhere!"

This didn't faze DC one bit, in fact he laughed.

"That may well end up being the case, he replied.

But... I think it's only fair to say all of us were in on that T-shirt gag."

Alfie blinked, huffed then stood up.

"Fucking Slags!! he roared, sweeping our drinks from the table...

All youse traitors are fucking fired!!"

THE VOICE OF METAL & ITCHY
LIP SYNCHING

NEW ROCHELLE NY 2014

"You're listening to Friday Night Rocks on KROC FM, with New York City's Metal Maven, Max Haven."

"And... we are back!"

Joining me in the studio tonight is Steve Steele, bassist for the New York City Metal band, Vertical Smile."

The Disc Jockey clearly hadn't done his homework my band weren't a metal band, plus I'd already exposed this self-proclaimed Maven of Metal as a charlatan during our preshow interview.

Max had professed to me earlier how he loved all the really heavy shit; cool I said and asked him what his favorite Slayer album was.

"Oh damn, that's a tough one, what it's called."

He snapped his fingers as if the action would magically fire his synapses and continued to dig himself deeper.

"You know the album I'm talking about; it's got Enter Sandman on it!"

Oh, very dear, he had mistaken Metallica's mega platinum black album as being authored by Slayer.

Haven's Father was the Radio stations president and once a week allowed the boy to play with Daddy's Trainset for a few hours.

There was one condition as K-ROC was a well-respected, family orientated station, Max wasn't permitted to broadcast on the FM channel and restricted to airing his show online.

I imagined the listenership for tonight's show must have measured in the tens of...tens.

For all his fakery he did at least let me pick the bulk of the show's playlist.

238

For the opening track, to use DJ parlance, I went to the back wall for a deep cut and played "Soldier Blue" by The Cult.

After three more songs, Max's intro, and some important messages from the station's sponsors.

He threw me an on-air curveball.

"So, tell me Steve, what's it like being known as The Voice of Metal?"

After allowing a few seconds of dead air to pass, I gave him a suitably ridiculous reply.

"Well, Max, I'm tempted to say thank you very much, but as I neither resemble nor do I resent that remark, I won't."

His face was one of utter bewilderment as I continued.

"Now, you come to mention it, I really should work out a way to *exploit* my voice for my own personal financial gain."

My placing emphasis on "Exploit" was a dig at Max, it predictably flew right over his dizzy head.

With glee he had rubbed his hands during our pre-screening interview, over the moon he was to have a guest on his show with such a voice like mine or as he'd called it The Accent of Evil.

"Man, your voice is badass, he raved.

All you British dudes sound like bad guys from a James Bond flick"

Max took full advantage of my dulcet tones, he had me spend an hour before the broadcast in a tiny recording studio, reading copy of an ad for one of the station's sponsors a fishing rod and bait store based in Mamaroneck.

That alone was a total tongue twister, which I kept mispronouncing, Mama-around-neck, Marrowroomwet..

And the script I had to recite was poorly written and incredibly cheesy.

"We've got rods, reels for all your heavy-duty tackle needs!"

Max's direction was for me to deliver it with a pious sense of authority, which caused me to crack myself up and blow even more takes.

Max was a couple of years older but behaved like an annoying teenager boasting of his previous celebrity guests, none of which I had heard of.

Halfway through the show, he had other guys join him to act as comedic foil for Max, in an upstate, bargain basement version of the Howard Stern show.

What I had thought would be a quick ten-minute interview ended up with my sitting in for the entire, four-hour show.

For the closing song he played my bands new single, the only reason I'd agreed to do the interview in the first place.

"Thank you for joining me, this evening, I'll leave you now with a K-ROC exclusive, the world premiere of my guest Steve Steele's band's brand-new single...

Keep on Rocking New York... good night!"

Much as it was thrill to hear a song I'd helped create being broadcast on the Radio.

Max had neglected to mention my bands name, the title of the song or its release date.

But that's just nitpicking it was after all good exposure or was it exploitation?

Midtown Manhattan, January 2010...

Oh man... what shit did I step into now?

It's a Tuesday afternoon, I'm in a small TV studio in Midtown Manhattan and I'm standing to the side of the set as a Production Assistant briefs me on what to expect when the director yells "Action."

Not that I'm actively listening, my dumbass has been celebrating his fortieth birthday for a week now,

I'm just hoping my hangover looks good on TV.

This afternoon, I'm at a taping for "That Metal Show" Don Dokken was supposed to be today's special guest but he cancelled thankfully, I'm not his replacement, Joe Lynn Turner is the last-minute sub.

Due to my big mouth, I am however about to make a brief appearance on camera.

The show's a half hour chat focused affair discussing Hard Rock & Heavy Metal, hosted by Veteran DJ Eddie Trunk and his co-hosts comedians Jim Florentine and Don Jameson.

It's fun, they chat with the guest, dissect a few albums and then there's a trivia section called "Stump the Trunk" which is where I come in.

Three of us have been chosen to fire a trivia question at Trunk, the goal is to catch him out, win a minor prize and then his co-hosts get to roast him for coming unstuck.

Two have gone before and both have failed to take Trunk down.

"Action!" Ugh, I'm totally bricking it, its boiling under the white-hot studio lights and here comes Jim Florentine with a microphone.

"What's your name and where are you from?"

Steve. er Brooklyn!

"And what's your question for Eddie?"

Years ago, Eddie had worked in Artist Relations at Mega force, I knew for a fact he was in the room when the artist I was about to mention got signed to the label

Ok, Bollocks or Bust, let's go.

"Ok, Eddie when the band Kings X were first signed to Mega force Records they had a different name, what was it?

Florentine started to chuckle; he knew I knew my shit ahead of

Ahead on the set, Eddie now leant forward in his chair and gasped

"Gaaaah, I know this, I know this, I know, I know it!!"

Jim was now laughing "No, you don't know Eddie, you don't know it" he turned to me

"You know Eddie was working for the label back then" I nodded, now grinning knowing Trunk was on the ropes.

Eddie, now pissed at himself gave up.

"Sneak Preview!" Florentine announced.

Stumped, his balls were busted and ass about to be roasted.

My prize a battery powered miniature Marshall Amp which now sits mostly silent on the windowsill and reminds me of when I bamboozled a bona-fide Maven of Metal on an internationally syndicated TV show.

584 8th, NYC 2016...

A relative flick of a guitar pick from Times Square on Eighth Avenue in Mid-town Manhattan.

Stands an unremarkable looking structure, the unimaginatively titled Music Building.

The largest rehearsal complex in the city with sixty-nine rooms over twelve floors, it had made a name for itself in the early eighties, when it could boast such monthly tenants as Billy Idol, Madonna, and The New York Dolls.

Nowadays one band would be on the hook for the lease and would sublet to several more acts, dividing up blocks of time to cover the rent.

My band, Vertical Smile rented two three-hour time slots a week from a group called the Black Tarts in a studio on the fifth floor.

Today the passenger elevator was out of order,

So, we took the one designated for freight only, the attendant hurried us inside as it was already occupied by a short impatient looking woman dressed in black.

She looked familiar, a holdover from the building's halcyon days, eighties pop minx Cyndi Lauper was heading to her studio on the 12th floor, and she didn't seem interested in our attempts at striking up a conversation.

Showing her true colors by coming across as fairly aloof, unlike, her biggest hit, Girls Just Wanna Have Fun, right now Miss Lauper clearly wasn't in the mood for any.

For all the buildings storied history, it wasn't maintained to more than a basic level, frequently the bogs would be out of order and honestly, I found the place to be a filthy, unhygienic shithole.

In fact, being confined to our room for more than three hours would cause me to itch.

There would be a whole lotta scratching going on today as it was the location for a day long video shoot.

When we arrived the director and crew had already spent three hours re-dressing the space, rigging the lighting, and disguising the room so that I didn't look anything like a rehearsal studio.

And....

Action!

Oh no, cut... hang on!

the lighting rig was in shot.

Ok, now, heavier, more intense and...

Action!

No, no... your eye line wasn't right.

Hell's Teeth this was a chore, after lip synching a performance of the song over and over and over again for hours I'm itching while I entertain the thought of taking a running jump out the window and making my mark on this life as a pavement pizza on eighth avenue.

85 Avenue A, Alphabet City, NYC, Four Months Later...

The stage is set, and a large screen hangs from the ceiling above the drum kit for the video release party/performance.

The end product has been craftily edited and shot in black and white to ensure it looks far more impressive than it cost to make.

This is the third song and second video the band has released since I joined the band, the first was offered as a free download, the accompanying video was mainly of Trick in an abandoned building with some arc lamps spliced with rehearsal footage of the band, the song was a Piano driven dramatic piece, that re-purposed lyrics from a children's nursery rhyme, it didn't exactly blow the band up but it did get played on the radio...once.

The second single had a catchier chorus with more focus on guitar, but we didn't make a video for it, or put it up for sale, it was given away as another loss leader.

For this third single,

I had written the bulk of the music on acoustic guitar; At the time I'd been listening to The Cult's "Sun King" then attempted to learn how to play Elton John's "Love Lies Bleeding" something I'd failed to do fairly spectacularly.

This is an odd method I've found can be useful when I'm trying to come up with something original,

Trying and failing to learn someone else's song, can often lead to me uncovering a new chord, lick or technique, I wouldn't have come up with by myself.

For the main guitar riff, Trick suggested I should instead play on bass, while the guitar played the chords.

I took minor offense to at first, I didn't want my playing to be the main focus of the song, but it actually worked a lot better.

As the guitar break is a simple, repeated melody my bass has ended up as the lead instrument.

The chorus uses a trick almost as old as the three-chord progression used in in twelve bar blues.

The "I-V-Vi-IV" sequence has been used in countless songs and all types of music genres.

I'd shared a good example of it in a song by Monster Magnet with Trick, which she had dismissed as formulaic and kind of dumb.

Not long after she didn't complain or even notice I'd used the same gag.

What makes it even more ironic is the final mix of the song was handled by one of Monster Magnets guitar players.

Last week Dad asked me to demonstrate how I played the bass line on Skype; it was one of my proudest moments when he complimented me on my nimble fingers and that my riff was the "hook" of the song.

Thanks to weeks of hustling, shameless self-promotion, social media saturation, the show is a success.

Both the audience and our musical peers fall in love with the video, the song, and my little trio.

Even if it's just for this one night only...

After our last song, we line up at the front of the stage to take our final bow... something I've never done at a show before

Trick leans close to my ear and tells me...

"From now on, whenever life get you down, think back to this night and remember how you felt in this moment."

She makes a valid point as for me it won't get any better than right now.

Quit while your ahead, always leave an audience wanting more, some have said and right then is when...

I should have quit the band.

MICK JAGGERS SISTER & THE LIBIDO TORPEDOS

READING UK 1992

Empire State's bassist, Jacob was going to art college and needed to leave the band, albeit temporarily.

DC tapped me to fill in for what he said with a wink would probably be for... "quite a while."

I jumped at the opportunity to play for a band I'd once loved to hate and playing bass in Empire State would become for me a nigh on perfect musical situation.

The band had no trouble getting gigs, having already cultivated a buzz on the local circuit with each show generating enough coin to cover rehearsals, a few after show beers and even the occasional taxi home.

My onstage debut was at a charity gig as part of a four-band bill.

The venue, The Irish club was a large hall in the town centre.

The rickety wooden stage brought to life the hoary old cliche of "treading the boards."

The planks creaked as we walked upon them, several felt loose, and a couple looked rotten.

Just before we went on, I made the utter rookie error of placing a full pint of lager on top of my bass amp as we kicked off our set, I was totally oblivious to the potential disaster in waiting.

I was buzzing, over excited and far too pre-occupied with how many rock star shapes I could throw busy having a riot interacting with the band.

After opening with two of our original tunes we busted out a cover of AC/DC's "Back in Black"

Just before going into the guitar solo, DC broke a string Adam took the beat down while he grabbed a backup axe and I attempted fill the guitar shaped hole with some, Red Hot Chili Peppers type slap bass over which Ski now started to scat.

"Yeah, funky bass" he beamed at me, then turned to face the crowd.

Check out me mate Steve man, he laughed.

Slapping... that... funky ass bass!!'

DC rejoined the song with a well-timed E chord and signaled for Adam to circle back to the start of the solo section.

Crisis averted, I thought breathing a sigh of relief as my legs gave way and I went arse over tit causing DC to laugh so hard he was unable to play the rest of the solo.

The deadly combination of my tread free cowboy boots, my pint of beer falling and shattering on the stage due to the vibration of the amp had caused a lake of lager to form on the uneven, wooden stage.

Now, as I lay on my back in a puddle of Fosters, feeling a total and utter twat my paranoia congratulated me...

Nice work, Steve,

First day on the job and...

DC's gonna fire your clumsy ass!

In moderate pain, I struggled to my feet and resumed playing.

After finishing the song, I noticed several streaks of blood running down my forearm from a gash on my elbow.

Pausing to admire my war wound under the glare of the stage lights, I could now see the bright side of the situation.

The jagged trails of vibrant red looked fabulous against my sleeveless white Judge Dredd T-shirt.

In a bid to get Empire State more exposure DC blagged the band a feature with Readings biggest local paper The Evening Post.

First came the photo shoot which for no reason at all was scheduled ridiculously early on a freezing cold Sunday morning on top of a multi-story car park.

Having been up all night at a house party, I hadn't bothered with a shower or a change of clothes.

My preening amounted to running my hand through my dyed black mane and chain-smoking Marlboro's to stave off the chill until the shutterbug shouted action.

Maybe, my look what the cat dragged in skanky look would make me appear more windswept and interesting.

The finished shot I didn't hate but as usual DC was the prettiest of us by far.

The reporter took us to a nearby bar for the interview, where I answered a bunch of questions in the finished piece my replies were wrongly attributed to Ski, the interviewer likely thought,

A bassist with half a brain?

No-one's gonna buy that,

his contributions should be felt, not heard.

The main point we were trying to get across in the article was how we'd never been happy with our demos and the only way to experience Empire State was in the flesh at a live show, in other words, get off your ass and come see us.

We continued to play regular shows at the Old Hatton's location now re-branded as the Granby Tavern, where Ski had a part time job hosting their weekly Karaoke nights.

DC secured us a few out-of-town support slots opening for national touring acts at a new venue The Phoenix Plaza, in Wokingham.

Our first show was opening for Killers, a new band fronted by former Iron Maiden vocalist Paul Di'Anno

We got a brief soundcheck and were assigned a small dressing room stocked with a handful of cheap beers.

We had run into Di'Anno's backing band in the hallway, but they didn't even acknowledge us, and their leader was nowhere to be seen.

I was quite nervous, sat in the dressing room waiting for showtime and sat quietly sipping on the piss weak lager the venue had provided us with, when a cheerful looking Paul D'Anno popped his head around the door.

"Awoight Lads!" he cheerfully asked.

His demeanor was a complete contrast to that of his band and he spent a few minutes giving us a little pep talk.

"You see lad's, this rock n roll lark, he sagely told us

You simply can't take shit too seriously, yah know coz, it ain't that noble a profession."

He noticed the beer we'd been allocated, a cheap supermarket brand bitter,

"Oh, dear oh dear, they gave you the shite booze, eh?"

D'Anno chuckled pulled out a note of decent denomination and slapped it on the table

"Here, you go boys, get yourselves a proper drink on me and while you're at it can you see if you can get me a fucking life!"

It was mind blowing to me that someone who was pretty famous could be so cool and generous, as he didn't know the band from Adam and had no real reason to be.

The following month back at the Plaza we opened for Tiger-tailz a Welsh glam rock band, they didn't do much for me, but their bassist Pepsi was friendly enough and popped to our dressing room to say hello.

Tonight, I'd had gone all out with my look for the show.

Black eyeliner a smudge of lipstick, glo in the dark Frankenstein's Monster shirt and a huge fabulous backcombed, hair sprayed to death goth-fro.

"Hey there boyo's do a good show, yeah" Pepsi smiled, then he looked my way and stopped himself and started to laugh, remarking in his lilting Welsh accent.

"Oh, I know you look like...

"You look like a cross between Mick Jagger and My Sister!!"

Back in Reading, one of its sleazier night clubs the After Dark hidden at the end of a narrow alley way off London Street had started hosting a hard rock/metal disco, on the slowest night of the week Tuesdays.

After attending a few times each week, noticing one guy who seemed to dominate the dance floor.

I hated him from the bar to me the man was a poseur with zero credibility.

Ironed straight blonde hair neatly trimmed fascial hair His overall look was a blend between Vim Fuego, lead singer/guitarist from Bad News, a fictional TV comedy metal band and Mantas the scary guitarist from black metal band, Venom.

Whenever he hit the dancefloor, I cringed as he performed perfect air guitar to Megadeth's "Hook in Mouth" and Pantera's "Cowboys from Hell."

He couldn't surely be a musician, must be a damn good bullshitter, I thought, however as usual I'd formed my opinion based on no information.

The next time I saw him was when his band Wages of Sin opened for Empire State at a local bar Cartoon's.

Sal's band were heavier with more complex songs than mine, one of their tunes "Thief of Tears" even exceeded the ten-minute mark.

Unlike Empire State and most local bands the five-piece line up didn't seem to have a group identity.

Guitarists Sal & Colin were full on Metal devotees, brandishing pointy shaped guitars from American manufacturers ESP & Jackson,

Colin had a perm tight, neat, and clean his Barnet looked like Darth Vader's helmet.

He worked out and ensured the girls got a gun show by dressing in tight pastel-colored T-shirts.

While a beast in the gym once he had a couple of drinks inside him Colin would transform into a full-on Metal Maniac,

His favorite band was Accept and when tanked up enough he'd deliver a complete solo vocal performance to the band's ode to a toxic personality acting out the lyrics

"Son of a bitch! Colin would roar as he stuck out his behind pointing to it aggressively.

"Kiss my ass, son of a bitch, you asshole!"

On bass was Norman who dressed like a primary school teacher and seemed totally out of place.

He looked terrified onstage and over the course of their set he developed a fascial twitch, I speculated his nerve endings were freaking out from being sandwiched between the sheer magnitude of metal of Sal and Colin's devastating dual axe attack.

Norm did have one redeeming quality to me as he played a Rickenbacker 4001 bass, a model favored by Rush's Geddy Lee and Cliff Burton from Metallica.

Lusting after it with envious eyes, I felt a four string that cool was an odd fit for one as awkward looking as him.

Behind the kit was T-Bone, whom I'd teamed up with previously in the band Incognito.

And then there was Bobby the man with the microphone, in his early forties he was twice the age of the rest of the band.

He had a lived in, slightly world-weary rock n roll look and a singing style from a different era.

His bluesy vocals were closer to Paul Rodgers from Free and Bad Company, than someone like Phil Anselmo from Pantera, who would have made for a much better fit.

It was impossible not to laugh as he crooned Sal's satanic lyrics lounge lizard style.

"Oh, yeah, Baby now, don't you know my name, I am death, the devil incarnates, oh woman, your end begins"!

I'd been hasty in my dismissal of Sal as an imposter the dude was legit, talking to him at the bar afterward using the time honored, cliched musician to musician stock opener...

Great set man.

Sal was a good bloke, an accomplished musician who wrote damn good progressive metal songs and we began to hang out.

He rented a large house with his two brothers and Colin on Northumberland Avenue, which had huge unfinished basement.

They had their gear set up downstairs and I started going over a couple of nights a week with my bass to jam and learn the bands setlist.

Sal was aware that Norm wasn't a good fit for the band so to get rid of him without hurting his feelings he took the quick, easy and somewhat cowardly route.

This was a method I'd employed before at some point or another, whoever was the weak link or the arsehole in the band, you arranged a meeting announce the band was splitting the up, waited a couple of weeks then re-formed the band with his or her replacement.

Maybe now, though I was stretching my four strings a little too thin playing bass for both Empire State and Wages of Sin.

Several times we played shows together, I'd have to pack extra stage clothes, working up a sweat during Wages support slot and not wanting to look like a wet gothic rat for Empire States always lengthy headline show.

Vocalist Bobby confided he was frustrated singing Sal's satanic metal lyrics, he didn't get all the doom and gloom and would have been much happier if he was just singing the blues, man.

He formed a side project called Seventy Ninety

The name representing that he hailed from the seventy's heyday of hard rock while the rest of the band were rooted in the nineties.

He asked me to join, quite why, I didn't refuse and now my four strings played in three bands.

Seventy-Ninety's debut was opening for Wages and Empire at the Granby, the fourth band who were set to kick off the night was a new band on the scene, Fractured Elbow.

That afternoon as we were loading the gear in, I was approached by their guitarist, Drew.

He looked terrified as he nervously asked if there was any chance, I could do the band a huge favor.

Their bassist had suddenly fallen ill and couldn't play the show could I please fill in for him.

Their set was due to start in three hours.

Fool for the Four String, well that was me, without even considering I was already playing in three bands already, I said yes.

But with such short notice where could we possibly rehearse, there was just one option available to us.

Two doors down from the Granby... The Cell.

No, please anywhere but there I thought.

I think I still had PTSD from my Commander Two Half Pints days.

Sucking it up I sweated the bands set to memory back up in the hotbox from hell studio four.

Joking that as I was spread so thin, for each of the four bands I would play just one string.

Then it was onto the show that never seemed to end, it was exhausting, mentally taxing but overall great fun.

The running gag between the bands when it came to introducing me onstage was to paraphrase Spinal Tap

"On the bass...for fucking everyone, Steve Steele!"

Paid for my trouble in alcohol the four sets became one long blur due to overindulgence.

Once the ringing in my ears had subsided.

I received an unexpected bonus of a head full of ants and a monstrous forty-eight-hour hangover.

Now it was Ski's turn to decide he was going to college,

His last show with the band was at the South Street Arts center, a venue run by the town council and being surrounded by a residential area equipped with a noise limiter.

If the band got too loud the device would cut the power, we got loud a lot as whenever DC went into a guitar solo, he boosted his signal with an effects pedal.

The limiter was housed in a tiny plastic ball on the ceiling.

Ski turned it into a gag and soon he had the audience rallying to our cause up in arms that the man was trying to shut the band down man.

Strange Behavior a band from out of town played after us they were really good, I felt at the even better than us, which invariably meant I got jealous.

Their singer Liam was great with the crowd, and he had a great look like Axl Rose crossed with Grizzly Adams.

DC's trademark gift of the gab ensured that he got Liam's number and a few weeks later he became our new front man.

Via DC's connections, we landed a few out door gigs playing for The local Boy Scouts meetings, it really wasn't as creepy as it sounds, we got paid a decent sum and played in front of a few hundred bored in dire need of rock n roll tweens.

The first was at a large international encampment in Wellington Country Park.

The site was a total mud bath on a par with Monsters of Rock Festival where I almost met my maker a few years back during Megadeth's set.

The organizers laid on transport to ferry the gear to the stage, so we rode proudly to the stage on a trailer towed by a clapped-out tractor.

Ahead of our set, the leader of the troupes took to the mic.

"Now, boys next up we have a special treat" the stuffy Scoutmaster announced.

"A musical group, who are going to play some pop songs for you!"

"But first..." he added.

"Join me as I lead you in our group prayer"

"Great" I deadpanned to DC "God"s the support act.

He started laughing..."oh mate, I got a great idea!"

We conferred with to change our planned opening number to a cover of an AC/DC Classic.

The prayer over, we took to the stage,

Liam grabbed the mic...

"All right Lads, hope you're having a good time."

Dib, Dib Dib!!

Dob, Dob, Dob!!

The crowd replied, Liam then told them."

"Your souls may belong to Jesus, but you'd better hold on tight as we're about to take you on a Highway to Hell!"

And we launched into the song of the same name.

The following month we got booked to play in the Queen's backyard, Windsor Great Park.

There wasn't a stage, just a roped off piece of grass near the food tent.

There wasn't too many of the scouts when we started but a few songs in a bunch of the older kids came over.

Our performance was subject to a strict no swearing policy which was a problem as Liam's stage banter was rife with profanity, plus some of our most popular covers such as Ice T's "Body count" and Rage Against the Machine's "Killing in The Name" were full of foul language.

We wouldn't curse, so Liam would get the audience to do it for us.

Whipping the crowd into an F-Bomb frenzy, Liam would ask after each song.

"All right boys, what's the word we ain't allowed to say?"

They roared their filthy reply.

"For Unlawful Carnal Knowledge? ...that's right you Muddy-funsters!"

The band now had enough cash in the band fund to book a studio make a demo of five songs.

We recorded over a couple of twelve-hour sessions at Alley cat Studios where DC and I had previously helped drink the bar dry with Incognito.

One song had an Aerosmith type swing, it seemed logical to add a saxophone solo to it and we tapped the only guy we knew you could play one, Gareth.

He worked in Making Music one of only two Musical Instrument stores in the town, recently he'd got me a sweet deal on a bass that had been used some of my early musical heroes in Siouxsie & The Banshee's, The Cure and The Cult.

A beautiful black Music man Stingray with a natural maple neck, handmade in San Luis Obispo California it had taken weeks to be delivered, I named her Sister Stella Sledgehammer, and she was making her recording debut during the sessions.

Gareth agreed to play sax for us for on the song and we could either pay him in cash or lager.

He reckoned that choosing the first option would likely cost the band a lot less.

On the last night of the sessions, he warmed up for ten minutes we got the beers in while he tracked a killer solo in two takes.

Afterwards he swiftly downed three pints and passed out.

Result, his contribution had cost us just six quid in Lager.

By this time both DC and I had steady girlfriends my Yoko Oh-No in particular become jealous of the female attention, she thought I was getting playing in the band,

This made little sense to me as it was the reason, she had been attracted to me in the first place.

One Friday night over a curry with our two Yoko Oh No's, DC told me he wanted to break up Empire State

He felt it had run its course, I wasn't happy with his decision and got a sense he wasn't either but both the Yoko's sure were.

Empire Played our last show at the Granby.

It was Friday night and packed,

We played two long sets, near the end of the second one Stella's battery for her active circuitry died and I hadn't packed a spare.

Screw it, I thought and picked DC back up guitar and played that for the rest of the show instead.

Soon afterwards I was put under house arrest by Yoko, there was a wedding to prepare for, invites to be sent and no more playing irresponsible carefree rock star for me.

Putting Stella Sledgehammer in her case, I slid her under the bed and considered myself pretty much retired at the ripe old age of twenty-five.

While the marriage didn't last but my desire to play did.

After licking my wounds, I dusted off Stella and rejoined the band... Incognito.

Alfie's new game plan wasn't much wiser me now being nearly ten years older, I did take the band more seriously second time around and even paid for most of my drinks.

Incognito's new guitarist was a well-heeled Doctor of Physics and the drummer only had one lung.

They pair had been in a band beforehand, so half of our set was re-written versions of their old tunes.

Alfie's vocals had improved, a little.

We played a few decent shows and made a botched attempts at recording in the guitarist's kitchen.

There was none of the old line-up's drunken high jinks, but Alfie's mindset hadn't changed, and he'd often bring up how he blamed me in part for the band not getting its big break.

"Yah, see with the classic line up, Steve..

He frowned.

We were on the cusp of getting get signed, but you and them other slags getting constantly shit faced, fucked it all up".

This time however he was adamant the band was gonna crack it and of course, we never did.

The Libido Torpedos
Stanton Street, NYC, Summer 2018...

Being in band was thought by many myself included to instantly make you irresistible to the opposite sex.

Going by my track record with the Ladies, I wasn't convinced If this necessarily applied in my case.

Well, maybe just once it did...

It was a very late on a hot New York night sometime in the summer my band had just played a show it had been a bit of a crappy one for me so afterwards I went outside to have a bit of a sulk and to be alone for a while.

"Your band is simply fabulous!" she had said.

"That's very nice of you to say so."

I replied with a forced smile.

"I'm glad you enjoyed our set, thanks for coming out.

"I'm willing to bet" she hedged "that you look great in the morning.

The subtle nature of her blatant come on was completely lost on me.

"I'm an early riser I said.

But I look like a nightmare when I first wake up."

"And that accent... she purred.

"I'm going to need you to stop talking right now...

. Otherwise... I'm going to have to go to the ladies' lounge and touch myself in a bad place.

Steady on, that's a bit unnecessary, I thought.

While she hadn't spotted my wedding ring, I'd certainly noticed her face which was no oil painting.

Without another word, I smiled gave her a thumbs up and it was goodnight sweetheart.

Palmer Park, Reading UK, 1992...

How about the rock star and the one-night stand?

I'd sort of had one but not quite, for me it was more a one-off performance...

After gatecrashing a random house party with DC on London Road and helping ourselves to their booze, we realized it wasn't our scene.

The place was full of pretentious students who had truly awful taste in music.

Drawing my attention to a pair of likely looking lasses, DC remarked they looked at least slightly rock n roll and so he steamed on in.

They were roommates, weren't digging the party either and sure, they were up for wasting some time with us.

We headed out across Palmer Park back to their apartment,

I latched onto the darker haired of the pair whose name was Jennifer Gunn

"Jen Gunn?" I asked, laughing.

As we passed under the glow of a lamppost, she cut me a look.

"What's so funny? she shot back with a poker face.

"You're a fine one to talk, she snorted.

I mean, Steve Steele, seriously?

At least mine isn't as implausibly ridiculous as yours, especially for a so called... rock star.

She sniggered sarcastically.

Up in her room we had a bit of a smooch until she pushed me away and whispered in my ear how she had something special to show me.

Bloody Hell, I thought, maybe this four-string lark is finally paying off, touching my hand gently she told me.

"Now, close your eyes...

And don't you dare peek until I say so."

I obliged, then I heard something being slid out from underneath the bed followed by the sound of her shuffling across the room and finally a low electronic hum.

"Ok, you can open your eyes, now" she whispered.

Miss Gunn was stood a few feet from me, in front of a small practice amp and still fully clothed.

Only now she now had strapped on a very expensive looking accessory...

A Gibson Les Paul.

Surprise...

She mouthed and proceeded to musically emasculate me with her vastly superior six string skills.

Her dazzling display of notes wordlessly shaming me for daring to call myself a musician.

With her having thoroughly gotten her rocks off, nothing more was written in the stars for me and Jen Gunn, but she did teach me how to play the verse riff to Metallica's "Orion" before she kicked me out.

Bull & Chequers, Woodley, UK 1988...

Penny was part of the gang up the Pub, we'd got friendly over time and gone on a handful of dates.

As a classically trained pianist, she could be a little snobbish when it came to popular music which she felt was often questionable, in its execution.

Freddy Mercury for example, well that was just cheating when he crossed his hands to reach the higher notes of the piano when he performed Bohemian Rhapsody.

Sitting at her father's piano one night she had played me a delicate rendition using the textbook correct technique.

I was suitably impressed, and it sounded beautiful.

But it was a bit too safe for my taste, so I came to Mercury's defense.

"Thing is, Penny, I said.

Freddy wasn't interpreting some ancient arrangement from a dusty old scroll, so those stuffy rules don't apply.

I argued.

He wrote it so surely; he can play it anyway he wants!

Besides, I ranted on,

"Wasn't the whole concept of rock music to defy convention, break a few rules and piss off your elders?

Penny was adamant, Freddy had cheated and taken the quick and easy path.

"That would also be the quick and easy way to a number one single then" I countered.

The Pianist wasn't playing around when it came to putting out and she would push me away whenever she got wind of my carnal rumblings.

My assumption was she found me a bit repulsive until I discovered she had a strange hang up.

The mere thought of touching a penis let alone having one rudely shoved inside her, she found utterly disgusting.

On the bright side, at least it was just a very small part of me that Penny found hideous.

But.... how was I going to get out of this one?

I racked my brain...

"Penny, sweetie, I'm so terribly sorry,
I'm dumping you for being a Penis Phobic Pianist!"

Being shitty boyfriend material, I did nothing of the sort and continued to string her along.

Another Friday night, another scenario of parents are out of town, swing by after the pub, bring a bunch of booze and try not to trash the house party.

From the sofa, Rick had been making eyes at Rose a highly educated and extremely well-spoken friend of the party's host.

Reverting to his stalking from afar technique didn't seem to be doing him any favors though, in fact Rose looked a bit perturbed by all his wide-eyed leering.

Bored and a bit buzzed, I headed upstairs to the Loo.

On my way back my path was blocked by Rose, she was stood next to an open bedroom door and looked absolutely fucking furious.

"Well...Hello... she began.

"I will have you know, as of right now, you are in very serious trouble."

Her clipped upper-class accent and condescending tone made me feel like an unruly pupil being admonished by a strict headmistress.

Before I could say anything close to...

"What the F...

She had shoved me through the open door and onto the bed.

Slamming the door behind her, Rose jumped on top of me and stuck herself to my face like something from an alien movie.

Suddenly Rick burst into the room, red faced, full of rage and brandishing fists of fury.

He came right for me; I rolled out of the way causing Rose to fall off me and onto the floor.

Punching the bed, throwing pillows he beat his fists against the wall.

"You bastard!" he screamed.

Cock blocking wanker!

You know I've been eyeing her up all night!"

Maybe, if Rick had slowed his row and appealed to Roses good breeding would have helped him woo her away from me.

He could have charmed her by saying something like her being in full bloom, ripe for the picking and his alone to de-flower...or maybe not.

In vain, I tried to explain how he'd got it all wrong and that she'd come on to me with zero provocation.

Rick was having none of it.

"Piece of shit, he yelled at me.

Don't you dare shag her!" he turned, ran downstairs and out the front door.

Rose was now sat back on the bed, giggling, she twirled a lock of her hair and put a hand on my knee.

"Oh, what fun, she gushed.

"Two naughty boys fighting over me, how delightfully flattering!"

Bollocks, I thought, this was a right old pickle.

Best mate hates me but this classy broad may just have the urge to merge.

Man, I could do with a slice of that right now.

Dammit Steve, what's it to be friendship or a quick...

"Fuck, I'm Sorry"

I told Rose and ran downstairs after the hot-headed bastard.

Rick ended up back at the boozer, where he refused to talk to me.

Ordering two pints and a double Jack Daniel's, I sat on my own and proceeded to get plastered

Rick was sat with The Sherry brothers on the far side of The Greenhouse, occasionally he glared in my direction.

Another round of drinks later, I was well on the way to getting blitzed when in walked Gemma, Rick's ex.

After spotting him, she came over and sat with me.

Helping herself to my Jack Daniels, I bent her ear with my tale of woe as she listened sympathetically.

It was weird, as if she somehow found this inebriated version of me, curiously intoxicating

She wanted to go out for a smoke and dragged me with her to a dark corner of the beer garden

I went to light her cigarette, she headed for my mouth kissing me with the finesse of a runaway lawn mower.

"Steve?"

A meek voice questioned,

Pulling away from Gemma's toothsome viciousness, a few feet behind us stood the Frigid Pianist.

"Oh shit... um hello Penny"

I'd been burying my head in the sand with her far too long and tonight I'd rudely shoved it in Gemma's chest.

"You fucking Pig!" she screamed stormed off, colliding with Rick who was walking out the side door

"What the fuck? he shouted at me.

"You're still going out with Penny you've just tried to hump Rose and now you're sucking on my ex's face? he asked open mouthed.

Fucking greedy prick!

After throwing several more insults in my direction, he left to walk a distraught looking Penny home.

Gemma told me to shake it off, they'd both get over it.

And she invited me on what sounded at lot like, but she made abundantly clear was for sure, deffo not, a date.

"Meet me up at the country club tomorrow afternoon we'll go canoeing, it'll be blast!" she smiled.

My thoughts slurred as I swayed in her arms,

What the fuck was I gonna do with a canoe?

The next day as expected I took to the water, like a duck shaped brick and capsized in five minutes flat.

Gemma found my plight hilarious, laughing as she rowed to my rescue.

Pulling me free of the vessel she dragged me onto the riverbank.

My dumb ass didn't need reviving, but she performed some toothsome mouth to mouth on me anyway.

After last night's personal disasters, Sex was the last thing on my mind. I mean, intercourse?

That was just something that happened between other people.

Sooner rather than later, my dalliance with this busty shelf stacker would inevitably go tits up.

A cheerful car horn caused her to release me,

"Oh, that my brother Carl, he can give us both a lift home."

Bloody Hell, he looked just like her, all that he was missing was a cracking rack.

My head spun, was he too feminine or his sister too masculine?

Rick was right, I was a greedy prick, possibly bi-sexual and maybe now running on dual fuel.

Declining the offer of a ride, I elected to walk home soaking wet, with my Libido utterly torpedoed.

Coopers Pub, Reading 1992...

The Coopers was one of the few bars in Reading that had a significant amount of rock and metal on its jukebox it also didn't attract the type of cliental that after having a few to many would start getting punchy with the likes of us rockers.

After rehearsals with Empire State, DC and I would spend most Saturday nights there.

For the past few weeks, a pair of imposing female goths had been showing up, DC had nicknamed them, The Gestapo Girls.

The younger Gestapo was Laura, unlike a lot of Goth Girls she wasn't aloof at all or especially self-absorbed, she was cute, friendly, and always keen to chat with me.

At six foot even she was significantly shorter than her older sister and the exact same height as me.

Her older sister, Lucinda was every inch a Giantess, towering above everyone in the bar, she was stood six foot six...in flats.

Unlike Laura, who I found sweet and charming, Lucinda terrified me.

Jet black hair to her waist, leather trench coat and thigh high boots

Like her younger sister she painted her face pale as a corpse and her eyes black as nightmares

But when I did pluck up the nerve to talk to her, she was just as sweet and approachable as Laura.

I became somewhat smitten with Lucinda, but unlike Laura who was alert and attentive, when I tried to talk to her, she was spaced out, distant and just didn't seem interested.

Once a month Laura and Lucinda would drive down to a London to a Club called that hosted a Goth night called "The Slimelight" Laura had told me how cool it was, and next time they went DC, and I cadged a lift with them.

The club was housed in a building called Electrowerkz a former scrap metal works in Islington and spread out three floors, it didn't have any of the frills you'd find in a a typical night club the entrance still had the old factory signs above it and once admitted through the heavy metal doors it felt like I was trapped in a decommissioned factory that had half of its light bulbs shot out.

Curious and sinister figures lurked in the corners, all manner of characters and not colorful at all, virtually everyone was toe to tip dressed in black.

Laura and Lucinda were in their element, I was casually terrified, DC he was more than happy to stand out, a carefree legend in double bleached light denim jeans, shirt, and crocodile skin boots.

Close by in the shadows was a curious beautiful creature of the night on the other side of the dance floor.

She had been making eye contact with me for a while now and I was very excited about it

"Man, check out that hot Gothess, over there she's been undressing me with her eyes for half an hour!"

DC took a quick butchers and burst out laughing.

"Nice one mate yeah, HE sure is one good looking geezer!"

What the?! I cried.

DC was wiping tears from his eyes when he asked.

"How does that Aerosmith song go again?

Oh yeah, DUDE looks like a Lady mate!!

The following Saturday after closing time at the Coopers we ended up at a House Party with the Gestapo Girls

Upon arrival, DC headed to the kitchen, where he wasted no time chatting up a few ladies, while I sat on the couch talking with Laura.

Lucinda sat on the floor in front of us with a guy she'd meet earlier at the Pub and were glued to the TV which was screening The Crow.

Around midnight, there was a sudden awkward silence between me and Laura, something weird and wicked was in the air, when she whispered

"Steve, would you mind if... oh fuck it.

Grabbing my head in both her hands she showered me with violent kisses.

A few minutes later, after coming up for air I opened my eyes...

Lucinda was no longer watching the movie.

Instead, she was glaring at me.

After giving Laura a brief icy glance, she got up and stormed out the front door.

"What the bloody hell, just happened? " I asked no one in particular as Laura raced off after her.

DC, a man renowned for being a goddamn girl whisperer, had observed the drama unfolding from the kitchen which he'd found hilarious and now sat down, next to me.

Between laughing like a strangled crow and gasping for breath he proceeded to enlightened me.

"Well played Squire,

That was entirely your fault,

Never mind though, eh?

"Why? What did I do now?

Mate, it's not what you did its

WHO... who you didn't do it to!

He could see I was none the wiser so spelt it out to me.

"Lucinda, yah daft bugger

She's got a crush on you!!

Hang on I thought, he's got to be winding me up.

Lucinda was a bit of a stunner; she could do so much better than me.

"No, no that can't be right,

I protested.

She hardly ever talks to me, and she's been ignoring me all night!"

DC handed me a tissue for my face which was plastered in Laura's black lipstick,

Trust me, she burns for you mate.

That bloke over there, the one from The Coopers, she ain't into him at all, it's just a ploy to make you jealous.

Meanwhile your dense dumbass decides to not only get off with her sister, but you do it right in front of her!

No wonder she threw all her toys out the pram,

Sorry mate but you really are a clueless fuck!

Over the next few weeks, I went on a couple of dates with Laura, sweet as her button nose was, I thought of her as more of a friend and of course I couldn't stop thinking about Lucinda.

Karma was going to bite me in the neck and drive a red-hot stake through my cold black heart for what I was about to do...

"You see, Laura it's not you, it's me...

Man, I was such an asshole she was more than smart enough to see through my bullshit.

Putting on a brave face, she smiled sadly as I broke her heart just a little bit.

Lucinda didn't say very much during our one and only extremely awkward date.

Interview With the Vampire would have been the perfect movie under different circumstances to woo a Lady Goth but my having just dated and dumped her sister made us being an item, impossible.

Not long after the Gestapo Girls stopped coming to the Pub.

Brixton Academy, London, UK 2001

So far, it had been a great show.

Just yesterday we had seen The Cult light up the Reading Festival on a rainy Sunday afternoon.

Tonight, the band were playing to a full house of diehard fans and totally on fire.

Over at the back bar, I was trying to get a quick beer in before the band came back on for the encore...

DC came running, he'd been down the front.

"Oh mate, you should have seen what just happened to T-Bone!

Apparently, The Cult's vocalist Ian Astbury had taken a dramatic swan dive off the stage and accidentally kicked him in the head.

"That's unfortunate, I laughed.

But I'm sure he deserved it!"

DC was more excited to share that he'd caught up with one of my old flames.

"Mate, I ran into Laura down there, Lady Gestapo!

Seriously?!

DC nodded frantically grinning like a maniac.

"Oh... *MY GOTH*" I exclaimed.

"Innit?! He laughed.

She was looking good, Squire, I told her I was here with you didn't look like she had a fella in tow so...you know.

She mentioned Lucinda's also in the building!

The band had just returned to the stage and kicked into my favorite song "Nirvana."

I hadn't heard them play live in decades....

Well shit, here's a dilemma...

Do I race down the front, rock til I'm crazy and lose a few more brain cells or...

Go find the only girl I'd ever regretted breaking up with

As I made my way down, I told myself she's long since over it, probably doesn't even remember me.

But then...

She might just be happy to see an old friend.

Nah, she probably still wants to justifiably kick my head in for what I did, fuck it.

The Cult wins this round.

After the show, I was unable to find Laura, instead I bumped into Lucinda, her long black hair was now platinum blonde and she seemed pretty out of it.

"Who's your name again?" she asked looking right through me.

Maybe it was just as well she couldn't remember me at all.

On the train home DC had some hot gossip he thought might cheer me up

It had been alleged Lucinda had shagged Iron Maiden's bassist Steve Harris backstage at some Festival.

"It's the truth mate, he galloped and frolicked with that leggy filly, traumatized the poor girl, she probably ended up walking like a racehorse for a week afterwards!"

We had a good old laugh about that.

Lucinda clearly still had a thing for four stringers and getting ridden by a bassist of Steve Harris's pedigree?

That Gestapo Girl had certainly gone up in the world!

THE GIG TRIANGLE

LONG ISLAND CITY, QUEENS
2019

It's been three years since my itchy video shoot with Vertical Smile at the Music Building and more than six since I joined the band.

Its early on a summer Sunday morning and I'm up on an abandoned stretch of elevated railway track where my band is shooting a video for our next single.

I'm dressed in a thrift store boiler suit with cut off sleeves and a pair of filthy work boots.

There's a video camera mounted on a tripod and a bunch of Go-Pros to capture my every move from several angles.

I mime to the playback throwing as many shapes as possible while trying not to trip on either the rails of the sleepers.

Trick has forked out for a cheap used drum kit for the shoot, which will be smashed to smithereens once we wrap.

As ever, there's a budget to consider and with Six being perennially broke, paying for the kit cost less than a cab to take Six and his own drum set to and from the location.

As this isn't a live performance, it doesn't matter if it sounds like shit, it only has to look good on camera.

Despite this, six is still having a shit fit.

"Fuck, he shouts.

This is totally un-fucking playable!"

I'm not in the best of moods today and he's been getting under my skin for weeks now so it's time to whack the hive.

"Look, you didn't pay for it" I begin.

No-one who sees this shit is gonna care, could you maybe just fake it, yeah?

This is met with the desired effect, and he squares me up with eyes of pugilistic intent.

Fuck you's and motherfuckers echo and bounce off the underbelly of the Long Island Expressway that passes overhead.

Trick prevents Six from solving his beef with his fists.

Both she and the video director will act as liaison between us for the rest of the shoot.

Back in 2013, I'd made a mental note on my way to audition for Vertical Smile.

If this doesn't play out then that's it, when the fun stops it's time to hang it up.

I'd given up on the dream of making a living as a musician twenty years ago when Empire State split up.

My thinking now was, I'm in my early forties and the chance of that particular opportunity kicking in my door was simply not gonna happen.

All I wanted to do was play a few gigs, have a laugh and if I was lucky, make enough scratch to cover drinks and maybe a cab home after the show.

There's an old concept known as the "Gig Triangle" a term coined I believe by session musicians, which can also be applied here.

When you have doubts about your current musical situation or are weighing up the pros and cons of a new one, just ask yourself three simple questions...

1/Do you like the material?

2/Are the people cool?

3/Are you getting paid?

Answer yes to two, then it's worth sticking with or pursuing.

When I joined the band, I'd have answered yes to numbers one and two, now it's just yes to number one and even that's not a definite, yeah, I like the songs but not nearly as much as I used to.

Long Island City, 4am, August 2019...

I've been up all night with Insomnia when I go over the events of lasts nights rehearsal it's a big fat fuck no to the whole gig triangle.

Another screaming match with Six, this time our most intense ever, it even bordered on fisticuffs.

The situation was diffused in the moment by Trick's begging and empty promises.

While six held the sticks that broke the camel's back, both are to blame in my mind.

The two of them still hold onto an impossible dream, the same one I'd given up on decades ago.

Trick's childlike optimism had infected me at times over the past six years, her sense of hope that maybe against astronomical odds the band may just have what it takes.

Over the past year, my joy for making music with the band has waned considerably.

I'm sick with shame that so many times I've put the band first, neglecting my other commitments, causing problems within my marriage and for several close friendships to fail.

Vertical Smile has now become a chore and at best an expensive hobby.

Maybe, I'd find an ally in Trick, she may see my side and fire Six for being a bitchy ball of bitterness.

After all, hadn't I been a good little rock soldier?

Loyal to her cause for years, contributing considerably more to the band than six ever had.

Along the way I'd turned down several offers and opportunities to join or collaborate with other bands which could have raised my musical profile.

But to stay laser focused on Vertical Smile, I'd said flat out no to them all.

I'd outlasted three of Six's predecessors, a diva of a lead guitarist who left, came back and finally was fired for good.

Staying too long at Trick's party when all that remained of the band was me and her playing bars with a couple of acoustic guitars

Maybe it was now me who was dreaming.

I mean, did I really expect, Trick a frequently a self-absorbed ice queen capable of discarding band members with the same clinical precision a hooker would her johns to reward me with the light of her gratitude?

West 125th Street, Harlem, February 2020...

Emerging from the Apollo Theatre, an icy blast of wind buffets 125th Street as I cower under the snow laced marquee.

Freezing, angry and very drunk, I'm typing a lengthy rage filled text.

Six months have passed since I quit Vertical Smile.

Not long afterwards, Trick had tried to take advantage of what was left of our friendship by convincing me to meet her at the band's producer's apartment.

She was seeking my feedback on a mix of the new single which featured my bass tracks and backing vocals.

Politely at first, I told her my opinion was worthless as I no longer had a horse in the race.

Her thinking was I'd be proud to hear how my contributions sounded on the completed song.

I wasn't and I felt used but as usual, I held my tongue.

Walking against the bitter wind towards the Subway my angry words beyond the litany of profanity amount to...

Delete all my bass tracks and backing vocals,

Even though I was no longer directly in contact with the band, I knew via loose friends that they had yet to settle on a permanent bassist.

My walking away hasn't sat well with me, I don't want my former band to benefit from my recordings and leave a road map for my replacement.

Having learnt my lesson years ago when Robby had gone ahead and released songs featuring my bass parts without my permission or crediting me.

It wasn't long before Trick responded.

What? was I crazy, she hadn't heard from me in months and the way I say hello is by screaming ridiculous demands?

Of course, she was going to give me full credit for my contributions, her thinking they would serve as a reminder that we had created some great music together.

But fine if that's what you want.

That was last night, and a considerable hangover ago, I'm much calmer now having just completed a two-mile run.

Pounding the pre-dawn streets of Long Island City.

Halfway down Skillman Avenue, I clamber up the overgrown embankment, reminding myself of the loose power cable beneath the tall grass, that once caused me to fall arse over tit.

Eight months ago, I'd shot a video I will never see on these rusty old rail tracks, this morning I'm up here once more to take back the Montauk Spur for myself.

A peaceful place to reflect get some clarity with just the odd stray cat for company.

Wading through the long grass between the rails, pausing to look at the sprawl of rail tracks beneath me and over to the Manhattan skyline.

As a much younger voice in my head now tells me.

You've been pretty lucky so far.

with that silly four string thing

My inner teen had a point, I had been lucky to have had a hand in writing some great songs more than a few truly terrible tunes and playing some great shows with the best of my friends and bandmates.

And... I'd been fortunate-ish to have created some of the best music with a handful of people, I'd prefer to forget.

THE SHED, THE BEAST & THE TABLE

LONDON ROAD, READING UK
2001

T-Bone was totally hammered.

His skinny frame swaying in the wind as he struggled to light a cigarette.

For the past ten minutes, I'd been trying to flag a cab to get his inebriated ass and drum kit home.

At last, a hackney carriage with its for-hire sign lit up pulled over.

With seating in the rear for five it was sizable enough to fit both T-Bone and all his disassembled shit.

Flicking the still unlit cigarette from his mouth, I shoved him into the far corner of the backseat and began loading.

Squashing him up against the window as I buried him behind a wall of stands, cymbals, and drums.

As I squeezed the door shut,

He slurred from behind his prison of percussion.

"Cheers, son"

"But... what am I going to do when I get home?"

He asked with a trace of concern.

I tapped the roof signaling the cabbie could pull away.

"You'll figure it out, fuck stick."

I helpfully replied.

In the decade since I'd first met T-Bone we'd developed a total mutual, disrespect for each other.

To the uninitiated it looked as if we absolutely detested each other, especially on stage where we did nothing to hide our open hostility toward each other.

To me, T-Bone was a caveman, the dipshit neanderthal who sat at the back dribbling as he gleefully hit shit with sticks.

Whenever he attempted to play something, he thought might impress me I'd listen attentively before offering some constructive criticism such as

"Shut the fuck up...it sounds like you're trying to build a shed back there"

In turn he dismissed everything I played as thwack a dang rubber band bollocks

However, if you came across the two of us in our natural habitat... any given dive bar, with some decent tunes on the jukebox and an ample supply of Fosters, it was a different story

We'd laugh the longest and get up to all manner of mischief via our drunken decisions.

Now, a pair of divorcees in our early thirties we had bonded over our relationship woes.

Unlike me, T-Bone had gotten shit on from a great height by his ex, taken to the cleaners financially and had been forced to take menial, low paying job.

He now lived in a single room bedsit, with just a box of clothes and constant hangover for company.

The Shed..London Street, Reading UK, 2001...

3AM, The following night...

Sunday morning was beating at the door.

With it came regrets, cringing embarrassment, and a bitch of a headache.

It had been eighties night at the After Dark Club and the pair of us had spent the last few hours making a right old mess on the dance floor.

To call it in fact dancing was a real stretch, setting two random people on fire and they would have busted better moves than our uncoordinated asses.

As ever our efforts to attract any female attention had failed miserably and now the harsh house lights came up...

It was chucking out time, sling yer bloody hook burnt baby burnt, this Disco Inferno is over.

No-one appeared as attractive as they had seemed in the shadows and the reflective shimmer of the mirror balls, especially, ugh I thought catching a glimpse of my reflection...me.

Next on the agenda, a long walk home with an empty heart and a throbbing head.

The shock of the cold outside the club was breathtaking as we trudged off into the night, boots crunching on a thin layer of frost.

In dire need of sustenance, we made our way toward the only place still open at such small an hour, Mr. Cod in Cemetery Junction.

Shivering in the frigid night air, sweat flash frozen to skin, we loped along as steam rose from our matted hair.

The combination of sufficient vodka red bulls to comatose an elephant along with the temperature change from sauna to subzero now hit T-Bone with the force of a frozen wrecking ball.

Each step he took looked like it was agony.

"Shit, my arms and legs are killing me" he whined.

Fuck me, mate I think I've been stabbed!"

T-Bone cried as his joints started to spasm uncontrollably.

Then slowly started to seize like a rusty robot.

Freezing and ravenous, I was in no mood for his poor me bollocks and prepared to verbally eviscerate him with a slew of insults until I caught sight of his twisted grimace under the streetlights and the sad sacks' agonizing attempts at movement thawed my blackened heart.

T-Bone sure knew how to put a smile on my face, my grin however didn't last very long though as it soon gave way to uncontrollable laughter.

"Stabbed? I asked between guffaws.

"Fucks sake...why would anyone want to stab you?

I was now gasping for breath.

Have a word mate... look at yourself.

You're a fucking mess!

"Fucking bollocks to you then!" he shouted.

Lurching at me with his arms outstretched and about as much finesse as Frankenstein's Monster

Willing his hands into fists he swung at me stiffly, one blow connecting weakly with my shoulder.

I countered his pathetic love tap with an overpowered knee to the nuts.

"Fuck-Gaah!" T-Bone gasped as he bent double and slurred insults.

I decided to leg it and sprinted up the street into an abandoned car park.

In the far corner stood a dilapidated wooden shed, I hid behind it and lay there in wait for what seemed like a very long time.

My trail had gone even colder than the air temperature when the tanked-up tin man finally wobbled and wheezed into the car park.

"Where you at, you skinny sack of shit!" he croaked,

Peeking from behind the shed,

"Fuck you tin tin!" I said and flipped him off.

After spotting a pile of wooden planks stacked to one side of the shack T-Bone grabbed one

Pissed up on booze and now royally fucked off, he started swinging unloading his rage on the defenseless shed.

A violent crash sounded from within, his bludgeoning likely dislodging a shelf full of supplies.

Another couple of blows shattered a window.

"Fuck you and fucking fuck this shit man! He yelled.

Damn, that looked like fun, I thought and grabbed my own wooden weapon.

Running to the other side of the shed, I joined T-Bone in his random act of senseless vandalism.

Two smashed windows, a split plank, and a few splinters each later we stood in the frigid morning air, catching our breath.

While the shack was still standing, it didn't look too clever our wailing having caused one side of it to partially cave in.

"Come on Brass, he smiled.

Me cod & chips is getting cold."

He paused to pick up another plank for one last whack.

After procuring our greasy deep-fried nosh we staggered down Cumberland Road toward my apartment

What a sight, we made two liquored up creatures of the night a pair of thirty something teenagers messily tucking into our takeaways as we struggled to walk in a straight line.

T-Bone reeled in his catch, biting down hard as hot grease spurted down his chin.

"Aahoo!" He screamed like Tom the cartoon cat as it singed his skin and half the filet of fish fell onto the pavement.

As for me, I was far beyond hungry chomping on a chicken burger, my mouth rouged with BBQ sauce leaving a trail of lettuce and globs of mayo in my wake.

A fire engine noisily rattled passed us, siren blasting and lights flashing,

T-Bone laughed, speculating that I'd left the oven on and how they were responding to my dinner invitation for a party of five.

We reached my street; the fire truck had stopped outside the pub car park at the end of the block.

The crew were responding to an abandoned car that had been set ablaze and a gang of firemen now dragged a hose toward it.

T-Bone, handed me what was left of his greasy supper,

"Ain't no fire T-Bones big old hose can't handle.

He declared and staggered toward the back of the Truck,

"Fucking choice" he exclaimed as he whipped out his personal extinguisher and put the invisible flames out.

The firemen had since put out the fire and were now making their way back to the truck and the pissed-up prick was about to get his ass arrested.

Despite it being extremely tempting to leave him there to get a good kicking, I dragged him, instead to my front door and shoved him inside.

In front of a James Bond flick, we consumed the rest of our feasts, washing it down with a couple of glasses of Wild Turkey, a pricy bourbon I'd been saving for a special occasion, this sure weren't it but it was the only booze I had in the house.

Exhausted, I crawled upstairs to bed leaving T-Bone to watch the rest of the flick, gibbering on about his hose pipe.

In the morning he was long gone along with my bottle of whiskey, pissed off, I realized it wasn't just the fire engine that T-Bone had hosed last night.

The Beast & The Table, London, UK 2001...

The UK's answer to "Tin Pan Alley" on Denmark Street in the West End of London was once the home of several music publishing houses and recording studios.

DC and I had been drawn to it over the years due to the handful of unique Musical Instrument stores that lined it.

Within their walls you could peruse mythical stringed instruments the likes of which, we'd only seen in grainy old concert footage, the price tags were astronomical, but it cost nothing to look and today for once, I had a decent amount of burnable income and was on a mission to get me a cool new four string.

T-Bone had temporarily laid down his drumsticks and taken up the bass for a new project, so he was also in the market for a new Axe, only he wanted something very metal, with plenty of pointy bits and sharp edges and he tagged along with me and DC.

"That's me new axe son" he said, pointing to the demonic dangerous looking four string hanging in the shop window.

We walked into the store.

"Hello Mate, can I give that big old bitch up there a whirl?" he asked the sales assistant, who obliged, handing him the aptly named BC Rich Beast

It certainly screamed metal with a goddamn vengeance.

The bloody thing was fucking enormous, in a none more black finish and a monstrous distortion of a four string

After he'd ensured the controls were all set to full, T-Bone plugged it into the nearest amp and gave the bottom E string a sturdy whack, the resulting rumble met with his approval.

"This I'll do" he told the salesman and asked if he had a box to carry it home in.

A few minutes later, he returned from out back, empty handed.

"We ain't got anything big enough in the building" the salesman, shrugged.

T-Bones only option he explained was to stump up the cash for a customized case they had in stock that may fit it.

"Fucks sake, go on then" he begrudgingly agreed.

"That's another two hundred" the salesman grinned.

T-Bone counted out the extra dosh, shelling out half as much more for the case as the cost of the beast.

The salesman now struggled as he brought a huge extra wide case from out back, it was covered in dust and looked more like a table with hinges, no legs, and a tiny handle.

DC quipped he should stick some green felt on it so we could play a game of pool.

Knocking the dust off, the salesman opened it up and secured the beast snugly in its case.

Far wider than any normal sized guitar case it was impossible to carry it by the handle horizontally.

So, T-Bone, the poor sod had to walk it upright through the narrow shop door, holding onto each side and twisting it back and forth as if he were moving a roll of carpet.

An hour later, having dragged T-Bone and his beast of burden in and out of three more stores, he was more than miffed that I'd yet to make a purchase.

Extremely pissed off, he told us we could go fuck ourselves bollocks and all this window-shopping shite, he was off to the pub up the street.

"You ladies go get your nails done" he told us.

"I'm gonna go get liquored up."

With the unwieldy case clutched close to his chest he wheezed as if in pain

Waddling back and forth he slowly crept away up the street, leaving the two of us to watch him laugh at his discomfort.

"Get the beers in, you bow legged Muppet!" DC shouted, after him

Since taking up the instrument fifteen years before hand I'd dismissed the industry standard four string, The Fender Precision bass as basic and utterly boring.

Invented by Leo Fender in 1951, as a more portable electric version alternative to an upright bass.

One of its first endorsees was Elvis's bass player, Bill Black who introduced it to a global audience when he played one in the 1957 Movie, "Jailhouse Rock"

Since then, the basic design had remained the same.

A solid body, four strings with a single coil, split pick up in and a rosewood or maple neck.

This simple, solid instrument had gone on become the most played and recorded bass guitar in musical history.

And stupid here had never even bothered to play one.

DC and I had now reached the last instrument store on Denmark Street, Andy's Music.

Upstairs, a Fender Precision finally caught my eye, it was black with a rosewood neck and a reflective mirrored scratch-plate.

The bass looked just like the one that Phil Lynott, Thin Lizzy's effortlessly cool vocalist/bassist had played in their seventy's heyday.

The eagle-eyed salesman noticed my interested and began to lay on his pitch.

"Ain't she a beauty, he said.

1979, all original, plays like butter" he grinned, an expression meant to denote playability, which I'd always thought was bloody stupid.

He brought it down from its hanger high up on the wall turned it to and fro so the mirror scratch plate caught and reflected the light, it was starting to dazzle me...maybe, just a little.

"This tall black guy with an afro and a tash brought it in, the salesman lied.

"Geezer, spoke with a thick Irish accent."

Yeah yeah, I thought, well that was a crock and like Thin Lizzy's hit single I... *Don't Believe a Word*

The sales assistant handed it to me, I plugged in, and it was love... at first note.

I told him I'd take it, but only if he knocked a hundred quid off the price and throw in a gig bag to carry it home in.

This was his penance for trying to bullshit me that it had once belonged to Phil Lynott

He hemmed, hawed then finally agreed.

We made the transaction he zipped it up into the bag, I hefted it over my shoulder and DC, and I headed to the pub.

Pool table shaped guitar case leant against his stool, T-Bone sat alone at the bar, he was already pretty stenciled.

I pointed and laughed.

"Now look here son, while you got yourself an oversized vanity plank of bullshit that you have to drag around in a tombstone"

I gestured to my gig bag "I on the other hand, just bought myself a total classic that's far easier to lug about.

Unzipping the gig bag, I revealed my new pride and joy.

"Oh, Sweet as mate, T-Bone remarked.

"Bit boring looking though ain't it?"

A few hours later DC and I were as plastered as T-Bone had been when we arrived.

As for T-Bone he was now seriously stenciled, barley coherent and swaying on his stool.

DC decided it was time to call it a night and we headed to the nearest Tube Station.

Fortunately for T-Bone, the stop for Tottenham Court Road was just across the street from the bar but once we got inside, he was shit out of luck.

The escalator was out of service and the only way to the platform was down a steep set of stationary, seemingly endless stairs.

"Oh mate, that's a blow now, innit? DC giggled.

Guess we'll just catch up with you at the bottom...

"Eventually" we both said in unison, laughed and merrily commenced our descent leaving T-Bone to whine, whinge and struggle with his unwieldy burden.

Once we reached the platform hundreds of feet below, I looked back up the dead escalator.

Obscured by his black monolith, T-Bone wasn't even halfway down, his progress agonizingly slow as he lifted the cumbersome case awkwardly down each step.

The station was deserted and silent except for the echoes of his huffing and puffing.

After ten more minutes DC offered him some encouragement "Hurry up you Twat!" he laughed

"Fuck off the pair of yah, T-Bone shouted back.

"I'm going as fast as...oh...fuck, ugh!"

T-Bone tripped and fell face down onto the case toppling it flat. Frantically he gripped onto the sides and screamed as his makeshift toboggan, slid, and banged down the last few steps.

Our roars of laughter almost drowning out his comedic yelling, with both of us being less concerned with T-Bones personal safety

The last thing we wanted was for his shiny spiky new toy to come to any harm and so positioned ourselves either side of the escalator to catch the table.

We successfully halted its progress but not T-Bone's who shot forward cleared the escalator and face planted the platform with a loud slap.

"Agh... fucking...ugh...shit...!" he cried and rolled onto his back, face already starting to swell from the impact.

His mashed mouth and bashed in chin made him look like Popeye, The Sailor Man Only T-Bone didn't have any sea legs and preferred to guzzle cans of Lager instead of tins of Spinach.

"Get me to the fucking hospital!!" he cried; his mangled speech about as coherent as Marlon Brando's in The Godfather.

Wiping away my tears of mirth I weighed in with some helpful advice.

Shut up mate, you don't need medical attention, get your busted ass back up... you're fucking embarrassing me man!"

"Would you two twats get your shit together, DC asked.

The next train is only a couple of minutes away."

Suddenly, T-Bone was on his feet and in my face like a deranged Elephant man as we started to fail quite spectacularly to have a proper rumble.

All that transpired was a totally uncoordinated shit show between two drunken tools with zero fighting skills.

After several wide swings at his bruised boat race, I managed to slap T-Bone on the cheek, he snorted and pushed me back sending me staggering as my Walkman and earbuds clattered to the floor,

Sniggering he now eyed what I'd just dropped with evil intent.

"No, no, NO! not my tunes man!" I screamed as

T-bone picked up my headphones.

"Oh, you wanna listen...then listen to this bitch!" He laughed as he ripped them apart, flung them onto the tracks and they disappeared under the wheels of the arriving Tube.

An hour later the three of us and our pair of new four strings sat safe and warm aboard the last train home.

T-Bone snored opposite DC and me, in a boozed-up stupor, drool on his swollen chin as DC and I split a can of Fosters.

The ticket inspector approached our seats "Tickets...please...er oh, what happened to him?" he asked gesturing at T-Bones bruised disfigured face.

"Oh, him, he had a fist fight with a Pool Table" DC Laughed

"Yeah" I added "But don't worry, I tapped the beast's oversized case that laid precariously on the luggage rack above our heads.

"The table's still in one piece!"

I leant over gave T-Bone a kiss on his swollen forehead "Wake up broken head, nearly home."

He opened one blackened eye and smiled "Fuck you son."

A week later over at DC's place, T-Bone produced a cassette, he put it in the deck.

"Check out this hair metal bollocks boys" he grinned.

The tape hiss and muffled sound quality initially made the songs unrecognizable then we realized he'd unearthed the unreleased demo DC and I had recorded with Empire State years ago and transferred it onto a cassette.

When the tape was over, we decided to form a band,

Like a bargain basement version of Rush, we'd be a power trio and share the vocals.

T-Bone would yell in and out of tune into his Tommy Lee type headset mic, if the bass part was simple, I'd try my best gravelly impression of Metallica's James Hetfield and if the guitar wasn't too nuts DC who could actually sing would belt it out.

It was unanimous though this band would be just for kicks, laughs and drinks as none of us were getting any younger and we no longer entertained any thoughts of making it.

THEATRICAL CUT & THE GRAND PRIZE

GRAMERCY THEATER NYC 2019

Revenge...

Very good eaten cold or so the vulgar said, to misquote its author, Eugene Sue.

Tonight, I'll get to dish it up in a deli on 38th & 8th Avenue.

While waiting for my sandwich order, a voice sheepishly questioned me from behind.

"Hey....Steve?"

It was Jake, producer of my former band, Devils Backbone after awkward niceties, I asked after the old band, he asked after my current one and I found my opportunity.

"Oh, you know, not much" I told him nonchalantly.

Rehearsing for our show at Gramercy next week"

Jakes face went white.

"Gramercy...Theatre?" he asked.

Wow, that's a pretty big room."

Judging by his reaction it seemed my old band were not yet in a position to play the venue, feeling mean, I added some salt to the dish.

"Yeah, I lied with a smirk.

I think, it's pretty much sold out."

Weather conditions can seriously impact a shows attendance, I knew only too well, having played a three-week Monday night residency at Arlene's Grocery back in March.

Each show had been blighted by extreme weather.

First night record low temperature for the time of year, a thunderstorm brought localized flooding for show two and the band played to an almost empty room after a foot of snow fell ahead of the last show.

I was fully expecting this next show at the biggest venue my band had played to date, to be subject to the same inclement elements.

Remarkably for a Saturday in the middle of January. Mother Nature has gifted the city with a perfect spring day.

The Gramercy Theater, one of my favorite venues in the city to catch a show and I'm stoked to stomp the same boards as the mighty King's X, Rival Sons and last night my TV crush Countess Luanne De Lesseps from the Real Housewives of New York

Like the Stone Pony who's stage I'd barged onto with Liquid Crowbar a few years back the Theater is a marquee venue, hosting national and international acts.

Nearly everywhere I've played in the city before, you can show up with your gear half an hour before the stage time at the front door but not here.

Load in is early afternoon, sound-checks must be performed, and backstage riders fulfilled, with a larger venue comes more staff things tend to go more smoothly but take a lot longer.

Tonight, Vertical Smile is playing second on a five-act bill, we won't be given the safety net of a sound-check, just a line check of the levels right before we begin.

Which a fancy way of saying...

Can, you hear yourselves?

Ok, you're go on in five minutes, we'll sort it out the mix from the board once you start playing.

Not an ideal situation but then we are low on tonight's musical totem pole.

Like most activities within the entertainment field, it goes a little something like this.

Weeks before the show a memo is sent to all the bands that everyone must be at the venue with all their gear at 2pm sharp.

Failure to comply means the schedule will go to shit and you may end up forfeiting your position on the bill.

Everyone shows up bang on time, to hurry up and wait. wait, on this occasion for two hours for anything to happen.

For the show, six has offered up his drum kit for all the bands to use.

His thinking or agenda, being such a generous offer might afford him or the band some preferential treatment.

It doesn't, all it does is raise his stress levels as he looks on helplessly while the other drummers pound the crap out of his prized pots and pans.

I'll spend most of the time until showtime trying to avoid his red-faced angry ass.

Both headliner and the direct support band get a soundcheck as torturous and tedious as the prep for a recording session.

Drums are first, each one has a separate microphone, and the levels have to match.

It goes something like this "ok bass drum, boom boom, boom" about twenty-five times, yep we got it, now snare, crack crack, crack" the whole kit has to be tested and tweaked individually, then theres a quick bash on the whole kit and next its each instrument in turn until the vocals and its rock n roll law that none shall deviate from the cliched soundcheck script of

"Check, check, one, two,one ONE...TWO... test test, test TEST" finally the band will play a song, maybe two and then it's onto the next act and all the way back to the bass drum.

Hours later when the doors open and people gradually trickle in, it feels like I've throw the biggest house party of my life as I anxiously await the first guests.

Trick is backstage getting her hair extensions worked on, six is stage left, fiddling with his phone, no doubt bitch posting on Facebook, never moving more than a few feet from his precious kit.

By default, I'm duty bound to to press the flesh, be glad to see those hands and thank folks for coming.

It not something, I've never been that good at, but I've learnt to fake it with enough authenticity to pull the wool over most people's eyes.

Showtime is now an hour away, I probably should be terrified but I feel almost relaxed, however that deep rooted fear, since my first show over thirty years ago that once again I'll break a string onstage is for the first time in years, a mild niggle at the back of my brain.

It must be ten years since I got over the fear and stopped bringing two basses to a show, the truth is the bigger the venue, the less anxious I'm likely to be.

The reason being, it's a lot easier to play to a room of a couple of hundred strangers than to a handful of people you know.

From the stage tonight, I'll only be able to pick out faces in the first couple of rows from the backwash of the stage lights other than that it will all be darkness and shadow.

In a smaller venue, I can see the whites of everyone's eyes, which is when the terror strikes, and my paranoia will intervene.

Look how they are all laughing at you.

You look utterly ridiculous up there!

I've since learnt to beat that irrational fear back by focusing my gaze on the middle of the back wall only occasionally making random eye contact with the audience.

Wandering backstage to chat with members of the other acts that I know, Anna the enigmatic vocalist for Temple V is swinging a censer of incense and passing out plastic shot glasses of turmeric.

Brian is also here, he's a fellow leftie, a good pal, and the only person I've ever met I'd call a true virtuoso.

A couple of years ago I'd been fortunate enough to man the low end for him in two tribute shows to the rarest of musicians, a six-string shredder, with a great sense of melody and song structure, Joe Satriani.

For Brian the shows had been a massive undertaking he'd already recorded a cover version of the entire album "Surfing with The Alien" single handedly but to have pulled it off live playing the album back-to-back twice, I still maintain he should have been paid for each note

Enter Joe happy go lucky bulldozer of a drummer who's playing tonight with the headliner.

He is the opposite to my drummer, Six.

Funny and great fun to watch onstage, he also enjoys yanking my chain.

Reminding me how he asked me to join one of his other bands not once but twice, what he doesn't know that I was asked a third time via my old guitarist, Dino.

I'm sure if I'd signed up via Dino's offer, he would have somehow parlayed it into me getting his band a support slot in return.

Of late I regret not taking Joe up on one of his invitations,

Right now, in the company of these cool musicians and more importantly good people, I'm having more fun than if I were hanging with my own band.

At Times like these it's easy to forget those that outnumber and surround us in all this noise.

The desperate, the entitled with their impossible dreams and rampant egos.

I think back on the wise words Paul D'Anno, imparted to me, DC, Adam, and Ski in a different dressing room decades ago and several thousand miles away.

How, we really shouldn't take this shit too seriously, it ain't that noble of a profession and not like you're saving anyone's life.

"Now, lads, best of luck tonight but don't let it go to your heads and disappear up your own arses coz, let me tell you...It stinks up there!"

London UK 1993

...You Fucking Muppet!"

Oh, dear what had I done now to incur DC's displeasure, opening my big mouth that was what.

What I should have said when the backstage assistant asked me if the band had been supplied with sufficient adult beverages was something like...

"NO!

Get me the manager of this establishment immediately this is a bloody outrage never in all my years, entertaining millions across the globe have I ever seen such a pitiful display of piss poor refreshment!"

Instead, clueless as usual I'd replied...

"Oh, yes everything's fine, thank you so very much."

Dazzled by the wide-eyed novelty of the band not only having a dressing room but one that was furnished with two cases of Stella, a six pack of Red Stripe and two bottles of Merlot.

In that moment I'd forgotten.

DC was planning a post-show party round his place, we weren't getting paid for the gig and he wanted at least make it pay by snagging as much free booze as possible

Eight hours earlier, the shrill ringing of the phone in the hallway had woken me from a fitful slumber and introduced me to a pretty horrific hangover.

Squinting, I began to piecing together who I was, oh bollocks, I'm still Steve...ok, where was I?

That's DC's home phone serenading my bitch of a headache and I'm lying on my second home,

Crashed out on his couch.

From the hallway I heard DC shuffling he coughed then picked up the phone.

"Hello. Huh?" he croaked.

"Oh, how's it going buddy?

"Er, oh, don't know really, I mean...could do.

Listen mate can I call you back in half an hour?"

He wandered into the living room in his dressing gown.

No matter how pissed up on booze either of us had gotten the night before, DC could annoyingly recall every minuscule detail of my frequently embarrassing behavior while I myself would have no recollection, whatsoever.

"Mate, you were in a right old state, last night!" he laughed from the kitchen as he boiled the kettle.

"Well, I moaned.

I'm sure you'll be thrilled to learn I'm paying in full for it now man, I look and feel like utter dog shit."

"Yeah, me too" he lied.

Those damn cheekbones of his had an uncanny knack of masking his multitude of sins.

All he needed was a hairbrush and a quick shave and he'd look fine.

Unlike me, mashed and mangled with Godzilla roller skating circles round my brain on a pair of Sherman tanks.

"That was Wally on the phone, the support band for Mike Fab-Gear just shat the bed and he's offered us the slot"

The band had recently scored a Top 40 hit with their cover of The Beatles "I am The Walrus."

"That's fantastic, where and when man?"

I asked, gratefully accepting the cup of industrial strength coffee he handed me.

"Clapham Grand, eight o'clock, tonight"

"Hang on... Clapham as in Clapham Junction... London?!"

"Fucking fuck yes! he laughed.

The Clapham Grand, a beautiful Victorian theatre built in 1900 with seating for 3,000, above the orchestra seating hung an ornate carved seated balcony flanked by a pair of ornate opera boxes.

More impressive to me personally was that Siouxsie & The Banshees had haunted its cavernous hall earlier this year.

Was this it, then, had I and we as a band arrived?

My rock n roll dream about to become reality?

The seemingly impossible goal I'd kept in my mind since witnessing The Cult decimate a packed to the rafters Hammersmith Odeon, six years ago just four miles north, across the River Thames from where I now sat.

Right now, it sure felt like it.

Assigned our own dressing room, access all areas lanyards even a dedicated soundman.

During soundcheck, he asked me if I had any specific sonic requirements?

The band had either used our own PA or operated the venues that provided one ourselves in the past.

I shrugged and asked if he could possibly maybe, make me a fraction louder.

Tonight, our playground for forty-five minutes was an enormous flat as a pool table nail and loose wooden board free stage.

The total square footage was six times deeper and four times wider than what we were used to usually performing on.

Due to us filling in at such short notice the headliner, allowed us use of their entire backline and drum kit.

I marveled at the volume, depth, and clarity when I plucked a single note. Feeling the vibration, from the towering Ampeg bass stack shifting the behind me.

Near the exit on stage left, DC grinned manically as he hit a huge Em chord, letting it ring out through his borrowed brace of Marshall stacks, the sound of an overdriven six string orchestra.

Adam's loaned drum kit behind me, set high upon a riser, his bludgeoning was like a stampede of regimented mammoth's and lastly Liam vocals soared to loosen the dust from the cut glass chandeliers above the balcony.

Wedge shaped monitors lined the lip of the stage, here is where we would rest our boots, smoldering as we stared right into the whites of the audience's eyes.

On this expansive playing field, we would throw all manner of shapes aping the moves and attitudes of our Rock Star hero's.

We pre-gamed backstage, toasting our sudden good fortune and that finally our time to shine had come.

A stagehand knocked on the door to let us know our showtime was in five minutes, we marched down the stairs, Adam took his place in the dark behind the kit, while the three of us stood behind the heavy curtain.

Liam clutched his cordless mic, DC blew dust from the neck of his Jackson while I checked that the cord from my jack socket and my wireless transmitter pack was secured to my strap for the last time.

The PA blasted our intro tape a mashup of the fanfare from the Rocky Horror Picture show soundtrack and a sample of Jesse Ventura's character Blaine from the movie Predator bellowing "It's Payback Time!"

Tonight, the band had landed on all eight feet, the four of us were ready, willing, and locked for rock.

South London had no idea what was about to hit it.

The curtain fell, we ran into position as the lighting rig exploded into life and we launched into our opening salvo.

For the next forty-five minutes my rock n roll dream came true performing on a proper grown-up stage, playing an utter belter of a show with my kick ass band...

To an audience of five people and one dog.

THAT'S L'AMORZ

BENSONHURST BROOKLYN 2002

Our yellow cab emerged from the Mid-town tunnel, into Manhattan and straight into gridlock.

"Hey, fuck you asshole!" a fractious motorist yelled from his open window, now this was more like it, the New York City I was after.

A powder keg of seething humanity liable to blow at any second dark, dangerous and filled with profanity.

The band, Rush hadn't toured the UK in a decade, so DC and I decided to go to them booking a flight, hotel, and a pair of tickets ever for their show at Madison Square Garden.

Our room number at the Skyline Hotel was 211, to show how much of a Rush geek I was I stuck a post it with #2 on it.

The legendary punk club, C.B.G. Bs on Bowery was our first nights port of call, made famous in the early seventies for launching careers of The Ramones, Talking Heads and Blondie, it was cool, dingy but didn't smell too great.

It was the toilets that had really put the place on the map there was no door on either the gents or ladies, the single "cubicle" in the men's room was just an exposed bowl and cistern set on a raised platform.

Dio forbid if you were ever caught short, not only would you be in full view of the boys but with the door free Ladies Room directly opposite you'd also be giving them a gross free show.

Rush's show the following night was well worth the four-figure outlay, the band delivered an unforgettable three-hour show.

Personally, it was a thrill to see them live for the first time in over ten years in such an exciting city and landmark venue.

Taking a windswept, ride on the Staten Island ferry the following afternoon, DC brought up again how he was wanted to go see the Thin Lizzy show in Brooklyn tonight.

From the rail of the vessel, I gazed toward the Borough's distant shoreline, with no knowledge of the neighborhood other than how it had been depicted in the 1979 classic gang movie "The Warriors" I assumed little had unchanged since and voiced my concerns to DC.

"Don't be daft mate!"

He laughed.

Not only is that flick some poncey hairdressers' idea of a gang movie, but it was made nearly twenty-five years ago!"

An icy blast of wind battered the ferry, I shivered and pulled my coat closer, looking again to the outline of the Brooklyn Navy Yard, I suppose he had a point, it couldn't surely still be that bad, could it?

Back at the hotel, the curt voice on the other end of the line told me nope the club wasn't near any landmarks and gave me some vague directions, slightly miffed, I hung up the phone.

The club was called L'Amour and located deep in the heart of Brooklyn, Bensonhurst to be precise.

Playing tonight was Thin Lizzy in a new line up fronted by fellow Readingensian, guitarist/vocalist John Sykes who originally, hailed like Aslan and T-Bone from Tilehurst.

DC had decided it would be rude not to go, but it sounded like getting there was going to be a nightmare.

Outside the hotel on 10th Avenue every cab we flagged flat out refused to take a fare beyond the safe environs of Manhattan

All their reactions to my requested destination where the same, I was given a look as if to say, "You're fucking kidding right?" before they took off at speed.

Neither of us were aware of the first rule of hailing a cab in NYC, that you never tell the driver your destination until your already sat inside.

For all I knew I could have been asking to venture into some desolate, lawless neighborhood,

A place stuck in a time capsule and still rife with gang warfare.

Where they still shot out the streetlights and the only illumination was provided by the stolen cars the gangbangers set ablaze.

Eventually a cheery cabbie pulled up, who was at least prepared to leave the island of Manhattan.

"I've got no clue where or what the place you're looking for is

He said with a grin.

But hop in and let's go find out!"

In pre-sat nav 2002, all bets were off once we crossed the Brooklyn Bridge.

Feeling myself tense up with fear I looked at my crumpled note pad of hastily scribbled directions.

Rolling off the exit ramp of the Bridge, we drove deep into the borough which covered a much wider area than the Island of Manhattan and home to more than two million people.

After nearly an hour traversing, highways and industrial areas our driver remarked.

"Man... these streets are all fucked up!"

Up ahead I spotted the elevated subway and a station, the only helpful tidbit I'd been given during my call to the club was that it was within reasonable walking distance of the New Utrecht N train stop.

We had the cabbie drop us at the intersection by a Corner Store, gregarious as always DC went inside to ask the shopkeeper how far we were from the club.

The guy behind the couldn't understand him... at all.

A long-haired British dude asking a Puerto Rican Bodega owner who knew pidgin English and more used to being addressed in a thick Brooklyn drawl, directions to a club with a French Name?

The accent barrier was utterly insurmountable.

We stood on the street corner and smoked cigarettes.

Looking up at the elevated subway as a Coney Island bound N train rattled by, I was reminded again of The Warriors and assumed riding it was still fraught with danger.

Whether we found the club or not it looked like it was our only way out of here.

On the other side of the street, a tall long-haired guy clad in a leather trench coat, moved with a purposeful stride.

"I bet he knows where it is."

DC said and immediately took off after him.

His name was Danny, and we were in luck.

"Shit, you limeys just won the fucking lottery man!

He laughed.

I'm heading there right now!"

I handed him my directions.

"Man, you never would have found it using these."

He screwed up the piece of paper and threw it over his shoulder.

The Joint is kind of off the grid, man"

He paused to crush a spent Marlboro under his cowboy boot and led us onto a dark, deserted stretch of 62nd Street.

Struggling to keep up with his frantic pace, I asked him what our best option was for getting back.

"Local car service he said lighting another cigarette.

Or you know, just take the N train back there"

Something in his voice implied that the second option should only be considered as a last resort.

If a hardboiled Brooklynite wasn't keen on riding it,

Then, we were seriously screwed.

The Rock Capital of Brooklyn, L'Amor pronounced "Lamorz" by the locals was smaller that I'd expected but unlike CBGB's the toilets at least had cubicles and doors.

A converted warehouse it had first opened in 1978 as a Discotheque, presumably to cash in on the success of the smash hit movie Saturday Night Fever.

Located in the same neighborhood depicted in the movie the venue that portrayed the 2001 Odyssey club where Tony Manero had cut a million-dollar dash was just a few blocks away on 64th Street.

By 1981 the club started transitioning to a rock and metal venue.

The old cliental rousted by a new 50,000-watt PA which was now more likely to blast Slayer than Sylvester.

During the early eighties it was the only dedicated metal club within a 500-mile radius and attracting many bands on the way up, Metallica, Megadeth and Slayer had all made their east coast debuts at L'Amors.

My only point of reference for the club was from Bensonhurst's finest doom/gothic metal group, the self-professed drab four, Type O Negative.

The band had played there so often they'd immortalized it in their scathingly hilarious twelve-minute epic "Unsuccessfully Coping with The Natural Beauty of Infidelity" or more commonly known as...

"I Know Your Fucking Someone Else"

The lyrics dealt with lead singer/bassist's Peter Steele reaction to his girlfriend cheating on him.

She had gone to L'Amour on a random Saturday night dressed in an outfit two sizes too tight to practice some freelance gynecology.

With Pete's ex where there's was a womb there was a way.

Like the best venue's/clubs that catered to our tribe it didn't smell too great and it was teeth rattling and brain meltingly loud.

To many it was place to avoid, to us, it almost felt like home.

Blissfully distracted by the bar maid's charm and impressive rack, DC suddenly nudged me drawing my attention to a short pretty girl with wavy, raven hair who'd just taken a seat at the end of the bar.

She was wearing a Rush T-shirt and asked the barmaid for a candle, to better read her book.

Eagle eyed DC picked out the title it was "Ghost Rider."

The memoir penned by Rush drummer Neil Peart.

"Oh, mate, this is total fate!" he grinned.

With zero seconds hesitation he steamed on over and struck up a conversation with the pretty confused looking book worm.

Her name was Kristin and duh... yeah of course she loved Rush, as did her best friend who was around here, somewhere.

Turning my attention back to the barmaid, I ordered another round.

I heard her before I saw her...

Once I'd got an eyeful who was making such a foul-mouthed racket, any designs I might have had on the busty barkeep went right out of my mind.

Tall, Blonde, with vivid red lipstick behind which lay a quick and vicious Tongue.

She looked like a cross between Drew Barrymore and the Groupie from Pink Floyd's The Wall flick.

DC handled the pleasantries.

"This is my best mate, Steve Steele he's a great bassist"

"So" Kristin's big mouthed best friend asked me.

"Your name is Steve Steele...and you're a bass player?"

I nodded, thinking there's no way she's gonna buy that and reached inside my jacket for evidence.

She glanced at my passport, smirked, then let me know in no uncertain terms

"Oh...You are so full of SHIT!"

Throwing caution and my four strings to the wind I accepted her invitation to hit the dance floor as the band struck up "The Boys Are Back in Town."

And the rest as they say is...

Geography!

CODA: THIRTY-SIX STRINGS

CHELSEA MANHATTAN 2022

I never bothered to learn music theory, figuring Lemmy from Motorhead couldn't read music and he didn't do too bad for himself.

Musician... it's such an unwieldy title and by my definition you should only refer to yourself as one if you make a living as one, instead I prefer to call myself an Obsessed Hobbyist.

Playing music after all is supposed to be fun, my approach today remains the same make sure I'm in tune, wing it and hope for the best.

DC has told me numerous times on how I should never sell anything with strings, put them in a closet and let their worth increase over time.

Sixteen four strings have passed through my sweaty paws since 1986 and as for years I didn't heed his advice I'm now down to a mere nine basses.

My combined 36 strings pale when you consider DC's extensive collection, who I don't think has sold anything...ever.

In fact, to call it a collection doesn't begin to cover a fraction of it, let's say instead he commands a Guitar Armada of FORTY-SEVEN six strings.

Too much?

I'm sure DC would say it's never enough.

Besides he should write his own book and call it

"I've only got 282 strings."

THANK YOU TO...

My wife, Punk & Personal Air Raid siren
Delores Jean Miller Steele for lighting a fire under my ass and
encouraging me to document this madness.
Mum & Dad, Keith & June Steele and my brother Chris for their
love, feedback & support.
Aunt Valerie Hansen for always being wonderful,
Cousin Michael Hansen for the free records and inspiration.
In-laws Ed, Julie, Corey & Erin Miller for their support
Musical families & friends for their support and inspiration
Robert William Appleton, Michael & Jo Ayres
Colin James Dunn, Malcom & Steve Berry
Chris & Judith Locke, Sean Harris, Graham Winter Goodwin,
Dave Shingleton, Alison Koilen, Angelina Snarey, Tim Martin, Nuj
Farrow, Bob & Sarah Guy
Ian & Kate Cocker, Adrian Ogden, Phil & Alison Stevens
Chris Hale, Pete Butterworth, Mike Hill & Lyz Rothman
Salina Steele Torrain, Ruby & Jesse
Max & Roisin Capshaw, Eric Grasso
Nikki Alcazar, Anjanette McGrath,
Andee Black, Lily Stephanie Paul Kane
Kevin & Stephanie Richardson, Kelly Clayton
Steve Steele

Ingram Content Group UK Ltd.
Milton Keynes UK
UKHW012158290523
422506UK00001B/74